Jung on Mythology

W9-CFA-412

CHICAGO PUBLIC LIBRARY

R0135152833

ENCOUNTERING JUNG

ENCOUNTERING JUNG

On Mythology

Selected and Introduced
by Robert A. Segal

Princeton University Press
Princeton, New Jersey

Introduction and Selection copyright © 1998 by Princeton University Press
Published by Princeton University Press, 41 William Street, Princeton,
New Jersey 08540

All Rights Reserved

This book is composed of texts selected from the following volumes of the
Collected Works of C. G. Jung: *The Psychogenesis of Mental Disease*, Volume
3, © 1960 by Bollingen Foundation, © renewed 1988 by Princeton University
Press; *Freud and Psychoanalysis*, Volume 4, © 1961 by Bollingen Foundation,
© renewed 1989 by Princeton University Press; *Symbols of Transformation*,
Volume 5, 2nd ed., © 1956 by Princeton University Press, © renewed 1984 by
Princeton University Press; *Psychological Types*, Volume 6, © 1971 by Prince-
ton University Press; *Two Essays on Analytical Psychology*, Volume 7, 2nd ed.,
© 1981 by Princeton University Press; *The Structure and Dynamics of the
Psyche*, Volume 8, 2nd ed., © 1969 by Princeton University Press; *The Arche-
types and the Collective Unconscious*, Volume 9 i, 2nd ed. © 1959 by Bollingen
Foundation, © renewed 1987 by Princeton University Press; *Aion*, Volume 9 ii,
2nd ed., © 1959 by Princeton University Press, © renewed 1987 by Princeton
University Press; *Civilization in Transition*, Volume 10, 2nd ed., © 1970 by
Princeton University Press; *Psychology and Religion: West and East*, Volume
11, 2nd ed., © 1958 by Bollingen Foundation, © renewed 1986 by Princeton
University Press; *Psychology and Alchemy*, Volume 12, © 1953 by Bollingen
Foundation, © renewed 1981 by Princeton University Press; *Alchemical
Studies*, Volume 13, © 1978 by Bollingen Foundation; *Mysterium Coniunc-
tionis*, Volume 14, © 1970 by Princeton University Press; *The Spirit in Man,
Art, and Literature*, Volume 15, © 1966 by Bollingen Foundation, © renewed
1971 by Princeton University Press; *The Practice of Psychotherapy*, Vol. 16,
2nd ed., © 1954 by Bollingen Foundation, © renewed 1982 by Princeton University Press; *The Development of Personality*, Volume 17, 2nd ed., © 1954 by
Bollingen Foundation; © renewed 1982 by Princeton University Press; *The
Symbolic Life*, Volume 18, © 1958 by Bollingen Foundation, © renewed 1986
by Princeton University Press. Other excerpts are taken from *C. G. Jung Speaking*, © 1977 by Princeton University Press; *The Collected Letters of C. G. Jung*,
Volumes 1 and 2, © 1953, 1955, 1961, 1963, 1968, 1971, 1972, 1974, 1975
by Princeton University Press; *Memories, Dreams, Reflections*, by C. G. Jung, ©
1961, 1962, 1963, and renewed 1989, 1990, 1991 by Random House, Inc. (reprinted here by arrangement with Pantheon Books, a division of Random House,
Inc.); *The Origins and History of Consciousness*, by Erich Neumann, © 1954 by
Bollingen Foundation, © renewed 1982 by Princeton University Press; *Creation
Myths*, by Marie-Louise von Franz, © 1972 (reprinted by arrangement with
Shambhala Publications Inc., Boston); *Re-visioning Psychology*, by James Hillman,
© 1975 by James Hillman (reprinted by arrangement with HarperCollins Pub-
lishers).

Library of Congress Cataloging-in-Publication Data
will be found on the last page of this volume

Princeton University Press books are printed on acid-free paper and meet the
guidelines for permanence and durability of the Committee on Production
Guidelines for Book Longevity of the Council on Library Resources

http://pup.princeton.edu

Printed in the United States of America

10 9 8 7 6 5 4 3 2 1

BL
304
.J86
1998

:SH

R01351 52833

Contents

CHICAGO PUBLIC LIBRARY
SOCIAL SCIENCES AND HISTORY
400 S. STATE ST.   60605

HE.

Part 2   Developments in the Jungian Theory of Myth

Chapter 11 **Erich Neumann**   231

Introduction to *The Origins and History
of Consciousness*   231

Chapter 12 **Marie-Louise von Franz**   240

From *Patterns of Creativity Mirrored in Creation Myths*   240

Chapter 13 **James Hillman**   256

From *Re-Visioning Psychology*   256

Jung on Mythology

Introduction

At least three major questions can be asked of myth: what is its subject matter, what is its origin, and what is its function? Theories of myth differ, first of all, on the answers they give to these questions. The subject matter, or referent, of myth can be anything. It can be the literal subject matter, which is most often gods and goddesses, or a symbolic subject matter, such as divinities as symbols of human traits. For most theorists, myth originates and functions to satisfy a need, but that need can be for anything—for example, for rain, for information, or for meaning in life. The need can be on the part of individuals or on the part of the community.

Theories of myth differ not only on the answers they give to the major questions but even more basically on the questions they seek to answer. Some theories concentrate on the subject matter of myth, others on the origin, still others on the function. The answer a theory gives to one question doubtless shapes the answer it gives to another, but most theories concentrate on just one or two of the questions. C. G. Jung's is one of the few theories that answers fully all three. A single statement summarizes his answer: "Myths are original revelations of the preconscious psyche, involuntary statements about unconscious psychic happenings, and anything but allegories of physical processes."[1] The subject matter is not literal but symbolic: not the external world but the human mind. Myth originates and functions to satisfy the psychological need for contact with the unconscious.

The Subject Matter of Myth

James Frazer, author of the anthropological classic *The Golden Bough*, deems the subject matter of myth physical processes. For Frazer, the chief myths of all religions describe the death

For their most helpful comments on this introduction, I want to thank John Beebe and Roderick Main.

[1] C. G. Jung, "The Psychology of the Child Archetype," in *The Archetypes and the Collective Unconscious*, Collected Works of C. G. Jung, ed. Sir Herbert Read et al., trans. R.F.C. Hull et al., vol. 9, pt. 1, 2d ed. (Princeton, N.J.: Princeton University Press, 1968 [1959]), 154.

and rebirth of vegetation, a process symbolized by the myth of the death and rebirth of the god of vegetation. Thus "the story that Adonis spent half, or according to others a third, of the year in the lower world and the rest of it in the upper world, is explained most simply and naturally by supposing that he represented vegetation, especially the corn, which lies buried in the earth half the year and reappears above ground the other half."[2]

By contrast, Jung interprets the myth of the death and rebirth of a god as a symbolic expression of a process taking place not in the world but in the mind. That process is the return of the ego to the unconscious—a kind of temporary death of the ego—and its reemergence, or rebirth, from the unconscious:

> I need only mention the whole mythological complex of the dying and resurgent god and its primitive precursors all the way down to the re-charging of fetishes and churingas with magical force. It expresses a transformation of attitude by means of which a new potential, a new manifestation of life, a new fruitfulness, is created.[3]

Jung does not deny that the psychological process of the death and rebirth of the ego *parallels* the physical process of the death and rebirth of vegetation. He denies that the physical process *accounts for* the psychological one, let alone for the mythic one. For Frazer, the leap from vegetation to god is the product of logic and imagination: "primitives" observe the course of vegetation and hypothesize the existence of a god to account for it—even if for Frazer himself the god is a mere symbol of vegetation. For Jung, the leap is too great for the human imagination to make. Humans generally, not merely primitives, lack the creativity required to concoct consciously the notion of the sacred out of the profane. They can only transform the profane into a sacred that already exists for them.[4] Humans must already have the idea of god within their minds and can only be projecting that idea onto vegetation and the other natural phenomena that they observe:

---

[2] James George Frazer, *The Golden Bough*, abridged ed. (London: Macmillan, 1922), 392.
[3] Jung, *Psychological Types*, Collected Works, vol. 6 (Princeton, N.J.: Princeton University Press, 1971), 193.
[4] Jung's reverence for the hiatus between the divine and the human is not always shared by his followers. For example, Jean Shinoda Bolen breezily effaces the line between the two, as her titles declare: *Goddesses in Everywoman* (New York: Harper & Row, 1984) and *Gods in Everyman* (New York: Harper & Row, 1989).

This latter analogy [between god and natural phenomenon] explains the well-attested connection between the renewal of the god and seasonal and vegetational phenomena. One is naturally inclined to assume that seasonal, vegetational, lunar, and solar myths underlie these analogies. But that is to forget that a myth, like everything psychic, cannot be solely conditioned by external events. Anything psychic brings its own internal conditions with it, so that one might assert with equal right that the myth is purely psychological and uses meteorological or astronomical events merely as a means of expression. The whimsicality and absurdity of many primitive myths often makes the latter explanation seem far more appropriate than any other.[5]

Even early Jung, who is prepared to give more weight to experience than later Jung, distinguishes between the experience of the sun itself and the experience of the sun as a god. Experience of the sun provides the *occasion* for the manifestation of the sun archetype but does not *cause* that archetype:

I have often been asked where the archetypes or primordial images come from. It seems to me that their origin can only be explained by assuming them to be deposits of the constantly repeated experiences of humanity. One of the commonest and at the same time most impressive experiences is the apparent movement of the sun every day. We certainly cannot discover anything of the kind in the unconscious, so far as the known physical process is concerned. What we do find, on the other hand, is the myth of the sun-hero in all its countless variations. It is this myth, and not the physical process, that forms the sun archetype. . . . The archetype is a kind of readiness to produce over and over again the same or similar mythical ideas.[6]

It is not only allegories of physical processes that Jung rejects as the real subject matter of myth. He also rejects literal interpretations of myth that still make the subject matter outer rather than inner. For example, the pioneering Victorian anthropologist Edward Tylor insists that the subject matter of myth is gods of nature rather than, as for Frazer, the natural

[5] Jung, *Psychological Types*, 193–94.
[6] Jung, "On the Psychology of the Unconscious," in *Two Essays on Analytical Psychology*, Collected Works, vol. 7, 2d ed. (Princeton, N.J.: Princeton University Press, 1966 [1953]), 69.

phenomena they control and even inhabit. For Tylor, myths are actual explanations of natural phenomena and not merely, as for Frazer, colorful descriptions of them. Gods are the purported agents behind natural processes and not simply allegories of those processes. As Tylor says in exasperation at those who would interpret myths allegorically, "When the Apache Indian pointed to the sky and asked the white man, 'Do you not believe that God, the Sun, . . . sees what we do and punishes us when it is evil?' it is impossible to say that this savage was talking in rhetorical simile."[7]

Jung conflates Tylor's theory with Frazer's, stating, for example, that "people are very loath to give up the idea that the myth is some kind of explanatory allegory of astronomical, meteorological, or vegetative processes."[8] The phrase "explanatory allegory" conflates Tylor's theory — myth as explanation — with Frazer's — myth as allegory. Jung asks rhetorically "why the sun and its apparent motions do not appear direct and undisguised as a content of the myths."[9] Tylor's answer would be that myths describe sun gods and not merely the sun because myths are about sun gods and not merely about the sun. Yet even if Jung were to distinguish Tylor's view from Frazer's, he would still invoke his fundamental claim that human beings cannot consciously invent gods. Humans can only project onto the world gods already in their minds. For Jung, myth is no more about gods than about the physical world. It is about the human mind. Myth must be read symbolically, as for Frazer, and the symbolized subject is a process, as likewise for Frazer, but the process is an inner rather than an outer one.

Jung interprets as projections not only nature myths but all other kinds of myths as well. He says that "in fact, the whole of mythology could be taken as a sort of projection of the collective unconscious. . . . Just as the constellations were projected into the heavens, similar figures were projected into legends and fairytales or upon historical persons."[10] Hero myths, of which

[7] Edward Burnett Tylor, *Primitive Culture*, 1st ed. (London: Murray, 1871), vol. 1, 262.

[8] Jung, "On Psychic Energy," in *The Structure and Dynamics of the Psyche*, Collected Works, vol. 8, 2d ed. (Princeton, N.J.: Princeton University Press, 1969 [1960]), 37–38.

[9] Jung, *Psychological Types*, 444.

[10] Jung, "The Structure of the Psyche," in *The Structure and Dynamics of the Psyche*, 152. For Jung, heroes are mythical because they are more than human. For Lord Raglan, who extends Frazer's theory of myth to heroes, heroes are mythical because they are not historical. That is, Raglan concentrates on disproving the historicity of hero stories in order to make them mythical, where Jung takes for granted that heroes cannot be historical because they are quasi-divine. See Lord Raglan, *The Hero*

Jungians are especially enamored, are projections onto mere human beings of a divine or quasi-divine status: "the hero myth is an unconscious drama seen only in projection, like the happenings in Plato's parable of the cave. The hero himself appears as a being of more than human stature."[11] Moderns, while often professed atheists, still create myths by projecting onto their fellow human beings exaggerated qualities that turn them into superhuman figures:

> [T]he archetypes usually appear in projection; and, because projections are unconscious, they appear on persons in the immediate environment, mostly in the form of abnormal over- or under-evaluations which provoke misunderstandings, quarrels, fanaticisms, and follies of every description. Thus we say, "He makes a god of so-and-so," or, "So-and-so is Mr. X's *bête noire.*" In this way, too, there grow up modern myth-formations, i.e., fantastic rumours, suspicions, prejudices.[12]

Once Jung differentiates a psychological interpretation of myth from a nonpsychological one, he must differentiate his particular psychological interpretation from Freud's. Jung grants the Freudian claim that there exist "fantasies (including dreams) of a personal character, which go back unquestionably to personal experiences, things forgotten or repressed, and can thus be completely explained by individual anamnesis [i.e., recollection]."[13] But he is far more concerned to vaunt his own claim that, in addition to these manifestations of the personal, Freudian unconscious, there exist "fantasies (including dreams) of an impersonal character, which cannot be reduced to experiences in the individual's past, and thus cannot be explained as something individually acquired."[14] These fantasies must emanate from a different unconscious, which, rather than the creation of an individual, must be inherited. Jung insists that myths are always the product of this distinctively Jungian, collective unconscious: "These fantasy-images [of an impersonal character] undoubtedly have their closest analogues in mythological types. . . . The products of this second category resemble the

(London: Methuen, 1936), pt. 2; reprinted in Otto Rank et al., *In Quest of the Hero* (Princeton, N.J.: Princeton University Press, 1990), 89–175.

[11] Jung, *Symbols of Transformation*, Collected Works, vol. 5, 2d ed. (Princeton, N.J.: Princeton University Press, 1967 [1956]), 391.

[12] Jung, "On the Psychology of the Unconscious," 95.

[13] Jung, "The Psychology of the Child Archetype," 155.

[14] Ibid.

types of structures to be met with in myth and fairytale so much that we must regard them as related."[15]

On the one hand Jung employs the collective unconscious to interpret myths. On the other hand he employs myths to interpret the collective unconscious:

> In order to interpret the products of the unconscious, I also found it necessary to give a quite different reading to dreams and fantasies. I did not reduce them to personal factors, as Freud does, but — and this seemed indicated by their very nature — I compared them with the symbols from mythology and the history of religion, in order to discover the meaning they were trying to express.[16]

Myths here steer one away from a Freudian diagnosis.

Going further, Jung uses myths to establish the collective unconscious. The first step in the proof is the demonstration of the universality of motifs, and myths provide evidence of that universality. As Jung says, "The material brought forward — folkloristic, mythological, or historical — serves in the first place to demonstrate the uniformity of psychic events in time and space."[17] The next step in the proof is the refutation of Freud's account of the universality of motifs. Jung cites the recurrence of mythic motifs that supposedly defy a Freudian account. For example, he continually appeals to the appearance in myths of the idea of birth from two mothers to refute Freud's analysis of Leonardo da Vinci's famous depiction of Jesus' being hovered over by Anne as well as Mary as a projection of Leonardo's own childhood experience:

> Freud interprets this remarkable picture in terms of the fact that Leonardo himself had two mothers. This causality is personal. We shall . . . simply point out that interwoven with the apparently personal psychology there is an impersonal motif well known to us from other fields. This is the motif of the *dual mother*, an archetype to be found in many variants in the field of mythology and comparative religion and forming the basis of numerous "représentations collectives." I might mention, for instance, the motif of the *dual descent*, that is,

[15] Ibid.

[16] Jung, "Introduction to Kraenfeldt's 'Secret Ways of the Mind,'" in *Freud and Psychoanalysis*, Collected Works, vol. 4 (Princeton, N.J.: Princeton University Press, 1961), 330.

[17] Jung, "On the Nature of the Psyche," in *The Structure and Dynamics of the Psyche*, 227.

descent from human and divine parents, as in the case of Heracles, who received immortality through being unwittingly adopted by Hera. . . . Now it is absolutely out of the question that all the individuals who believe in a dual descent have in reality always had two mothers, or conversely that those few who shared Leonardo's fate have infected the rest of humanity with their complex. Rather, one cannot avoid the assumption that the universal occurrence of the dual-birth motif together with the fantasy of the two mothers answers an omnipresent human need which is reflected in these motifs.[18]

It is a testimony to the confidence of both Jungians and Freudians in their psychologies that mythology since the time of the masters has come to be taken by depth psychologists less as evidence of the unconscious and more as an expression of it.

Jung maintains that because the collective unconscious is inherently unconscious, "in the last analysis, therefore, it is impossible to say what [its contents] refer to. Every interpretation necessarily remains an 'as-if.' The ultimate core of meaning may be circumscribed, but not described."[19] It is not merely Freud but other theorists as well who thus wrongly assume the subject matter, or referent, of myth to be specifiable. If one heeds Jung, "there is no longer any question whether a myth refers to the sun or the moon, the father or the mother, sexuality or fire or water; all it does is to circumscribe and give an approximate description of an *unconscious core of meaning*."[20]

Jung is by no means abandoning the attempt to interpret myth. He is simply cautioning against would-be definitive interpretations of myth. More precisely, he is cautioning against would-be definitive *Jungian* interpretations of myth. He is prepared to rule out all non-Jungian interpretations, but he is not prepared to rule in any one Jungian interpretation. Insofar as the contents of the collective unconscious are archetypes, the definitive meaning of myths is the expression of archetypes. But because archetypes are innately unconscious, they can express themselves only obliquely, through symbols. Furthermore, not

---

[18] Jung, "The Concept of the Collective Unconscious," in *The Archetypes and the Collective Unconscious*, 44–45. On the case of Leonardo see also, for example, "On the Psychology of the Unconscious," 65; "Concerning the Archetypes, with Special Reference to the Anima Concept," in *The Archetypes and the Collective Unconscious*, 68 n. 27.

[19] Jung, "Archetypes of the Collective Unconscious," in *The Archetypes and the Collective Unconscious*, 156.

[20] Ibid.

only does every myth contain multiple archetypes, but every archetype harbors inexhaustible meanings. No symbol can convey even obliquely the array of meanings of the archetype it expresses. As Jung says of the difficulty a poet faces in trying to express an archetypal experience:

> [T]he primordial experience is the source of his creativeness, but it is so dark and amorphous that it requires the related mythological imagery to give it form. In itself it is wordless and imageless, for it is a vision seen "as in a glass, darkly." It is nothing but a tremendous intuition striving for expression. . . . Since the expression can never match the richness of the vision and can never exhaust its possibilities, the poet must have at his disposal a huge store of material if he is to communicate even a fraction of what he has glimpsed, and must make use of difficult and contradictory images in order to express the strange paradoxes of his vision.[21]

For some theorists, myths are difficult to interpret because their meaning is symbolic rather than literal. For Jung, the greatest difficulty is not that myths are encrypted symbolically but that the symbols used to convey their meaning do so both indirectly and, worse, inadequately. The issue is epistemological, and Jung continually invokes Immanuel Kant to differentiate what we can know from what we cannot. Kant's distinction between the unknowable, noumenal reality and the knowable, phenomenal one becomes for Jung not only the distinction between metaphysics and psychology but also the distinction within psychology between the unconscious and consciousness. It becomes as well the distinction between archetypes and symbols.

For Jung, interpreting myths poses a double difficulty. The initial but less weighty difficulty is the need to recognize the motifs in myths as symbols. Jung is impatient with those who read myths literally, for they thereby mistake the symbols for the symbolized. Once motifs are recognized as symbols, the weightier difficulty is deciphering their meaning. Symbols are the only medium for conveying archetypes, but they are an imperfect medium. Nothing can bridge the divide between the unconscious and consciousness. Indeed, Jung dismisses Freud's view of the unconscious precisely because Freud seemingly bridges

---

[21] Jung, "Psychology and Literature," in *The Spirit in Man, Art, and Literature*, Collected Works, vol. 15 (Princeton, N.J.: Princeton University Press, 1966), 96–97.

the divide by deriving the unconscious from consciousness. For Jung, myths, as a symbolic manifestation of archetypes, can never be deciphered exhaustively. It is not merely that one can never be sure of the correctness of the interpretation — a problem that would hold even if myths referred entirely to conscious processes. It is that no myth can convey fully the meaning invested in it by the archetypes it conveys. The point is not simply that a myth can harbor a plurality of meanings — again, a problem that would hold even if myths referred wholly to conscious processes. The point is that any myth is limited in what it can convey. In stressing that myth falls short of conveying the meanings invested in it, Jung is by no means disparaging it. On the contrary, he declares myth the best medium for conveying the unconscious: "Myth is the primordial language natural to these psychic processes, and no intellectual formulation comes anywhere near the richness and expressiveness of mythical imagery."[22]

For Jung, interpreting myths poses a third difficulty as well. Myths for him do not merely convey meanings. They convey meanings to adherents. Myths are intended by the unconscious to reveal its contents to those whose myths they are. To reach their intended audience, myths must be translatable into a language the audience knows. Just as archetypes must be translated, however insufficiently, into myths, so myths must be translated, however insufficiently, into the language of those whose myths they are. Just as archetypes are dependent on myths to convey their meaning, so myths are dependent on interpretations to convey *their* meaning. Even if the meaning of a myth is the expression of the archetypes it harbors, the myth must still be interpreted by whoever is to benefit from it. As Jung says,

And whatever explanation or interpretation does to it [i.e., the myth], we do to our own souls as well, with corresponding results for our own well-being. The archetype — let us never forget this — is a psychic organ present in all of us. A bad explanation means a correspondingly bad attitude to this organ, which may thus be injured. But the ultimate sufferer is the bad interpreter himself.[23]

[22] Jung, "Introduction to the Religious and Psychological Problems of Alchemy," in *Psychology and Alchemy*, Collected Works, vol. 12, 2d ed. (Princeton, N.J.: Princeton University Press, 1968 [1953]), 25.
[23] Jung, "Archetypes of the Collective Unconscious," 160.

Tracking the relationship of archetypes to myths to interpretations is like tracking the translation of a message from one
language into a second language which lacks many of the
equivalents of the first, and then into a third language which
lacks many of the equivalents of the second. Yet the second
language must be translated into the third if the indispensable
message of the first language is not to be lost. To be cut off
from that original message is for Jung to be cut off from one's
own unconscious — a psychological disaster:

> In reality we can never legitimately cut loose from our arche-
> typal foundations unless we are prepared to pay the price of
> a neurosis, any more than we can rid ourselves of our body
> and its organs without committing suicide. If we cannot deny
> the archetypes or otherwise neutralize them, we are con-
> fronted, at every new stage in the differentiation of con-
> sciousness to which civilization attains, with the task of find-
> ing a new *interpretation* appropriate to this stage, in order to
> connect the life of the past that still exists in us with the life
> of the present, which threatens to slip away from it.[24]

Insofar as a new interpretation of a myth conveys some aspect
of the myth and (in turn of an archetype) not previously conveyed, we "dream the myth onwards."[25]

By nature, all theorists of myth, not just Jung, are interested
in the similarities rather than the differences among myths. To
encompass all cases of myth, theorists not only identify overt
similarities among them but also uncover similarities beneath
apparent differences. Jung, however, goes further. He repeatedly
declares myths to be not merely similar but outright identical —
an identity that he attributes to their identical origin:

> It is the same as with myths and symbols, which can arise
> autochthonously in every corner of the earth and yet are
> identical, because they are fashioned out of the same world-
> wide human unconscious, whose contents are infinitely less
> variable than are races and individuals.[26]

By the identity of myths worldwide, Jung must mean the identity of the archetypes they manifest. He cannot mean that

[24] Ibid., 157.
[25] Ibid., 160.
[26] Jung, *Psychological Types*, 120–21.

myths themselves are identical. He may be downplaying the differences as insignificant, but he cannot be denying them.

Yet for all his insistence on the universal identity of the archetypal contents of myths, Jung is also attentive to the differences. When he analyzes specific myths, the identification of archetypes becomes only the first, not the last, step in the process. One must analyze the specific symbols used to convey those archetypes, the meaning of those archetypes in the specific myth in which they appear, and the meaning of that myth in the life of the specific adherent to the myth. A myth is not merely a myth in its own right. It is a myth for someone. The meaning of a myth is more than its general meaning for all humanity. One must understand the person or the society to understand the myth: "So it is with the individual images [in a myth]: they need a context, and the context is not only a myth but an individual anamnesis."[27] Hence for Jung the analysis of myth is best undertaken as part of therapy. The frequent characterization of Jung as oblivious to the particulars of a myth and its adherents is inaccurate and unfair. Undeniably, for many Jungians, including Erich Neumann and the Jungian-oriented Joseph Campbell, the meaning of a myth is exclusively the universal one. But for Jung himself and for Jungian analysts practicing today, the meaning is the particular one as well as the universal one.[28]

The Origin of Myth

As a theorist of myth, Jung is concerned with accounting for the similarities among myths. There are two possible explanations: diffusion and independent invention. Diffusion means that myths originate in one society and spread elsewhere. Independent invention means that every society invents myths on its own. The prime argument of diffusionists is that the similarities among myths are too precise to have arisen independently. The prime argument of independent "inventionists" is that the similarities are too widespread geographically to be the product of diffusion. Additionally, inventionists argue that diffusion, even when granted, fails to explain either the origin of the myth in

---

[27] Jung, "The Psychological Aspects of the Kore," in *The Archetypes and the Collective Unconscious*, 189.

[28] While not in fact a Jungian, Campbell is often deemed one, and not merely because he interprets myths psychologically but also because he usually stresses only the similarities among myths. See my *Joseph Campbell: An Introduction*, rev. ed. (New York: Penguin/New American Library, 1990 [1987]), chaps. 9, 12.

the society in which it arises or the acceptance of the myth by the societies to which it spreads.

Jung is staunchly committed to independent invention as the origin of myth. Making the standard argument of independent inventionists, he asserts that there is no evidence and indeed no possibility of contact among all of the societies with similar myths:

> Every endeavour has been made to explain the concordance of myth-motifs and -symbols as due to migration and tradition; Goblet d'Almellas' *Migration of Symbols* is an excellent example of this. But this explanation, which naturally has some value, is contradicted by the fact that a mythologem [i.e., archetype] can arise anywhere, at any time, without there being the slightest possibility of any such transmission.[29]

Jung makes the same argument in the case of individuals. His most famous example, that of the "Solar Phallus Man," is of an institutionalized patient who believed that the sun had a phallus and that the movement of the sun's phallus was the cause of wind. Jung then came upon a comparable fantasy in a book describing the vision of a member of the ancient cult of Mithras. Assuming that the patient could not have known of the book, Jung forever after cited the similarity as concrete evidence of independent invention:

> The patient was a small business employee with no more than a secondary school education. He grew up in Zurich, and by no stretch of imagination can I conceive how he could have got hold of the idea of the solar phallus, of the vision moving to and fro, and of the origin of the wind. I myself, who would have been in a much better position, intellectually, to know about this singular concatenation of ideas, was entirely ignorant of it and only discovered the parallel in a book of Dieterich's which appeared in 1910, four years after my original observation (1906).[30]

[29] Jung, "The Significance of Constitution and Heredity in Psychology," in *The Structure and Dynamics of the Psyche*, 111.
[30] Jung, *Symbols of Transformation*, 157–58. See also Jung, "The Structure of the Psyche," 150–51; "The Concept of the Collective Unconscious," 50–52; "The Tavistock Lectures" [*Analytical Psychology: Its Theory and Practice*], in *The Symbolic Life*, Collected Works, vol. 18 (Princeton, N.J.: Princeton University Press, 1976), 41–42; "The 'Face to Face' Interview," in *C. G. Jung Speaking*, ed. William McGuire and R.F.C. Hull (Princeton, N.J.: Princeton University Press, 1977), 434–35. Sonu Shamdasani coined the term "Solar Phallus Man" in his "A Woman Called Frank," *Spring* 50 (1990): 40. The first challenge to Jung's assumption that this patient could

More important, Jung further uses this example as evidence of the distinctively Jungian version of independent invention: through heredity rather than through experience. Independent invention as experience means that every society creates myths for itself. Independent invention as heredity means that every society — and individual — inherits myths. Of the Solar Phallus Man, Jung thus says,

> This observation [of independent invention] was not an isolated case: it was manifestly not [to be sure] a question of inherited ideas, but of an inborn disposition to produce parallel thought-formations, or rather of identical psychic structures common to all men, which I later called the archetypes of the collective unconscious.[31]

For Tylor, Frazer, and Freud, for example, the similarities among myths stem from independent invention through experience. For Tylor, everyone is born with a need to explain the world, but the explanations themselves are not innate. Where moderns invent science to explain baffling experiences, primitives invent myths. Because all primitives for Tylor experience the same perplexing phenomena, and because all primitives sensibly postulate gods to account for them, myths are bound to be similar. But each primitive society invents gods and in turn myths on its own, in response to the similar experiences of its members.

Likewise for Frazer, everyone is born with a need to eat, but the explanations of the source of food are not innate. Where moderns invent science to explain the source of food, primitives invent myths. Because all primitives experience hunger, and because all primitives postulate gods to account for the source of food, myths are bound to be similar. But each primitive society invents gods and in turn myths on its own, in response to the similar experiences of its members. Frazer provides the quintessential statement of independent invention through experience:

> [T]he resemblance which may be traced in this respect between the religions of the East and West is no more than what we commonly, though incorrectly, call a fortuitous co-

not previously have known of the idea of the sun's having a phallus is to be found in Henri F. Ellenberger, *The Discovery of the Unconscious* (New York: Basic Books, 1970), 743 n. 140. For a more recent challenge see Richard Noll, "Jung the Leontocephalus," *Spring* 53 (1992): 17–18, 48 n. 15; Noll, *The Jung Cult* (Princeton, N.J.: Princeton University Press, 1994), 181–84.

[31] Jung, *Symbols of Transformation*, 158.

incidence, the effect of similar causes acting alike on the similar constitution of the human mind in different countries and
under different skies.[32]

For Freud, everyone is born with an incestuous drive that
surfaces at age three to five. Everyone experiences that drive
individually. From one's forebears one inherits only the drive
itself, not their experiences of it. Because everyone in society
also experiences frustration in trying to satisfy that drive, myths
are invented as one indirect, disguised, compensatory outlet for
the blocked drive. Again, similar experiences are bound to give
rise to similar myths. In his classic application of Freud's theory, Otto Rank maintains that all hero myths, if not all myths,
even have a similar plot, yet it is still one invented by each
society on its own.[33]

   In contrast to Tylor, Frazer, and Freud alike, Jung contends
that everyone is born not merely with a need of some kind that
the invention of myth fulfills but with myths themselves. More
precisely, we are all born with the raw material of myths — but
material already elevated to the mythic level.

   For Tylor, the myth makers of each society start with the
impersonal forces of the physical world and proceed to hypothesize gods to account for those forces and to invent myths to
describe the actions of gods. For Frazer, the same is true. For
Freud, myth makers start with a child and the child's parents
and proceed to transform the child into a hero, the child's parents into royalty or nobility, and the conflicts between children
and parents into hero myths.

   For Jung, myth makers start with the archetypes themselves — for example, the archetype of the hero. The archetype
does not symbolize something else in turn but is itself the symbolized. In every society myth makers invent specific stories
that express those archetypes, but the myth makers are inventing only the manifestations of already mythic material. The figure Odysseus, for example, gets either invented or appropriated
to serve as a Greek expression of heroism. But heroism is not
itself invented, the way it is for Tylor, Frazer, and Freud. For
Jung, heroism, like divinity, constitutes so superhuman a status
that humans could not consciously have invented the idea.
They must, then, have inherited it. What are invented are the
myths expressing heroism. The myth of Odysseus is passed on

[32] Frazer, 448.
[33] See Otto Rank, *The Myth of the Birth of the Hero*, trans. F. Robbins and Smith Ely
Jelliffe (New York: Journal of Nervous and Mental Disease, 1914). Reprinted in
Rank et al., *In Quest of the Hero*, 3–86.

from generation to generation by acculturation, but the hero archetype that it expresses is passed on by heredity.

For Tylor, Frazer, and Freud, experience, even if it is of innate needs, provides the impetus for the creation of myths. For Freud, for example, the experience of one's parents' reaction to one's incestuous drives spurs the creation of myth. For Jung, by contrast, experience provides only the occasion for the expression of already mythical material. Rather than transforming parents into gods or heroes, myths merely articulate the archetypal experience of them *as* gods or heroes. The archetype of the Great Mother does not, as Freud would assume, result from the magnification of one's own mother but, on the contrary, expresses itself through her and thereby shapes one's experience of her. The archetype forms the core of one's "mother complex." Jung's insistence on the existence of innate fantasies that are projected onto the mother rather than derived from her is much like the emphasis of the Kleinian school of psychoanalysis.[34]

The Function of Myth

For Jung, myth serves many functions, not all of them psychological. But the prime function of myth is psychological: to reveal the unconscious. As already quoted, "Myths are original revelations of the preconscious psyche, involuntary statements about unconscious psychic happenings."[35] Myth does not inadvertently reveal the unconscious. Insofar as its creation is guided by the unconscious, it intentionally seeks to reveal the unconscious. What is "involuntary" is on the part of consciousness, the recipient of the revelation. For Jung, the unconscious seeks to communicate its presence to consciousness as clearly as possible. It does not, as for Freud, speak in code to elude detection. It simply speaks its own distinct language:

> My idea is that the dream does not conceal; we simply do not understand its language. For instance, if I quote to you a Latin or a Greek passage some of you will not understand it, but that is not because the text dissimulates or conceals; it is because you do not know Greek or Latin.[36]

[34] See, for example, Melanie Klein, *Narrative of a Child Analysis* (London: Hogarth, 1975 [1961]).
[35] Jung, "The Psychology of the Child Archetype," 154.
[36] Jung, "The Tavistock Lectures," 82–83. See also Jung, *Memories, Dreams, Reflections*, recorded and ed. Aniela Jaffé, trans. Richard and Clara Winston (New York: Vintage Books, 1962), 161–62.

The analyst is bilingual and thus able to translate the language of the unconscious into the language of consciousness, at least as far as the language of the unconscious is translatable. The lay person takes the language of the unconscious either as mere gibberish or as the language of consciousness. In the case of dreams, the lay inclination is to dismiss the content as gibberish; but in the case of myths, which are the product of conscious as well as unconscious elaboration, the lay inclination is to take the content at face value. By contrast, a Jungian analyst takes the content symbolically, recognizing mythic speech as a foreign language rather than the native language.

Myth for Jung functions not merely to announce the existence of the unconscious but actually to enable humans to experience it. Myth provides not only information about the unconscious but also entrée to it:

> The protean mythologem and the shimmering symbol express the processes of the psyche far more trenchantly and, in the end, far more clearly than the clearest concept; for the symbol not only conveys a visualization of the process but—and this is perhaps just as important—it also brings a re-experiencing of it, of that twilight which we can learn to understand only through inoffensive empathy, but which too much clarity only dispels.[37]

The telling of myths "causes these processes to come alive again and be recollected, thereby re-establishing the connection between conscious and unconscious."[38]

For all his scorn for those psychologically benighted theorists who take the subject matter of myth to be the external world, Jung himself often waxes romantic about the external function of myth. Myth for him links the inner world to the outer one by personifying the impersonal outer world:

> Primitive man is not much interested in objective explanations of the obvious, but he has an imperative need—or, rather, his unconscious psyche has an irresistible urge—to assimilate all outer sense experiences to inner, psychic events. It is not enough for the primitive to see the sun rise and set; this external observation must at the same time be a psychic god

[37] Jung, "Paracelsus as a Spiritual Phenomenon," in *Alchemical Studies*, Collected Works, vol. 13 (Princeton, N.J.: Princeton University Press, 1968), 162–63.
[38] Jung, "Background to the Psychology of Christian Alchemical Symbolism," in *Aion*, Collected Works, vol. 9, pt. 2, 2d ed. (Princeton, N.J.: Princeton University Press, 1968 [1959]), 180.

or hero who, in the last analysis, dwells nowhere except in the soul of man.[39]

Personifying the external world gives it meaning and relevance. The world is believed to operate responsively, in reaction to the purposes of gods, rather than mechanically. To cite Jung's favorite example,

The Pueblo Indians believe that they are the sons of Father Sun, and this belief endows their life with a perspective (and a goal) that goes far beyond their limited existence. . . . Their plight is infinitely more satisfactory than that of a man in our own civilization who knows that he is (and will remain) nothing more than an underdog with no inner meaning to his life.[40]

The function of myth here is not explanatory but existential. Myth makes humans feel at home in the world, even if it does so by explaining events in the world.

Modern myths for Jung are for the most part nonprojective. They presuppose the withdrawal of projections from the outer world, which is now experienced as impersonal and mechanical: "We have stripped all things of their mystery and *numinosity*; nothing is holy any longer."[41] Put another way, modern myths for Jung are nonreligious. They cannot do what religious myths used to do: "The religious myth is one of man's greatest and most significant achievements, giving him the security and inner strength not to be crushed by the monstrousness of the universe."[42] Myths for moderns do not function to connect the inner world with the outer world, which remains impersonal and mechanical. Instead, modern myths function to connect— better, to reconnect—moderns to the inner world. Modern myths still provide meaning, but that meaning now lies entirely within humans rather than also within the world. While Jung bemoans the effect of "de-deification" on the modern experience of the world, he recognizes the necessity of the process for the development of consciousness.

Yet the characterization of the external world as in fact meaningless really holds for only the earlier Jung. Once Jung, in collaboration with the physicist Wolfgang Pauli, proposes the

---

[39] Jung, "Archetypes of the Collective Unconscious," 6.
[40] Jung, "Approaching the Unconscious," in Jung et al., *Man and His Symbols* (New York: Dell Laurel Editions, 1968 [1964]), 76.
[41] Ibid., 84.
[42] Jung, *Symbols of Transformation*, 231.

concept of synchronicity, the world for him regains its meaning-fulness even without its personality. Indeed, that meaningfulness is now inherent in the world rather than imposed on it through projection: "Synchronistic experiences serve our turn here. They point to a latent meaning which is independent of [our] consciousness."[43] Meaningfulness for later Jung stems not from the existence of god, or personality, in the world but from the symmetry between human beings and the world. Rather than alien and indifferent to humans, the world proves to be akin to them — not because gods respond to human wishes or because human wishes directly affect the world but because human thoughts correspond to the nature of the world. As Jung says of his favorite example of synchronicity, that of a resistant patient who was describing a dream about a golden scarab when a scarab beetle appeared, "at the moment my patient was telling me her dream a real 'scarab' tried to get into the room, as if it had understood that it must play its mythological role as a sym-bol of rebirth."[44] Here the world seemingly responds to the pa-tient's dream, but more exactly the world merely, if fortuitously, matches the patient's dream. It is the patient's conscious atti-tude that is "out of sync" with the world.

Synchronicity is not itself myth. Synchronicity is the experi-ence of the world as meaningful. Myth would be an account of that experience. Synchronicity is an acausal nexus between the inner, human world and the outer, natural one. Myth is a causal account of events in the outer world, and the cause is divine rather than human. Since, however, the payoff of myth for Jung is not an account of the world but the feeling of at-homeness in it, synchronicity offers an existential benefit comparable with that offered by myth. With the concept of synchronicity Jung thus restores to the world a meaningfulness that the withdrawal of projections still demanded by Jung partly removes.[45]

For Jung, myth serves other functions as well. Parallels in myths to elements in a patient's dream can serve heuristically to suggest archetypal interpretations of that dream: "For this rea-son it is particularly important for me to know as much as

---

[43] Jung, *Letters*, ed. Gerhard Adler and Aniela Jaffé, trans. R.F.C. Hull, vol. 2 (Prince-ton, N.J.: Princeton University Press, 1976), 495.

[44] Ibid., 541.

[45] On synchronicity see above all Jung, "Synchronicity: An Acausal Principle" and "On Synchronicity," in *The Structure and Dynamics of the Psyche*, 417–519 and 520–31. Of the many books on Jung's concept of synchronicity, see esp. Robert Aziz, C. G. Jung's Psychology of Religion and Synchronicity (Albany: State University of New York Press, 1990); Roderick Main, introduction to *Jung on Synchronicity and the Paranormal*, ed. Main (London: Routledge, 1997), 17–36.

possible about primitive psychology, mythology, archaeology, and comparative religion, because these fields offer me invaluable analogies with which I can enrich the associations of my patients."[46]

Occasionally, Jung attributes to myth a social function: providing a guide for behavior. The lives of characters in myth become models to be emulated:

> For instance, the way in which a man should behave is given by an archetype. That is why primitives tell the stories they do. . . . Our ancestors have done so and so, and so shall you. Or such and such a hero has done so and so, and this is your model. Again, in the teachings of the Catholic Church there are several thousand saints. They show us what to do, they serve as models. They have their legends and that is Christian mythology.[47]

There are theorists of myth for whom the prime function of myth is the inculcation of correct behavior. In the classic statement by the anthropologist Bronislaw Malinowski, "The myth comes into play when rite, ceremony, or a social or moral rule demands justification, warrant of antiquity, reality, and sanctity."[48] Jung's occasional social functionalism runs less counter than askew to his focus on the individual rather than the social utility of myth.

Myths and Dreams

Every theorist assumes some analogue to myth. For Tylor, the analogue is science. Myth for him is the primitive counterpart to modern scientific theory, and it is by analogy to modern scientific theory that he elucidates myth. For Frazer, the analogue is also science, though less scientific theory than applied science. Myth for him is the primitive counterpart to modern technology, and it is by analogy to modern technology that he explicates myth.

For both Freud and Jung, dream provides the analogue. Like dreams, myths arise from the unconscious, serve to restore con-

[46] Jung, "The Aims of Psychotherapy," in *The Practice of Psychotherapy*, Collected Works, vol. 16, 2d ed. (New York: Pantheon Books, 1966 [1954]), 45.
[47] Jung, "The Houston Films," in *C. G. Jung Speaking*, 292–93.
[48] Bronislaw Malinowski, "Myth in Primitive Psychology" [1926], in *Magic, Science and Religion and Other Essays* (Garden City, NY: Doubleday Anchor Books, 1954), 107.

nection to the unconscious, and must be interpreted symbolically. For Jung, "The conclusion that the myth-makers thought
in much the same way as we still think in dreams is almost self-
evident."[49]

Yet Jung and Freud alike also recognize the differences between myths and dreams. Dreams are not usually projected
onto the world, whereas myths are: myths purport to be about
the world, not merely about oneself. Ordinarily, dreams are
dreamed by individuals, whereas myths are believed by a group.
Dreams are created anew by each dreamer; myths are passed on
from one generation to the next. Myths no less than dreams are
manifestations of the unconscious, but myths are consciously
created, even if their creators are in fact guided by the unconscious.

To be sure, Jung regularly declares that "the primitive mentality does not *invent* myths, it *experiences* them."[50] He even
states that

> We can see almost daily in our patients how mythical fanta-
> sies arise: they are not thought up, but present themselves as
> images or chains of ideas that force their way out of the un-
> conscious, and when they are recounted they often have the
> character of connected episodes resembling mythical dramas.
> That is how myths arise, and that is the reason why the fan-
> tasies from the unconscious have so much in common with
> primitive myths. . . . [M]yth is nothing but a projection from
> the unconscious and not a conscious invention at all.[51]

Doubtless Jung is overstating his point. Surely he means
merely that primitives, living so close to primordial unconsciousness, subject their myths to less conscious reworking than
moderns do to theirs in, say, writing a novel or a screenplay. He
cannot mean that primitive myths, let alone modern ones, involve no conscious reworking by their tellers.

Indeed, Jung considers myths a less pristine manifestation of
the unconscious than dreams: the "manifestation" of an archetype, "as we encounter it in dreams and visions, is much more
individual, less understandable, and more naïve than in myths,
for example."[52] A myth as heard or read is coherent, whereas a
dream as dreamed or remembered is not:

[49] Jung, *Symbols of Transformation*, 24.
[50] Jung, "The Psychology of the Child Archetype," 154.
[51] Jung, "On Psychic Energy," 38.
[52] Jung, "Archetypes of the Collective Unconscious," 5.

The medium in which [myths and dreams] are embedded is, in the former case [i.e., myths], an ordered and for the most part immediately understandable context, but in the latter case [i.e., dreams] a generally unintelligible, irrational, not to say delirious sequence of images which nonetheless does not lack a certain hidden coherence.[53]

Consequently, the interpretation of myths requires more reconstruction than the interpretation of dreams.

There is a final difference for Jung between myths and dreams. Where many dreams for Jung come from the personal unconscious, all myths emanate from the collective unconscious. Jung even identifies archetypal dreams by their mythological content:

The collective unconscious influences our dreams only occasionally, and whenever this happens, it produces strange and marvellous dreams remarkable for their beauty, or their demoniacal horror, or for their enigmatic wisdom — "big dreams," as certain primitives call them. . . . In many dreams and in certain psychoses we frequently come across archetypal material, i.e., ideas and associations whose exact equivalents can be found in mythology. From these parallels I have drawn the conclusion that there is a layer of the unconscious which functions in exactly the same way as the archaic psyche that produced the myths.[54]

In this respect, myths are closer to the unconscious than dreams.[55]

Myth as a Way of Thinking

While some theorists of myth are concerned with only the function or even only the origin of myth, most are concerned with the content of myth. Some theorists stress the similarities between the content of myth and the content of science. For Tylor and Frazer, for example, myth and science are explanations of

[53] Jung, "The Psychology of the Child Archetype," 153.
[54] Jung, "Analytical Psychology and Education," in *The Development of Personality*, Collected Works, vol. 17, 2d ed. (Princeton, N.J.: Princeton University Press, 1966 [1954]), 117–19.
[55] Jung even states that "archetypes were originally derived, not from dreams, but from mythological material, like fairy tales, legends, and religious forms of thought" (*Dream Analysis*, ed. William McGuire [Princeton, N.J.: Princeton University Press, 1983], 550).

the same physical events. Other theorists stress the distinctiveness of the content of myth. For the theologian Rudolf Bultmann and the philosopher Hans Jonas, for example, myth describes not the external world but the human experience of that world.[56]

A few theorists go beyond the distinctiveness of the content of myth to the distinctiveness of mythic thinking. Where for Tylor and Frazer myth involves the same processes of observation, inference, and generalization as science, for the philosopher Lucien Lévy-Bruhl mythic thinking is the opposite of scientific thinking. It involves the projection of mystical qualities onto the world and is oblivious to contradictions.[57] For the anthropologist Claude Lévi-Strauss, by contrast, mythic thinking is as rigorous as modern scientific thinking and is preoccupied with identifying logical contradictions. Mythic thinking here, too, involves projection, but what is projected onto the world are contradictions which myth then seeks to overcome.[58]

For both Freud and Jung, mythic thinking is dream thinking, but on the nature of dream thinking they differ. For Freud, myths, like dreams, represent a compromise between primary process thinking, which operates according to the pleasure principle, and secondary process thinking, which operates according to the reality principle. Male hero myths, for example, conventionally express Oedipal wishes, but in disguised form. Manifestly, the hero is a victim, a victim of fate and of his parents; latently, the hero is the culprit. Manifestly, the hero seeks power; latently, the hero seeks sex. Manifestly, the hero is the named historical or legendary figure; latently, the hero is the myth maker or any reader grabbed by the myth. The expression of Oedipal wishes in disguised form is a compromise between the pleasure principle, which seeks to vent the wishes outright, and the reality principle, which opposes the satisfaction of them altogether. While the wishes contained in myths evince the primary process thinking of the pleasure principle, the disguise that transforms the latent wishes into the manifest myth represents censorship rather than primary process thinking. What Freud calls "dream work" — the elaborate process by which the

---

[56] See Rudolf Bultmann, "New Testament and Mythology" [1941], in *Kerygma and Myth*, ed. Hans-Werner Bartsch, trans. Reginald H. Fuller (London: SPCK, 1953), vol. 1, 1–44; Hans Jonas, *Gnosis und spätantiker Geist*, 1st ed., vol. 2, pt. 1 (Göttingen: Vandenhoeck & Ruprecht, 1954).

[57] See Lucien Lévy-Bruhl, *How Natives Think*, trans. Lilian A. Clare (London: Allen & Unwin, 1926).

[58] See Claude Lévi-Strauss, *Introduction to a Science of Mythology*, trans. John and Doreen Weightman, 4 vols. (New York: Harper & Row, 1969–81).

latent meaning is converted into the manifest one — is not, then, an expression of primary process thinking but, on the contrary, the conversion of primary process thinking into secondary process thinking.[59]

For Jung, as for Freud, there are two kinds of thinking: "fantasy" thinking, which is like primary process thinking, and "directed," or "logical," thinking, which is like secondary process thinking. Where directed thinking is deliberate, organized, and purposeful, fantasy thinking is spontaneous, associative, and directionless: "What happens when we do not think directedly? Well, our thinking then lacks all leading ideas and the sense of direction emanating from them. We no longer compel our thoughts along a definite track, but let them float, sink or rise according to their specific gravity." Fantasy thinking "leads away from reality into fantasies of the past or future."[60] By contrast, directed thinking turns outward to the world. While Jung would certainly not say that fantasy thinking operates by the pleasure principle, he does say that directed thinking operates by the reality principle:

> To that extent, directed or logical thinking is reality-thinking, a thinking that is adapted to reality, by means of which we imitate the successiveness of objectively real things, so that the images inside our mind follow one another in the same strictly causal sequence as the events taking place outside it. We also call this "thinking with directed attention."[61]

For Jung, as for Freud, mythic thinking is fantasy thinking. But where for Freud myths, like most dreams, represent a compromise between primary and secondary process thinking because they represent a compromise between the pleasure principle and the reality principle, for Jung myths and dreams are the outright expression of fantasy thinking — the rough equivalent of primary process thinking. When, as noted, Jung declares that "myth is nothing but a projection from the unconscious and not a conscious invention at all," he is insisting that myth is an untampered manifestation of fantasy thinking.[62] Rather than a defense against the naked expression of the unconscious, as for Freud, myth for Jung *is* the naked expression of the uncon-

---

[59] See Sigmund Freud, *The Interpretation of Dreams*, trans. James Strachey (New York: Basic Books, 1955), chap. 6.
[60] Jung, *Symbols of Transformation*, 17.
[61] Ibid., 11.
[62] Jung, "On Psychic Energy," 38.

scious. Myths and dreams must still be interpreted, but because they are like hieroglyphics rather than because they are like a secret code. They await, even beckon, interpretation rather than stymie it. For Freud, the manifest level of a myth or a dream hides, if also reveals, the latent level, and the process of interpretation is the use of the manifest level to uncover the latent one masked by it. For Jung, the latent level *is* manifest — for those who have ears to hear. Consequently, myths and dreams for Jung evince a distinctive way of thinking, whereas myths and dreams for Freud evince a distinctive way of masking a distinctive way of thinking.

Freud and Jung agree that myths go beyond dreams to project fantasy thinking onto the world. Myths transform the outer world into an extension of the inner one. Mythic thinking is thus not merely a way of thinking but a way of thinking about the world — and in turn a way of experiencing the world:

> We move in a world of fantasies which, untroubled by the outward course of things, well up from an inner source to produce an ever-changing succession of plastic or phantasmal forms. . . . Everything was conceived anthropomorphically or theriomorphically, in the likeness of man or beast. . . . Thus there arose a picture of the universe which was completely removed from reality, but which corresponded exactly to man's subjective fantasies.[63]

More than a story, myth becomes a world view.

Insofar as Jung parallels myths with fantasies, myths would hardly be limited to "primitives." Yet insofar as Jung contrasts fantasy thinking to directed thinking, myths would seem to be largely primitive. For Jung, primitives are ruled entirely by fantasy thinking. Although scarcely absent among moderns, fantasy thinking has been supplemented and considerably supplanted by directed thinking, which is to be found above all in modern science. At the least, then, one would expect moderns to have far fewer myths than primitives. Certainly Jung accepts the conventional assumption of his day, summed up in Ernst Haeckel's Law of Recapitulation, that the biological development of the individual (ontogeny) duplicates that of the species (phylogeny): "The supposition that there may also be in psychology a correspondence between ontogenesis and phylogenesis therefore seems justified."[64] The child is therefore the

[63] Jung, *Symbols of Transformation*, 21.
[64] Ibid., 23.

counterpart to the primitive, and vice versa. The adult is the counterpart to the modern and vice versa. Just as the child is governed wholly by fantasy thinking and only the adult guided substantially by directed thinking, so the primitive is governed completely by fantasy thinking and only the modern guided significantly by directed thinking. Myths would therefore seem to be a predominantly primitive phenomenon. As Jung says, "These considerations tempt us to draw a parallel between the mythological thinking of ancient man and the similar thinking found in children, primitives, and in dreams."[65] Yet Jung argues forcefully that moderns as well as primitives have and even must have myths, though perhaps not to the same degree.

Kinds of Myths

Jung's key essay on myth is "The Psychology of the Child Archetype," where he uses myths of the child to set forth his overall theory of myth. Typically presenting his theory by distinguishing it from Freud's, Jung contends that the figure of the child in mythology symbolizes not, as for Freud, the actual child but the archetypal child. Further, Jung contends that the figure of the child points not merely back to childhood, as for Freud, but also on to adulthood. Because myths for Freud serve to fulfill the lingering childhood wishes of neurotic adults, they perpetuate a childhood state. Because myths for Jung serve to spur normal adults to recognize their unconscious and to integrate it with ego consciousness, they advance rather than retard psychological growth. As he says of myths of the child,

> One of the essential features of the child motif is its futurity. The child is potential future. . . . It is therefore not surprising that so many of the mythological saviours are child gods. This agrees exactly with our experience of the psychology of the individual, which shows that the "child" paves the way for a future change of personality. In the individuation process, it anticipates the figure that comes from the synthesis of conscious and unconscious elements in the personality.[66]

The child somehow symbolizes a specific archetype on the one hand and, even more, the whole personality in its development from primordial unconscious to ego consciousness to self

---

[65] Ibid., 22–23.
[66] Jung, "The Psychology of the Child Archetype," 164.

on the other. Thus the mythic child is less human than divine. While remaining literally a child, the mythic child symbolizes the lifelong process of psychological maturation. Child myths depict children as both youngsters and future adults. The child is truly father to the man.

By definition, theories of myth purport to cover all kinds of myths. In practice, few do. At the least, every theory is best suited to a particular kind of myth. The subject matter determines the suitability. For example, Frazer's theory, which assumes the symbolic subject matter of the chief myths to be the course of vegetation, best fits myths that literally describe the death and rebirth of gods. Tylor's wider-ranging theory, according to which the subject matter of myth is the cause of any event in the physical world, still fits only myths that literally describe the decisions of gods to bring about events in the physical world. The theory of the historian of religions Mircea Eliade, for whom the subject matter of myth is the legacy of the past actions of gods or heroes, fits only myths about the past, and really only myths about the introduction in the hoary past of cultural and natural phenomena that still exist today—for example, marriage and thunder.[67]

Freudian and Jungian theories best fit hero myths, for the subject matter of myth for both is striving and accomplishment. For both, heroism can evince itself at varying stages of psychological development. For Freudians, the hero can, like Oedipus, be the stereotypical rebel against the tyrannical father. Here the hero symbolizes the adult still neurotically tied to the Oedipal stage of development.[68] But the Freudian hero can also, like Moses vis-à-vis God, be the heir of the father, identifying himself with the father and thereby forging psychological maturity.[69] Alternatively, myths for Freudians can go back to pre-Oedipal states. The Freudian hero can even be the creator god himself, thereby accomplishing the same feat as the female: giving birth.[70]

Hero myths for Jungians begin not even with creation but with the state prior to creation, and they carry the process of psychological development all the way forward from the prenatal state to the state beyond the development of ego consciousness, which is the classic Freudian end. In Jungian terms, myths

---

[67] See Mircea Eliade, *The Sacred and the Profane*, trans. Willard R. Trask (New York: Harcourt, Brace, 1959), chap. 2.
[68] See Rank, *The Myth of the Birth of the Hero*.
[69] See Jacob A. Arlow, "Ego Psychology and the Study of Mythology," *Journal of the American Psychoanalytic Association* 9 (1961): 371–93.
[70] See Alan Dundes, "Earth-Diver: Creation of the Mythopoeic Male," *American Anthropologist* 64 (1962): 1032–51.

deal with the second, distinctively Jungian half of life as well as with the first, Freudian half. The key psychological feat for Freudians is the establishment of independence of one's parents. Jungians, too, seek to liberate their patients from their parents, but for them the key feat of the first half of life is the establishment of a measure of independence from the unconscious. The feat of the second half is, almost paradoxically, the restoration of contact with the unconscious. In Freudian myths the hero, who can be divine or human, is the son who either defeats his father or, better, reconciles himself with his father. In Jungian myths the hero, who can similarly be divine or human, is ego consciousness, which in the first half of life must defeat the unconscious out of which it has emerged and which in the second half of life must return to the unconscious and reconcile itself with it. The classic Jungian hero, no less than the classic Freudian one, is male, but his conventional nemesis is the mother rather than the father. The subject matter of hero myths for Jungians is realms of the mind rather than members of the family, but relations between those realms are mythically depicted in familial terms: ego consciousness is the son and the unconscious the Great Mother, herself most often depicted as a dragon. Like Freudians, Jungians subsume creation myths under hero myths by making creation itself a heroic act, which symbolizes the birth not of the external world but of ego consciousness: "Now we know that cosmogonic myths are, at bottom, symbols for the coming of consciousness."[71]

Myths of the child, of the hero, and of creation are group myths, as myths for Jung have traditionally been. But the decline of religion has obliged moderns to seek their own, private myths. Jung had the creativity to forge—or to find—his own myth, and he announces at the outset of his autobiography, *Memories, Dreams, Reflections*, that he will proceed to "tell my personal myth,"[72] which refers either to his whole life or, more narrowly, to his speculations about life after death. Far from an inferior alternative to a group myth, a personal myth for Jung is the ideal, for it alone is geared to the uniqueness of one's psyche. A personal myth seeks to nurture those particular aspects of one's personality that have been neglected. At times, Jung even defines myth as personal: "Myth is more individual and expresses life more precisely than does science. Science works with concepts of averages which are far too general to

---

[71] Jung, "The Fish in Alchemy," in *Aion*, 148.
[72] Jung, *Memories, Dreams, Reflections*, 3.

do justice to the subjective variety of an individual life."[73] Jung's emphasis here on the individuality of myths "balances" — to use the prized Jungian epithet — his emphasis elsewhere on the similarity, even identity, of myths worldwide.

Myths and Primitives

For Jung, myths serve primarily to open adults up to their unconscious, from which, in the course of growing up, they have ineluctably become severed. Myths "compensate or correct, in a meaningful manner, the inevitable one-sidednesses and extravagances of the conscious mind."[74] But for Jung it is only the ego consciousness of moderns that is sufficiently developed to be severed from the unconscious. As he says, "Since the differentiated consciousness of civilized man has been granted an effective instrument for the practical realization of its contents through the dynamics of his will, there is all the more danger, the more he trains his will, of his getting lost in one-sidedness and deviating further and further from the laws and roots of his being."[75] In that case it is hard to see how myths "compensate" primitives, who for Jung hover so close to unconsciousness that their ego consciousness has barely begun to develop:

> Primitive mentality differs from the civilized chiefly in that the conscious mind is far less developed in scope and intensity. Functions such as thinking, willing, etc. are not yet differentiated; they are pre-conscious, and in the case of thinking, for instance, this shows itself in the circumstances that the primitive does not think *consciously*, but that thoughts appear. . . . Moreover, he is incapable of any conscious effort of will.[76]

The primitive mind for Jung is really no less one-sided than the modern one. It is simply one-sidedly unconscious rather than, like the modern one, one-sidedly conscious.

Nevertheless, Jung considers myths to be as indispensable for primitives as for moderns. Indeed, he is referring to primitives, if not to them alone, when, as quoted, he states that "myths are original revelations of the preconscious psyche, involuntary

[73] Ibid.
[74] Jung, "The Psychology of the Child Archetype," 162.
[75] Ibid., 162–63.
[76] Ibid., 153.

statements about unconscious psychic happenings, and anything but allegories of physical processes."[77] Primitives may live far closer to the unconscious than moderns do, but even the primitive unconscious is still unconscious and still seeks to reveal itself to primitives. Just as primitives as well as moderns have dreams, so primitives as well as moderns have myths. Surely Jung's linkage of mythic thinking to fantasy thinking to children's thinking to primitive thinking dictates that primitives will have at least as many myths as moderns — and may well rely on them even more.

Jung assumes that primitives interpret their myths literally, as referring to the outer world. But he still maintains that primitive myths function to reveal to primitives their own inner world. The myths merely do so circuitously, via projection onto the outer world:

All the mythologized processes of nature, such as summer and winter, the phases of the moon, the rainy seasons, and so forth, are in no sense allegories of these objective [i.e., external] occurrences; rather they are symbolic expressions of the inner, unconscious drama of the psyche which becomes accessible to man's consciousness by way of projection — that is, mirrored in the events of nature.[78]

Despite Jung's own association of mythic with childish with primitive, he castigates Freudians for making the same associations:

The first attempts at myth-making can, of course, be observed in children, whose games of make-believe often contain historical echoes. But one must certainly put a large question-mark after the [Freudian] assertion that that myths spring from the "infantile" psychic life of the race. . . . [T]he myth-making and myth-inhabiting man was a grown reality and not a four-year-old child. Myth is certainly not an infantile phantasm, but one of the most important requisites of primitive life.[79]

Since Jung's own linkage of myths to children to primitives does not denigrate myths, the supposed Freudian denigration must stem from more than the linkage.

[77] Ibid., 154.
[78] Jung, "Archetypes of the Collective Unconscious," 6.
[79] Jung, *Symbols of Transformation*, 24–25.

Myths and Moderns

Moderns for Jung have largely withdrawn their forebears' projections from the physical world. Moderns experience the world itself, largely unfiltered by their unconscious. That world is natural rather than supernatural. It is the world explained by science. In "de-deifying" the world, moderns have demythicized it: "Only in the following centuries, with the growth of natural science, was the projection withdrawn from matter and entirely abolished together with the psyche. . . . Nobody, it is true, any longer endows matter with mythological properties."[80] Moderns still project, but their projections are chiefly onto other human beings: "Projection is now confined to personal and social relationships."[81]

Yet Jung hardly denies the continued existence of myths. Myths in modernity can take several forms. Minimally, there is the invocation of traditional myths by artists:

Dante decks out his experience in all the imagery of heaven, purgatory, and hell; Goethe brings in the Blocksberg and the Greek underworld; Wagner needs the whole corpus of Nordic myth, including the Parsifal saga; Nietzsche resorts to the hieratic style of the bard and legendary seer; Blake presses into his service the phantasmagoric world of India, the Old Testament, and the Apocalypse.[82]

Artists often update traditional myths by recasting them in modern garb:

Mythological motifs frequently appear, but clothed in modern dress; for instance, instead of the eagle of Zeus, or the great roc, there is an airplane; the fight with the dragon is a railway smash; the dragon-slaying hero is an operatic tenor; the Earth Mother is a stout lady selling vegetables; the Pluto who abducts Persephone is a reckless chauffeur, and so on.[83]

More significant for Jung has been the outright revival of traditional myth, of which his grandest example is the revival of the worship of Wotan in twentieth-century Germany:

---

[80] Jung, "The Philosophical Tree," in *Alchemical Studies*, 300.
[81] Ibid.
[82] Jung, "Psychology and Literature," 97.
[83] Ibid.

But what is more than curious—indeed, piquant to a degree—is that an ancient god of storm and frenzy, the long quiescent Wotan, should awake, like an extinct volcano, to new activity, in a civilized country that had long been supposed to have outgrown the Middle Ages.[84]

Wotan was considered no mere literary metaphor but a real god "out there," worshiped with the slaughtering of sheep. Here myth is lived out, not merely interpreted.

Still more significant for Jung has been the creation of new, distinctively modern myths, of which his best example is the belief in flying saucers. Because flying saucers are a technologically advanced phenomenon, they fit the modern scientific self-image and make for an ideal kind of modern myth: "It is characteristic of our time that the archetype . . . should now take the form of an object, a technological construction, in order to avoid the odiousness of mythological personification. Anything that looks technological goes down without difficulty with modern man."[85] Even though the belief in flying saucers is not tied to a story, the belief still qualifies as a myth, for it is a belief in something superhuman in the external world, and it is a widely shared belief.

What interests Jung about the belief in flying saucers is what interests him about myths generally: the psychology of their adherents. At the same time, Jung appreciates that the myth of flying saucers, like earlier myths, serves not only psychological needs but also existential ones. The myth personifies the external world and thereby makes it akin to the human one. About the possible reality of flying saucers, Jung remains typically open-minded.[86] The reality of them would not dissolve the psychology of them, for they already belong to what he calls "the reality of the psyche." The outer reality of them would constitute synchronicity.

For some theorists, such as Tylor and Frazer, myth is an exclusively primitive phenomenon. Whenever found among moderns, it is either a mere "survival" or an atavism. For other theorists, such as Bultmann, myth can be made acceptable to

---

[84] Jung, "Wotan," in *Civilization in Transition*, Collected Works, vol. 10, 2d ed. (Princeton, N.J.: Princeton University Press, 1970 [1964]), 180. For a less negative, more balanced view of Wotan, who turns out to have traditionally been a god of life and not just a god of death, see Margrit Burri, "Repression, Falsification, and Bedeviling of Germanic Mythology," trans. Wolfgang Giegerich, *Spring* (1978): 88–104. I thank John Beebe for this reference.

[85] Jung, "Flying Saucers," in *Civilization in Transition*, 328.

[86] See Jung, "Flying Saucers," 413–17; "Letter to Keyhoe," in *The Symbolic Life*, 632.

moderns. For still other theorists, notably Eliade and Campbell, myth is panhuman. While less insistent on this point than Eliade or Campbell, Jung certainly considers myth to be a continuing phenomenon, even if not quite a panhuman one:

> Has mankind ever really got away from myths? . . . One could almost say that if all the world's traditions were cut off at a single blow, the whole of mythology and the whole history of religion would start all over again with the next generation. Only a very few individuals succeed in throwing off mythology in epochs of exceptional intellectual exuberance — the masses never.[87]

Earlier Psychological Interpretations of Myth

For Jung, the recognition of the psychological nature of myth comes gradually. The stages are not simply primitive and modern. While Jung takes for granted that primitives are oblivious to the psychological meaning of their myths, he points to a "philosophical interpretation of myths . . . already grown up among the Stoics, which today we should not hesitate to describe as psychological."[88] Jung sees the continuation of that tradition in the Church Fathers and down into the medieval and Renaissance periods. The tradition that he traces from Gnosticism to alchemy to modern science involves ever more psychological self-consciousness, though he fluctuates in the degree of self-consciousness he finds. At his most charitable, he is prepared to say that

> Since all cognition is akin to recognition, it should not come as a surprise to find that what I have described as a gradual process of development had already been anticipated, and more or less prefigured, at the beginning of our era. . . . The alchemists . . . in their own way knew more about the nature of the individuation process than we moderns do. . . . The same knowledge, formulated differently to suit the age they lived in, was possessed by the Gnostics. The idea of an unconscious was not unknown to them.[89]

---

[87] Jung, *Symbols of Transformation*, 25.
[88] Jung, "The Personification of the Opposites," in *Mysterium Coniunctionis*, Collected Works, vol. 14, 2d ed. (Princeton, N.J.: Princeton University Press, 1970 [1963]), 142.
[89] Jung, "Gnostic Symbols of the Self," in *Aion*, 184, 190. On Gnostic self-conscious-

More typically, Jung traces a sharp progression in self-consciousness from the Gnostics to, especially, the later alchemists:

The older alchemists were still so unconscious of the psychological implications of the opus that they understood their own symbols as mere allegories — or semiotically — as secret names for chemical combinations, thus stripping mythology, of which they made such copious use, of its true meaning and using only its terminology. Later this was to change, and already in the fourteenth century it began to dawn on them that the lapis was more than a chemical compound.[90]

Myth and Religion

There are theorists of myth who subsume myth under religion. For Tylor and Frazer, for example, all myths are religious myths. For them, a secular myth would be a contradiction in terms. For other theorists, such as Eliade, there can be secular as well as religious myths. For Eliade, myths prior to modernity are religious myths; modern myths are secular ones. Jung is here like Eliade.

For Jung, myth and religion have traditionally worked in tandem. Religion has preserved myth, and myth has sustained religion. The heart of religion for Jung is neither belief nor practice but experience, and myth provides the best entrée to the experience of God, which means to the unconscious. Jung thus praises early Christianity for both adopting and adapting various pre-Christian myths: "The fact that the myth [of the phoenix] was assimilated into Christianity by interpretation is proof, first of all, of the myth's vitality; but it also proves the vitality of Christianity, which was able to interpret and assimilate so many myths." A religion that fails to reinterpret its myths is dead. The "spiritual vitality" of a religion "depends on the continuity of myth, and this can be preserved only if each age translates the myth into its own language and makes it an essential content of its view of the world."[91]

In contrast to early Christianity, modern Christianity, according to Jung, has failed to update its myths. That failure is an aspect of its overall failure to reinvigorate itself. Sometimes

ness see the introduction to my edited The Gnostic Jung (Princeton, N.J.: Princeton University Press; London: Routledge, 1992), 33–35.
[90] Jung, "The Conjunction," in Mysterium Coniunctionis, 475.
[91] Jung, "Rex and Regina," in Mysterium Coniunctionis, 336 n. 297.

Jung says that modern Christianity has gone astray by severing belief from experience and trying in vain to rely on sheer belief. Jung's objection here is twofold: that belief without experience is empty and that the belief is often incompatible with modern knowledge. Other times Jung says that modern Christianity has gone awry in seeking to meet the challenge of modern knowledge by turning belief into faith severed from knowledge. Jung's objection here is that even faith requires experience to sustain itself. As Jung sums up his criticisms of both options:

> The Churches stand for traditional and collective convictions which in the case of many of their adherents are no longer based on their own inner experience but on *unreflecting belief*, which is notoriously apt to disappear as soon as one begins thinking about it. The content of belief then comes into collision with knowledge, and it often turns out that the irrationality of the former is no match for the ratiocinations of the latter. Belief is no adequate substitute for inner experience, and where this is absent even a strong faith which came miraculously as a gift of grace may depart equally miraculously.[92]

While these particular criticisms do not involve myth, still other times Jung says that modern Christianity has erred in its attempt to update itself by eliminating myth — as if myth were a gangrenous limb that must be amputated to save the patient. Jung is here referring to Bultmann's "demythologization" of the New Testament. Jung's first objection is that the supposed incompatibility of myth with modern knowledge stems from a false, literal interpretation of myth: "Theology [wrongly] rejects any tendency to take the assertions of its earliest records as written myths and, accordingly, to understand them symbolically."[93] Jung's second objection is that myth is indispensable to experience and thereby to religion:

> Indeed, it is the theologians themselves who have recently made the attempt — no doubt as a concession to "knowledge" — to "demythologize" the object of their faith while drawing the line [between myth and religion] quite arbitrarily at the crucial points. But to the critical intellect it is only too obvious that myth is an integral component of all religions

---

[92] Jung, "The Undiscovered Self," in *Civilization in Transition*, 265.
[93] Ibid., 285.

and therefore cannot be excluded from the assertions of faith without injuring them.[94]

Here Christianity has sought to overcome the opposition between faith and knowledge by discarding belief at odds with knowledge. But in eliminating myth, it has eliminated experience as well.

Finally, at yet other times Jung says that modern Christianity has rightly turned to myth to resurrect itself but has still failed to reinterpret myth symbolically and thereby to make it palatable to moderns:

[R]eligions have long turned to myths for help. . . . But you cannot, artificially and with an effort of will, believe the statements of myth if you have not previously been gripped by them. If you are honest, you will doubt the truth of the myth because our present-day consciousness has no means of understanding it. Historical and scientific criteria do not lend themselves to a recognition of mythological truth; it can be grasped only by the intuitions of faith or by psychology.[95]

Ironically, Bultmann, despite the misleading term "demythologization," strives to do the same as Jung: not to eliminate myth from the New Testament but, on the contrary, to reinterpret myth symbolically in order to make it acceptable to moderns. And Bultmann, also like Jung, contends that the true meaning of the New Testament has always been symbolic, though Bultmann's symbolic interpretation is existential rather than psychological.

By Christian mythology, Jung means the life of Christ. Read literally, the Gospels are incompatible with both history and science. But if, says Jung, "the statement that Christ rose from the dead is to be understood not literally but symbolically, then it is capable of various interpretations that do not conflict with knowledge and do not impair the meaning of the statement."[96] Read psychologically, the life of Christ becomes a symbol of the archetypal journey of the hero from primordial unconscious (birth) to ego consciousness (adulthood) to return to the unconscious (crucifixion) to reemergence from it to form the self (resurrection). Understood symbolically, Christ serves as a model for Christians seeking to cultivate their relation to the self.

[94] Ibid.
[95] Jung, "The Conjunction," 528.
[96] Jung, "The Undiscovered Self," 266.

Without denying the historicity of Christ, Jung maintains that Christ can be inspirational even as a mythical hero. Indeed, for Jung the prime appeal of Christ's life has always been psychological:

> Christ lived a concrete, personal, and unique life which, in all essential features, had at the same time an archetypal character. This character can be recognized from the numerous connections of the biographical details with worldwide mythmotifs. . . . The life of Christ is no exception in that not a few of the great figures of history have realized, more or less clearly, the archetype of the hero's life with its characteristic changes of fortune. . . . Since the life of Christ is archetypal to a high degree, it represents to just that degree the life of the archetype. But since the archetype is the unconscious precondition of every human life, its life, when revealed, also reveals the hidden, unconscious ground-life of every individual.[97]

Jung argues, further, that the Gospels themselves present a combined mythical and historical figure:

> In the gospels themselves factual reports, legends, and myths are woven into a whole. This is precisely what constitutes the meaning of the gospels, and they would immediately lose their character of wholeness if one tried to separate the individual from the archetypal with a critical scalpel.[98]

Just like Bultmann, to whom he is in fact so close, Jung thus claims to be explicating the symbolic meaning intended by the Gospels all along. For both, the obstacles that modernity poses to a literal rendition of Christ's life become an opportunity to make clear for the first time the meaning intended from the start. A virtue is truly made out of a necessity.

Jung never faults Christian mythology itself for its outdatedness, only its interpreters: "Our myth has become mute, and gives no answers. The fault lies not in it as it is set down in the Scriptures, but solely in us, who have not developed it further,

---

[97] Jung, "Psychology and Religion," in *Psychology and Religion: West and East*, Collected Works, vol. 11, 2d ed. (Princeton, N.J.: Princeton University Press, 1969 [1958]), 88–89. Like a child in myth, Christ symbolizes at once an archetype—the self—and the developing ego. On Christ as a symbol of the self see Jung, "Christ, a Symbol of the Self," in *Aion*, chap. 5. On Christ as a symbol of the ego in relation to the self see Edward F. Edinger, *Ego and Archetype* (Baltimore: Penguin, 1973 [1972]), chap. 5.

[98] Jung, "Psychology and Religion," 88.

who, rather, have suppressed any such attempts."[99] Jung does lambaste mainstream Christianity for its one-sidedness — above all, for its failure to give sufficient credence to evil: "The old question posed by the Gnostics, 'Whence comes evil?' has been given no answer by the Christian world."[100] But this limitation is a separate issue. Even if one-sided, Christian mythology can still be interpreted anew by each generation. In fact, Jung hopes that modern Christians will not only psychologize their mythology but also broaden it to include evil, as epitomized by nuclear war.

Yet for all Jung's efforts to make Christianity acceptable to moderns by psychologizing it, he recognizes that religion has simply ceased to be an option for many moderns, surely including to some degree Jung himself.[101] Nonreligious moderns must either adopt secular myths such as the myth of flying saucers or else forge their own, personal myths, as Jung himself was able to do.

Terms

Jung uses various terms which must be distinguished: instinct, archetype, image, symbol, sign, allegory, "mythological motif," "mythologem," and myth. Instincts and archetypes are related but distinct. An instinct is a reflex action. An archetype is the emotional and intellectual significance of that action:

> What we properly call instincts are physiological urges, and are perceived by the senses. But at the same time, they also manifest themselves in fantasies and often reveal their presence only by symbolic images. These manifestations are what I call the archetypes. . . . The unconscious . . . seems to be

---

[99] Jung, *Memories, Dreams, Reflections*, 332.
[100] Ibid.
[101] Jung's ambiguous position on Christianity has spawned contrary interpretations. Some maintain that Jung seeks to replace dying Christianity with psychology: see esp. Raymond Hostie, *Religion and the Psychology of Jung*, trans. G. R. Lamb (New York: Sheed and Ward, 1957); Howard L. Philp, *Jung and the Problem of Evil* (London: Rockliff, 1958). Others contend that Jung seeks to resurrect Christianity through psychology: see esp. Hans Schaer, *Religion and the Cure of Souls in Jung's Psychology*, trans. R.F.C. Hull (New York: Pantheon, 1950); David Cox, *Jung and Saint Paul* (London: Longmans, Green; New York: Association Press, 1959); Victor White, *God and the Unconscious* (London: Collins, 1952); Murray Stein, *Jung's Treatment of Christianity* (Chicago: Chiron, 1985). Still others argue for a middle ground: see esp. Peter Homans, *Jung in Context* (Chicago: University of Chicago Press, 1979).

guided chiefly by instinctive trends, represented by corresponding thought forms — that is, by the archetypes.[102]

Shutting one's eyes upon looking at the sun is clearly instinctual. Even feeling terrified or fascinated by the sight is still instinctual. By contrast, experiencing the sun as a god is archetypal. An archetypal experience is not any emotional event but only an overwhelming one, the extraordinariness of which stems exactly from the power of the archetype encountered through projection. Many, though certainly not all, phenomena experienced archetypally are experienced as gods. The key evidence of the modern withdrawal of projections from the physical world is the experience of the world as natural rather than divine.

Despite Jung's somewhat misleading synonym "primordial images," archetypes are not themselves pictures but rather the inclination to form them in typical ways. Symbols are the actual pictures formed. Symbols are the means by which archetypes, themselves unconscious, communicate to consciousness. Each archetype requires an infinite number of symbols — as many symbols as there are dimensions of the archetype. Archetypes are transmitted by heredity; symbols, by acculturation. Archetypes are the same universally; symbols vary from culture to culture:

> Again and again I encounter the mistaken notion that an archetype is determined in regard to its content, in other words that it is a kind of unconscious idea. . . . It is necessary to point out once more that archetypes are not determined as regards their content, but only as regards their form and then only to a very limited degree. . . . Its form . . . might perhaps be compared to the axial system of a crystal, which, as it were, preforms the crystalline structure in the mother liquid, although it has no material existence of its own. This first appears according to the specific way in which the ions and molecules aggregate. The archetype in itself is empty and purely formal, nothing but a *facultas praeformandi*, a possibility of representation which is given *a priori*. The [symbolic] representations themselves are not inherited, only the forms.[103]

[102] Jung, "Approaching the Unconscious," 58, 67.
[103] Jung, "Psychological Aspects of the Mother Archetype," in *The Archetypes and the Collective Unconscious*, 79.

For example, a specific savior like Buddha would be a symbol. The archetype manifested through the Buddha would be the category saviors. Through the Buddha, Buddhists would encounter those aspects of the savior archetype captured by the symbol. Other saviors like Jesus would capture other aspects of the savior archetype. Any symbol, however rich, is capable of capturing only a limited number of aspects of its archetype. Which symbol is employed by the archetype depends on which aspects of the archetype the subject, whether individual or group, needs to cultivate.

An archetype for Jung is not the symbol of something else but the symbolized itself. The archetype of the child, for example, refers not to any actual children but to itself. The archetype is irreducible. An actual child can symbolize the child archetype but not vice versa:

It may not be superfluous to point out that lay prejudice is always inclined to identify the child motif [i.e., archetype] with the concrete experience "child," as though the real child were the cause and pre-condition of the existence of the child motif. In psychological reality, however, the empirical idea "child" is only the means (and not the only one) by which to express a psychic fact that cannot be formulated more exactly. Hence by the same token the mythological idea of the child is emphatically not a copy of the empirical child but a *symbol* clearly recognizable as such: it is a wonder-child, a divine child, begotten, born, and brought up in quite extraordinary circumstances, and not — this is the point — a human child.[104]

Identifying archetypes is not easy. First, the number of archetypes is unlimited: "There are as many archetypes as there are typical situations in life."[105] Second, archetypes can take the most disparate of forms: natural objects like the moon and fire, artifacts like rings and weapons, human beings like mothers and children, superhuman figures like gods and witches, legendary figures like heroes and monsters, abstractions like circles and squares, ideas like the anima and the self, and events like birth and death. Third, the same entity can be both a symbol and an archetype. For example, Zeus may be a clear-cut symbol, but sky gods can be both an archetype and a set of symbols

---

[104] Jung, "The Psychology of the Child Archetype," 161 n. 21.
[105] Jung, "The Concept of the Collective Unconscious," 48.

in turn of the god archetype, which itself can be both an archetype and a set of symbols of the self archetype.

Jung vigorously distinguishes symbols from mere "signs" or "allegories" — terms he uses interchangeably. A sign or allegory has only a single meaning. A symbol has multiple meanings. The meaning of a sign or allegory is denotative. The meaning of a symbol is connotative. The meaning of a sign or allegory is conscious. The deepest meaning of a symbol is unconscious. A sign or allegory is consciously chosen to convey its meaning. A symbol may arise spontaneously, as in dreams, and even a conscious choice is directed by the unconscious. A sign or allegory conveys fully the signified or allegorized, so that to know the meaning of a sign or allegory is to know the complete meaning of the signified or allegorized. A symbol conveys only a portion of what it symbolizes, so that to know the meaning of a symbol is to gain only a glimpse of the symbolized.

Jung never makes clear what accounts for the limitations of symbols. Seemingly, the finiteness of any symbol, however rich, restricts the number of aspects of an archetype it can convey. For example, Homer's Helen can convey only the erotic and seductive aspects of the anima archetype; the Virgin Mary, only the motherly, compassionate ones. Alternatively, the limits may lie in the ability of human beings to decipher the array of meanings of any symbol. Perhaps for Jung both limitations hold.

Presumably, the Freudian unconscious expresses itself through signs and allegories because its contents were originally conscious and are therefore in principle wholly retrievable. But when Jung says that "an allegory is a paraphrase of a conscious content, whereas a symbol is the best possible expression for an unconscious content whose nature can only be guessed, because it is still unknown," he is seemingly excluding Freudian meanings as allegories and is confining allegories to the signified of, say, nature mythology.[106] As he states, "Symbols are not signs or allegories for something known; they seek rather to express something that is little known or completely unknown."[107] But by "unknown" Jung doubtless means forever, not just presently, unknown. Therefore only the Jungian unconscious expresses itself through symbols because only its contents are inherently unconscious and so cannot be directly accessed by conscious effort.

Jung also calls archetypes "mythological motifs" and "my-

---

[106] Jung, "Archetypes of the Collective Unconscious," 6 n. 10.
[107] Jung, *Symbols of Transformation*, 222.

thologems." But sometimes he applies these terms to the symbols expressing archetypes. Still other times he applies the terms neither to archetypes nor to symbols but to parts of myths — for example, to the virgin birth portion of the myth of Jesus. The terms never refer to whole myths. As he says, "These products [i.e., mythologems] are never (or at least very seldom) myths with a definite form, but rather mythological components."[108]

Myths are more than archetypes. They are stories that, read symbolically, contain archetypes. Archetypes are "mythological components which, because of their typical nature, we can call 'motifs,' 'primordial images,' types or — as I have named them — archetypes."[109] An archetype is not merely a motif within a myth but a motif within many myths. A motif found in only one myth would not be an archetype. Any myth ordinarily contains multiple archetypes, though one archetype is often dominant. The plot of myth is not only the manifestation of one or more archetypes but also the development of them and their interaction. On the literal level the subject of a myth is a particular like Zeus. On the symbolic level the subject is the archetype symbolized by Zeus — for example, sky gods. The activities of Zeus symbolize the development of the archetype of the sky god and its relationship to other archetypes, as symbolized by Hera and other gods.

Developments in Jungian Theory

The most influential Jungian theorists of myth after the master himself have been Erich Neumann (1905–1960), Marie-Louise von Franz (1915–), and James Hillman (1926–). One might consider adding Joseph Campbell (1904–1987), the greatest popularizer of myth of this century, but Campbell is too eclectic to qualify as a full-fledged Jungian. Neumann systematizes the developmental, or evolutionary, aspect of Jungian theory. Jung himself certainly correlates myths with stages of psychological development, but Neumann works out the stages, beginning with the "uroboric" state of sheer unconsciousness and proceeding to the incipient emergence of the ego out of the unconscious, the development of an independent ego consciousness, and the eventual return of the ego to the unconscious to create the self. Like Jung, Neumann characterizes the course of psychological development as one of continuing heroism. Neu-

---

[108] Jung, "The Psychology of the Child Archetype," 153.
[109] Ibid.

mann concentrates on heroism in the first half of life, both in *The Origins and History of Consciousness* (1949, tr. 1954), from which the selection here is taken, and even more in *The Great Mother* (1955), which indeed focuses on the primordial unconscious itself as the matrix of all subsequent development. Neumann's emphasis on heroism in the first half of life complements Campbell's devotion to heroism in the second half in *The Hero with a Thousand Faces* (1949).

Von Franz is best known for her many books on fairy tales — among them *An Introduction to the Psychology [or Interpretation] of Fairy Tales* (1970, rev. 1996), *A Psychological Interpretation of "The Golden Ass" of Apuleius* (1970, rev. 1980), *Problems of the Feminine in Fairytales* (1972), *Shadow and Evil in Fairy Tales* (1974, rev. 1995), *Individuation in Fairy Tales* (1977, rev. 1990), and *The Psychological Meaning of Redemption in Fairytales* (1980). But she is also the author of the fullest Jungian book on creation myths, *Patterns of Creativity Mirrored in Creation Myths* (1972, rev. 1995), from which the selection here is taken. For von Franz, creation myths symbolize the same process of the emergence and development of the ego out of the primordial unconscious as hero myths of the first half of life do for Neumann. But for her, creation myths are far more abstract and impersonal than hero myths since their literal subject matter is the birth of the whole world rather than of a single figure within it. No less than Neumann does von Franz deem the act of creation heroic, but she focuses on myths of creation of the cosmos itself. Rather than classifying stages in the process of creation like Neumann, she classifies means of creation — for example, creation by two figures instead of one. Like Neumann, von Franz stresses the difficulty of creation, which likewise represents the incipient ego's difficulty in breaking free of the unconscious. Myths that present creation as a long and arduous effort better fit the development of the psyche than those that depict it as a quick, effortless act.

By far the most radical development in the Jungian theory of myth has been the emergence of "archetypal" psychology, which in fact considers itself post-Jungian. The chief figure in this movement is Hillman, whose main theoretical works include *The Myth of Analysis* (1972); *Loose Ends* (1975); *Re-Visioning Psychology* (1975), from which the selection here is taken; *The Dream and the Underworld* (1979); *Puer Papers* (ed. 1979); *Archetypal Psychology* (1983); and (with Karl Kerényi) *Oedipus Variations* (1991). Another important figure in the movement is David Miller, perhaps best known for *The*

New Polytheism (1979). Archetypal psychology faults classical Jungian psychology on multiple grounds. By emphasizing the compensatory, therapeutic message of mythology, classical Jungian psychology purportedly reduces mythology to psychology and gods to concepts. In espousing a unified self (or "Self") as the ideal psychological authority, Jungian psychology supposedly projects onto psychology a Western, specifically monotheistic, more specifically Christian, even more specifically Protestant, outlook. The Western emphasis on progress is purportedly reflected in the primacy that Jungian psychology accords both hero myths and the ego, even in the ego's encounter with the unconscious: the encounter is intended to abet development. Finally, Jungian psychology is berated for placing archetypes in an unknowable realm distinct from the known realm of symbols.

As a corrective, Hillman and his followers advocate that psychology be viewed as irreducibly mythological. Myth is still to be interpreted psychologically, but psychology is itself to be interpreted mythologically. One grasps the psychological meaning of the myth of Saturn by imagining oneself to be the figure Saturn, not by translating Saturn's plight into clinical terms like depression. Moreover, the depressed Saturn represents a legitimate aspect of one's personality. Each god deserves its due. The psychological ideal should be pluralistic rather than monolithic — in mythological terms, polytheistic rather than monotheistic. Hillman takes his mythic cues from the Greeks rather than from the Bible, however simplistic his equation of Greece with polytheism and of the Bible with monotheism may be. Insisting that archetypes are to be found *in* symbols rather than outside them, Hillman espouses a relation to the gods in themselves and not to something beyond them. The ego becomes but one more archetype with its attendant kind of god, and it is the "soul" rather than the ego that experiences the archetypes through myths. Myth serves to open one up to the soul's own depths. The payoff is aesthetic rather than moral: one gains a sense of wonder and contemplation, not a guide to living. The most apposite myths for the archetypal school become those of the playful puer and of the receptive anima rather than those of the striving hero and of the fully integrated wise old man.

Robert A. Segal

Part 1. Jung on Myth

Chapter 1. Jung vis-à-vis Freud on Myth

(a) Jung's Freudian Interpretation of Myth

Jung here offers an orthodox Freudian analysis of myth in the course of analyzing the case of an eleven-year-old girl who had been treated by an assistant of his. While Jung's use of myth-
ological parallels to amplify the meaning of the girl's dreams might seem Jungian, the meaning Jung accords the parallels is Freudian. The long work in which the case appears, "The The-ory of Psychoanalysis," represents Jung's final attempt to revise Freud's theory without breaking with it.

From "The Theory of Psychoanalysis," CW 4, pars. 475–86

THIRD INTERVIEW

475   The girl related a dream she had had when she was five years old, which made an unforgettable impression on her. "I'll never forget the dream as long as I live," she said. I would like to add here that such dreams are of quite special interest. The longer a dream remains spontaneously in the memory, the greater is the importance to be attributed to it. This is the dream: "*I was in a wood with my little brother, looking for strawberries. Then a wolf came and jumped at me. I fled up a staircase, the wolf after me. I fell down and the wolf bit me in the leg. I awoke in deadly fear.*"

476   Before we take up the associations given us by the little girl, I will try to form an arbitrary opinion as to the possible content of the dream, and then see how our results compare with the associations given by the child. The beginning of the dream reminds us of the well-known fairytale of Little Red Ridinghood, which is, of course, known to every child. The wolf ate the grandmother first, then took her shape, and afterwards ate Lit-

tle Red Ridinghood. But the hunter killed the wolf, cut open
the belly, and Little Red Ridinghood sprang out safe and sound.
477   This motif is found in countless myths all over the world,
and is the motif of the Bible story of Jonah. The meaning immediately lying behind it is astro-mythological: the sun is swallowed by the sea monster and is born again in the morning.
Of course, the whole of astro-mythology is at bottom nothing
but psychology—unconscious psychology—projected into the
heavens; for myths never were and never are made consciously,
they arise from man's unconscious. This is the reason for the
sometimes miraculous similarity or identity of myth-forms
among races that have been separated from each other in space
ever since time began. It explains, for instance, the extraordinary distribution of the cross symbol, quite independently of
Christianity, of which America offers specially remarkable examples. It is not possible to suppose that myths were created
merely in order to explain meteorological or astronomical processes; they are, in the first instance, manifestations of unconscious impulses, comparable to dreams. These impulses were
actuated by the regressive libido in the unconscious. The material which comes to light is naturally infantile material—fantasies connected with the incest complex. Thus, in all these so-
called solar myths, we can easily recognize infantile theories
about procreation, birth, and incestuous relations. In the fairytale of Little Red Ridinghood it is the fantasy that the mother
has to eat something which is like a child, and that the child is
born by cutting open the mother's body. This fantasy is one of
the commonest and can be found everywhere.
478   From these general psychological considerations we can conclude that the child, in this dream, was elaborating the problem
of procreation and birth. As to the wolf, we must probably put
him in the father's place, for the child unconsciously attributed
to the father any act of violence towards the mother. This motif, too, is based on countless myths dealing with the violation
of the mother. With regard to the mythological parallels, I
would like to call your attention to the work of Boas,[1] which
includes a magnificent collection of American Indian sagas;
then the book by Frobenius, *Das Zeitalter des Sonnengottes*;
and finally the works of Abraham, Rank, Riklin, Jones, Freud,
Maeder, Silberer, and Spielrein, and my own investigations in
Symbols of Transformation.

---

[1] [The anthropologist Franz Boas (1858–1942); see especially his *Indianische Sagen*
(1895).—EDITORS.]

479   After these general reflections, which I give here for theoretical reasons but which naturally formed no part of the treatment, we will go on to see what the child has to tell us about her dream. Needless to say, she was allowed to speak about her dream just as she liked, without being influenced in any way. She picked first on the bite in the leg, and explained that *she had once been told by a woman who had had a baby that she could still show the place where the stork had bitten her.* This expression is, in Switzerland, a variant of the widespread symbolism of copulation and birth. Here we have a perfect parallelism between our interpretation and the association process of the child. For the first association she produced, quite uninfluenced, goes back to the problem we conjectured above on theoretical grounds. I know that the innumerable cases published in the psychoanalytic literature, which were definitely not influenced, have not been able to quash our critics' contention that we suggest our interpretations to the patients. This case, too, will convince no one who is determined to impute to us the crude mistakes of beginners — or, what is worse, falsification.

480   After this first association the little patient was asked what the wolf made her think of. She answered, "I think of my father when he is angry." This, too, coincides absolutely with our theoretical considerations. It might be objected that these considerations were made expressly for this purpose and therefore lack general validity. I think this objection vanishes of itself as soon as one has the requisite psychoanalytic and mythological knowledge. The validity of a hypothesis can be seen only on the basis of the right knowledge, otherwise not at all.

481   The first association put the stork in the place of the wolf; the association to the wolf now brings us to the father. In the popular myth the stork stands for the father, for he brings the children. The apparent contradiction between the fairytale, where the wolf is the mother, and the dream, where the wolf is the father, is of no importance for the dream or the dreamer. We can therefore dispense with a detailed explanation. I have dealt with this problem of bisexual symbols in my book.[2] As you know, in the legend of Romulus and Remus both animals, the bird Picus and the wolf, were raised to the rank of parents.

482   Her fear of the wolf in the dream is therefore her fear of the father. The dreamer explained that she was afraid of her father because he was very strict with her. He had also told her that we have bad dreams only when we have done something

---

[2] [Cf. *Symbols of Transformation*, particularly par. 547.]

wrong. She then asked her father, "But what does Mama do wrong? She always has bad dreams."

483   Once her father slapped her because she was sucking her finger. She kept on doing this despite his prohibition. Was this, perhaps, the wrong she had done? Hardly, because sucking the finger was simply a rather anachronistic infantile habit, of little real interest at her age, and serving more to irritate her father so that he would punish her by slapping. In this way she relieved her conscience of an unconfessed and much more serious "sin": *it came out that she had induced a number of girls of her own age to perform mutual masturbation.*

484   It was because of these sexual interests that she was afraid of her father. But we must not forget that she had the wolf dream in her fifth year. At that time these sexual acts had not been committed. Hence we must regard the affair with the other girls at most as a reason for her present fear of her father, but that does not explain her earlier fear. Nevertheless, we may expect that it was something similar, some unconscious sexual wish in keeping with the psychology of the forbidden act just mentioned. The character and moral evaluation of this act are naturally far more unconscious to a child than to an adult. In order to understand what could have made an impression on the child so early, we have to ask what happened in her fifth year. *That was the year in which her younger brother was born.* So even then she was afraid of her father. The associations already discussed show us the unmistakable connection between her sexual interests and her fear.

485   The problem of sex, which nature connects with positive feelings of pleasure, appears in the wolf dream in the form of fear, apparently on account of the bad father, who stands for moral education. The dream was therefore the first impressive manifestation of the sexual problem, obviously stimulated by the recent birth of a younger brother, when as we know all these questions become aired. But because the sexual problem was connected at all points with the history of certain pleasurable physical sensations which education devalues as "bad habits," it could apparently manifest itself only in the guise of moral guilt and fear.

486   This explanation, plausible though it is, seems to me superficial and inadequate. We then attribute the whole difficulty to moral education, on the unproven assumption that education can cause a neurosis. This is to disregard the fact that even people with no trace of moral education become neurotic and suffer from morbid fears. Furthermore, moral law is not just an

evil that has to be resisted, but a necessity born from the inner-most needs of man. Moral law is nothing other than an out-ward manifestation of man's innate urge to dominate and con-trol himself. This impulse to domestication and civilization is lost in the dim, unfathomable depths of man's evolutionary his-tory and can never be conceived as the consequence of laws imposed from without. Man himself, obeying his instincts, cre-ated his laws. We shall never understand the reasons for the fear and suppression of the sexual problem in a child if we take into account only the moral influences of education. The real reasons lie much deeper, in human nature itself, perhaps in that tragic conflict between nature and culture, or between individ-ual consciousness and collective feeling.

From "The Theory of Psychoanalysis," CW 4, pars. 506–10

NINTH INTERVIEW

506   This interview contributed some important details to the his-tory of her sexual problem. First came a significant dream frag-ment: "*I was with other children in a clearing in a wood, sur-rounded by beautiful fir-trees. It began to rain, there was thunder and lightning, and it grew dark. Then I suddenly saw a stork in the air.*"

507   Before we start analysing this dream, I must mention its par-allels with certain mythological ideas. To anyone familiar with the works of Adalbert Kuhn and Steinthal, to which Abraham[3] has recently drawn attention, the curious combination of thun-derstorm and stork is not at all surprising. Since ancient times the thunderstorm has had the meaning of an earth-fecundating act, it is the cohabitation of Father Heaven and Mother Earth, where the lightning takes over the role of the winged phallus. The stork in flight is just the same thing, a winged phallus, and its psychosexual meaning is known to every child. But the psy-chosexual meaning of the thunderstorm is not known to every-one, and certainly not to our little patient. In view of the whole psychological constellation previously described, the stork must unquestionably be given a psychosexual interpretation. The fact that the thunderstorm is connected with the stork and, like it, has a psychosexual meaning seems difficult to accept at first. But when we remember that psychoanalytic research has al-ready discovered a vast number of purely mythological connec-tions in the unconscious psychic products, we may conclude

---

[3] [See *Symbols of Transformation*, index, s.vv. — EDITORS.]

that the psychosexual link between the two images is present also in this case. We know from other experiences that those unconscious strata which once produced mythological formations are still active in modern individuals and are unceasingly productive. Only, the production is limited to dreams and to the symptomatology of the neuroses and psychoses, as the correction by reality is so strong in the modern mind that it prevents them from being projected upon the real world.

508   To return to the analysis of the dream: the associations that led to the heart of this image began with the idea of *rain during a thunderstorm*. Her actual words were: "I think of water — my uncle was drowned in the water — it must be awful to be stuck in the water like that, in the dark — but wouldn't the baby drown in the water, too? Does it drink the water that is in the stomach? Queer, when I was ill Mama sent my water to the doctor. I thought he was going to mix something with it like syrup, which babies grow from, and Mama would have to drink it."

509   We see with unquestionable clearness from this string of associations that the child connected psychosexual ideas specifically relating to fertilization with the rain during the thunderstorm.

510   Here again we see that remarkable parallelism between mythology and the individual fantasies of our own day. This series of associations is so rich in symbolical connections that a whole dissertation could be written about them. The symbolism of drowning was brilliantly interpreted by the child herself as a pregnancy fantasy, an explanation given in the psychoanalytic literature long ago.

(b) Jung's Rejection of Freud's Theory of Myth

Jung soon comes to reject altogether Freud's view of the origin, function, and subject matter of myth. For Freud, myth originates and functions to vent sexual wishes lingering from childhood. Myth thereby stymies psychological development. For Jung, myth originates and functions to abet psychological growth. Freud and Jung agree that myth must be interpreted symbolically, but they disagree on what myth symbolizes. For Freud, a myth about a hero and a female dragon would ordinarily symbolize the fantasized sexual relationship between a male myth maker and his mother. For Jung, the myth, depending on the specific relationship described, would symbolize the past, present, or potential relationship between the ego of the myth maker and his unconscious, symbolized as a terrible mother threatening his autonomy.

From "The Significance of the Father in the Destiny of the Individual," CW 4, par. 738

738   This little example shows what goes on in the psyche of an eight-year-old child who is over-dependent on his parents, the blame for this lying partly on the too strict father and the too tender mother. (The boy's identification with his mother and fear of his father are in this individual instance an infantile neurosis, but they represent at the same time the original human situation, the clinging of primitive consciousness to the unconscious, and the compensating impulse which strives to tear consciousness away from the embrace of the darkness. Because man has a dim premonition of this original situation behind his individual experience, he has always tried to give it generally valid expression through the universal motif of the divine hero's fight with the mother dragon, whose purpose is to deliver man from the power of darkness. This myth has a "saving," i.e., therapeutic significance, since it gives adequate expression to the dynamism underlying the individual entanglement. The myth is not to be causally explained as the consequence of a personal father-complex, but should be understood teleologically, as an attempt of the unconscious itself to rescue consciousness from the danger of regression. The ideas of "salvation" are not subsequent rationalizations of a father-complex; they are, rather, archetypally performed mechanisms for the development of consciousness.)[1]

---

[1] [*Orig.*: The infantile attitude, it is evident, is nothing but infantile sexuality. If we now survey all the far-reaching possibilities of the infantile constellation, we are obliged to say that *in essence our life's fate is identical with the fate of our sexuality*. If Freud and his school devote themselves first and foremost to tracing out the individual's sexuality, it is certainly not in order to excite piquant sensations but to gain a deeper insight into the driving forces that determine the individual's fate. In this we are not saying too much, but rather understating the case. For, when we strip off the veils shrouding the problems of individual destiny, we at once widen our field of vision from the history of the individual to the history of nations. We can take a look, first of all, at the history of religion, at the history of the fantasy systems of whole peoples and epochs. The religion of the Old Testament exalted the paterfamilias into the Jehovah of the Jews, whom the people had to obey in fear and dread. The patriarchs were a stepping-stone to the Deity. The neurotic fear in Judaism, an imperfect or at any rate unsuccessful attempt at sublimation by a still too barbarous people, gave rise to the excessive severity of Mosaic law, the compulsive ceremonial of the neurotic. Only the prophets were able to free themselves from it; for them the identification with Jehovah, complete sublimation, was successful. They became the fathers of the people. Christ, the fulfiller of their prophecies, put an end

From "Introduction to Kranefeldt's 'Secret Ways
of the Mind,'" CW 4, par. 761

761   In order to interpret the products of the unconscious, I also
found it necessary to give a quite different reading to dreams
and fantasies. I did not reduce them to personal factors, as
Freud does, but—and this seemed indicated by their very nature—I compared them with the symbols from mythology and
the history of religion, in order to discover the meaning they
were trying to express. This method did in fact yield extremely
interesting results, not least because it permitted an entirely
new reading of dreams and fantasies, thus making it possible to
unite the otherwise incompatible and archaic tendencies of the
unconscious with the conscious personality. This union had
long seemed to me the end to strive for, because neurotics (and
many normal people, too) suffer at bottom from a dissociation
between conscious and unconscious. As the unconscious contains not only the sources of instinct and the whole prehistoric
nature of man right down to the animal level, but also, along
with these, the creative seeds of the future and the roots of all
constructive fantasies, a separation from the unconscious
through neurotic dissociation means nothing less than a separation from the source of all life. It therefore seemed to me that
the prime task of the therapist was to re-establish this lost connection and the life-giving co-operation between conscious and
unconscious. Freud depreciates the unconscious and seeks
safety in the discriminating power of consciousness. This approach is generally mistaken and leads to desiccation and rigid-
ity wherever a firmly established consciousness already exists;
for, by holding off the antagonistic and apparently hostile elements in the unconscious, it denies itself the vitality it needs for
its own renewal.

to this fear of God and taught mankind that the true relation to the Deity is love.
Thus he destroyed the compulsive ceremonial of the law and was himself the expo-
nent of the personal loving relationship to God. Later, the imperfect sublimations of
the Christian Mass resulted once again in the ceremonial of the Church, from which
only those of the numerous saints and reformers who were really capable of sublimation were able to break free. Not without cause, therefore, does modern theology
speak of the liberating effect of "inner" or "personal" experience, for always the
ardour of love transmutes fear and compulsion into a higher, freer type of feeling.]
    [*Orig. footnote: Cf. Freud, Zeitschrift für Religionspsychologie (1907).] [I.e.,
"Obsessive Acts and Religious Practices."—EDITORS.]

From "The Concept of the Collective Unconscious," CW 9 i, pars. 92–96

92 The hypothesis of the collective unconscious is, therefore, no more daring than to assume there are instincts. One admits readily that human activity is influenced to a high degree by instincts, quite apart from the rational motivations of the conscious mind. So if the assertion is made that our imagination, perception, and thinking are likewise influenced by inborn and universally present formal elements, it seems to me that a normally functioning intelligence can discover in this idea just as much or just as little mysticism as in the theory of instincts. Although this reproach of mysticism has frequently been levelled at my concept, I must emphasize yet again that the concept of the collective unconscious is neither a speculative nor a philosophical but an empirical matter. The question is simply this: are there or are there not unconscious, universal forms of this kind? If they exist, then there is a region of the psyche which one can call the collective unconscious. It is true that the diagnosis of the collective unconscious is not always an easy task. It is not sufficient to point out the often obviously archetypal nature of unconscious products, for these can just as well be derived from acquisitions through language and education. Cryptomnesia should also be ruled out, which it is almost impossible to do in certain cases. In spite of all these difficulties, there remain enough individual instances showing the autochthonous revival of mythological motifs to put the matter beyond any reasonable doubt. But if such an unconscious exists at all, psychological explanation must take account of it and submit certain alleged personal aetiologies to sharper criticism.

93 What I mean can perhaps best be made clear by a concrete example. You have probably read Freud's discussion[2] of a certain picture by Leonardo da Vinci: St. Anne with the Virgin Mary and the Christ-child. Freud interprets this remarkable picture in terms of the fact that Leonardo himself had two mothers. This causality is personal. We shall not linger over the fact that this picture is far from unique, nor over the minor inaccuracy that St. Anne happens to be the grandmother of Christ and not, as required by Freud's interpretation, the mother, but shall simply point out that interwoven with the apparently personal psychology there is an impersonal motif

[2] *Leonardo da Vinci and a Memory of His Childhood*, sec. IV.

well known to us from other fields. This is the motif of the *dual mother*, an archetype to be found in many variants in the field of mythology and comparative religion and forming the basis of numerous "représentations collectives." I might mention, for instance, the motif of the *dual descent*, that is, descent from human and divine parents, as in the case of Heracles, who received immortality through being unwittingly adopted by Hera. What was a myth in Greece was actually a ritual in Egypt: Pharaoh was both human and divine by nature. In the birth chambers of the Egyptian temples Pharaoh's second, divine conception and birth is depicted on the walls; he is "twice-born." It is an idea that underlies all rebirth mysteries, Christianity included. Christ himself is "twice-born": through his baptism in the Jordan he was regenerated and reborn from water and spirit. Consequently, in the Roman liturgy the font is designated the "uterus ecclesiae," and, as you can read in the Roman missal, it is called this even today, in the "benediction of the font" on Holy Saturday before Easter. Further, according to an early Christian-Gnostic idea, the spirit which appeared in the form of a dove was interpreted as Sophia-Sapientia — Wisdom and the Mother of Christ. Thanks to this motif of the dual birth, children today, instead of having good and evil fairies who magically "adopt" them at birth with blessings or curses, are given sponsors — a "godfather" and a "godmother."

94   The idea of a second birth is found at all times and in all places. In the earliest beginnings of medicine it was a magical means of healing; in many religions it is the central mystical experience; it is the key idea in medieval, occult philosophy, and, last but not least, it is an infantile fantasy occurring in numberless children, large and small, who believe that their parents are not their real parents but merely foster-parents to whom they were handed over. Benvenuto Cellini also had this idea, as he himself relates in his autobiography.

95   Now it is absolutely out of the question that all the individuals who believe in a dual descent have in reality always had two mothers, or conversely that those few who shared Leonardo's fate have infected the rest of humanity with their complex. Rather, one cannot avoid the assumption that the universal occurrence of the dual-birth motif together with the fantasy of the two mothers answers an omnipresent human need which is reflected in these motifs. If Leonardo da Vinci did in fact portray his two mothers in St. Anne and Mary — which I doubt — he nonetheless was only expressing something which countless millions of people before and after him have believed.

The vulture symbol (which Freud also discusses in the work mentioned) makes this view all the more plausible. With some justification he quotes as the source of the symbol the *Hiero-glyphica* of Horapollo,[3] a book much in use in Leonardo's time. There you read that vultures are female only and symbolize the mother. They conceive through the wind (*pneuma*). This word took on the meaning of "spirit" chiefly under the influence of Christianity. Even in the account of the miracle at Pentecost the pneuma still has the double meaning of wind and spirit. This fact, in my opinion, points without doubt to Mary, who, a virgin by nature, conceived through the pneuma, like a vulture. Furthermore, according to Horapollo, the vulture also symbolizes Athene, who sprang, unbegotten, directly from the head of Zeus, was a virgin, and knew only spiritual motherhood. All this is really an allusion to Mary and the rebirth motif. There is not a shadow of evidence that Leonardo meant anything else by his picture. Even if it is correct to assume that he identified himself with the Christ-child, he was in all probability representing the mythological dual-mother motif and by no means his own personal prehistory. And what about all the other artists who painted the same theme? Surely not all of them had two mothers?

96   Let us now transpose Leonardo's case to the field of the neuroses, and assume that a patient with a mother complex is suffering from the delusion that the cause of his neurosis lies in his having really had two mothers. The personal interpretation would have to admit that he is right — and yet it would be quite wrong. For in reality the cause of his neurosis would lie in the reactivation of the dual-mother archetype, quite regardless of whether he had one mother or two mothers, because, as we have seen, this archetype functions individually and historically without any reference to the relatively rare occurrence of dual motherhood.

From C. G. Jung Speaking, p. 44

The aetiology of the neuroses is the great divide between my theory and that of Sigmund Freud, from whom I parted company some fifteen years ago because of this opposition. My sojourns among the natives of East Africa and the Pueblo Indians of New Mexico proved to me that the causes of neurosis do not necessarily lie in the repression of the sexual instinct; the re-

---

[3] [Cf. the trans. by George Boas, pp. 63ff., and Freud, *Leonardo*, sec. II. — EDITORS.]

pression of any other primary instinct, say of hunger, can produce it just as well. Freud's way and mine also diverge very
widely in the matter of dream interpretation. Whereas he will
always look for sexual causes, I trace the origin of dreams back
to age-old mythological influences. Deriving from our remotest
ancestors, there slumber in all of us subconscious memories
which awaken at night and seek to compensate the false attitude modern man has towards nature. A schizophrenic in my
clinic once explained to me that there was a tube in the sun
from which it blew out the wind. Many years later a papyrus
was discovered that told the scientific world for the first time of
an age-old myth about the wind from the sun-tube,[4] a myth
that had not only been recorded in the ancient papyrus but also
inherited from generation to generation in the deepest layers of
the conscious mind. Then, in a single case, the enchained fantasy was allowed to burst forth, at first in inexplicable form.
What fell below the threshold of consciousness during the day
both in our own lives and those of our ancestors awakens in
dreams to posthumous reality.

[4] See "The 'Face to Face' Interview," C. G. *Jung Speaking*, pp. 434f.

Chapter 2. The Origin of Myth

(a) The Similarities among Myths

The first step in Jung's argument for his view of the origin of myth is the establishment of the similarities among myths worldwide. Jung recognizes that the similarities can be accounted for in various ways, but he assumes that the more widespread and the more exact the similarities are, the more plausible his account of them will be. He therefore asserts that myths—more precisely, the motifs in myths—are not merely widespread but universal and are not merely similar but identical.

From "Schiller's Ideas on the Type Problem," CW 6, par. 193

193   It could easily be objected that the analogy between Schiller's train of thought and these apparently remote ideas is very far-fetched. But it must not be forgotten that not so long after Schiller's time these same ideas found a powerful spokesman through the genius of Schopenhauer and became intimately wedded to Germanic mind, never again to depart from it. In my view it is of little importance that whereas the Latin translation of the Upanishads by Anquetil du Perron (published 1801–2) was available to Schopenhauer, Schiller took at least no conscious note of the very meagre information that was available in his time.[1] I have seen enough in my own practical experience to know that no direct communication is needed in the formation of affinities of this kind. We see something very similar in the fundamental ideas of Meister Eckhart and also, in some respects, of Kant, which display a quite astonishing affinity with those of the Upanishads, though there is not the faintest trace of any influence either direct or indirect. It is the same as with myths and symbols, which can arise autochthonously in

[1] Schiller died in 1805.

every corner of the earth and yet are identical, because they are fashioned out of the same worldwide human unconscious, whose contents are infinitely less variable than are races and individuals.

From "On the Psychology of the Unconscious," CW 7, par. 101

101   There are present in every individual, besides his personal memories, the great "primordial" images, as Jacob Burckhardt once aptly called them, the inherited possibilities of human imagination as it was from time immemorial. The fact of this inheritance explains the truly amazing phenomenon that certain motifs from myths and legends repeat themselves the world over in identical forms. It also explains why it is that our mental patients can reproduce exactly the same images and associations that are known to us from the old texts. I give some examples of this in my book *Symbols of Transformation.*[2] In so doing I do not by any means assert the inheritance of ideas, but only of the possibility of such ideas, which is something very different.

From "The Relations between the Ego and the Unconscious," CW 7, par. 235

235   But equally, just as the individual is not merely a unique and separate being, but is also a social being, so the human psyche is not a self-contained and wholly individual phenomenon, but also a collective one. And just as certain social functions or instincts are opposed to the interests of single individuals, so the human psyche exhibits certain functions or tendencies which, on account of their collective nature, are opposed to individual needs. The reason for this is that every man is born with a highly differentiated brain and is thus assured of a wide range of mental functioning which is neither developed ontogenetically nor acquired. But, to the degree that human brains are uniformly differentiated, the mental functioning thereby made possible is also collective and universal. This explains, for example, the interesting fact that the unconscious processes of the most widely separated peoples and races show a quite remarkable correspondence, which displays itself, among other things, in the ex-

[2] Cf. also "The Concept of the Collective Unconscious."

traordinary but well-authenticated analogies between the forms and motifs of autochthonous myths. The universal similarity of human brains leads to the universal possibility of a uniform mental functioning. This functioning is the *collective psyche*. Inasmuch as there are differentiations corresponding to race, tribe, and even family, there is also a collective psyche limited to race, tribe, and family over and above the "universal" collective psyche. To borrow an expression from Pierre Janet,[3] the collective psyche comprises the *parties inférieures* of the psychic functions, that is to say those deep-rooted, well-nigh automatic portions of the individual psyche which are inherited and are to be found everywhere, and are thus impersonal or suprapersonal. Consciousness plus the personal unconscious constitutes the *parties supérieures* of the psychic functions, those portions, therefore, that are developed ontogenetically and acquired. Consequently, the individual who annexes the unconscious heritage of the collective psyche to what has accrued to him in the course of his ontogenetic development, as though it were part of the latter, enlarges the scope of his personality in an illegitimate way and suffers the consequences. In so far as the collective psyche comprises the *parties inférieures* of the psychic functions and thus forms the basis of every personality, it has the effect of crushing and devaluing the personality. This shows itself either in the aforementioned stifling of self-confidence or else in an unconscious heightening of the ego's importance to the point of a pathological will to power.

From "Commentary on 'The Secret of the Golden Flower,'" CW 13, par. 11

11   In order to make this strange fact more intelligible to the reader, it must be pointed out that just as the human body shows a common anatomy over and above all racial differences, so, too, the human psyche possesses a common substratum transcending all differences in culture and consciousness. I have called this substratum the collective unconscious. This unconscious psyche, common to all mankind, does not consist merely of contents capable of becoming conscious, but of latent predispositions towards identical reactions. The collective unconscious is simply the psychic expression of the identity of brain structure irrespective of all racial differences. This ex-

---

[3] *Les Névroses* (1898).

·   plains the analogy, sometimes even identity, between the various myth motifs and symbols, and the possibility of human communication in general. The various lines of psychic development start from one common stock whose roots reach back into the most distant past. This also accounts for the psychological parallelisms with animals.

From "The Philosophical Tree," CW 13, par. 352

352   The third possibility is much less rare than one might suppose. On the contrary, it occurs so frequently that comparative research into symbols becomes unavoidable in elucidating the spontaneous products of the unconscious. The widely held view that mythologems or myth motifs[4] are always connected with a tradition proves untenable, since they may reappear anywhere, at any time, and in any individual regardless of tradition. An image can be considered archetypal when it can be shown to exist in the records of human history, in identical form and with the same meaning. Two extremes must be distinguished here: (1) The image is clearly defined and is consciously connected with a tradition. (2) The image is without doubt autochthonous, there being no possibility let alone probability of a tradition.[5] Every degree of mutual contamination may be found between these two extremes.

From "Fundamental Questions of Psychotherapy," CW 16, par. 254

254   The practical need for a deeper understanding of the products of the unconscious is sufficiently obvious. In pursuit of this, I am only going further along the path taken by Freud, though I certainly try to avoid having any preconceived metaphysical opinions. I try rather to keep to first-hand experience, and to leave metaphysical beliefs, either for or against, to look after themselves. I do not imagine for a moment that I can stand above or beyond the psyche, so that it would be possible to judge it, as it were, from some transcendental Archimedean point "outside." I am fully aware that I am entrapped in the psyche and that I cannot do anything except describe the expe-

[4] Including figures of speech.
[5] It is not always easy to prove this, because the tradition is often unconscious yet is recalled cryptomnesically.

riences that there befall me. When, for instance, one examines the world of fairytales, one can hardly avoid the impression that one is meeting certain figures again and again, albeit in altered guise. Such comparisons lead on to what the student of folklore calls the investigation of motifs. The psychologist of the unconscious proceeds no differently in regard to the psychic figures which appear in dreams, fantasies, visions, and manic ideas, as in legends, fairytales, myth, and religion. Over the whole of this psychic realm there reign certain motifs, certain typical figures which we can follow far back into history, and even into prehistory, and which may therefore legitimately be described as "archetypes."[6] They seem to me to be built into the very structure of man's unconscious, for in no other way can I explain why it is that they occur universally and in identical form, whether the redeemer-figure be a fish, a hare, a lamb, a snake, or a human being. It is the same redeemer-figure in a variety of accidental disguises. From numerous experiences of this kind I have come to the conclusion that the most individual thing about man is surely his consciousness, but that his shadow, by which I mean the uppermost layer of his unconscious, is far less individualized, the reason being that a man is distinguished from his fellows more by his virtues than by his negative qualities. The unconscious, however, in its principal and most overpowering manifestations, can only be regarded as a collective phenomenon which is everywhere identical, and, because it never seems to be at variance with itself, it may well possess a marvellous unity and self-consistency, the nature of which is at present shrouded in impenetrable darkness. Another fact to be considered here is the existence today of parapsychology, whose proper subject is manifestations that are directly connected with the unconscious. The most important of these are the ESP[7] phenomena, which medical psychology should on no account ignore. If these phenomena prove anything at all, it is the fact of a certain psychic relativity of space and time, which throws a significant light on the unity of the collective unconscious. For the present, at any rate, only two groups of facts have been established with any certainty: firstly, the congruence of individual symbols and mythologems; and secondly,

---

[6] The concept of the archetype is a specifically psychological instance of the "pattern of behaviour" in biology. Hence it has nothing whatever to do with inherited ideas, but with modes of behaviour.
[7] Rhine, *Extra-Sensory Perception.*

the phenomenon of extra-sensory perception. The interpretation of these phenomena is reserved for the future.

(b) Independent Invention Rather Than Diffusion as the Source of the Similarities

Having argued for the uncanny similarities among myths worldwide, Jung seeks next to account for them. There are only two possible explanations: either cultures on their own invent similar myths (independent invention), or else myths are invented by one culture and carried to others (diffusion). Jung argues uncompromisingly for independent invention, and he does so by arguing against diffusion. Strictly, the issue is over the similarities among mythic motifs in myths and not over the similarities among whole myths, which even Jung would concede are the result of diffusion.

From "The Significance of Constitution and Heredity in Psychology," CW 8, par. 228

228   There is nothing strange about these observations, at least to begin with; they become perplexing only when we discover how far even the individual consciousness is infected by this uniformity. Astounding cases of mental similarity can be found in families. Fürst published a case of a mother and daughter with a concordance of associations amounting to thirty per cent.[1] A large measure of psychic concordance between peoples and races separated from one another in space and time is generally regarded as flatly impossible. In actual fact, however, the most astonishing concordances can be found in the realm of so-called fantastic ideas. Every endeavour has been made to explain the concordance of myth-motifs and -symbols as due to migration and tradition; Goblet d'Almellas' *Migration of Symbols* is an excellent example of this. But this explanation, which naturally has some value, is contradicted by the fact that a mythologem can arise anywhere, at any time, without there being the slightest possibility of any such transmission. For instance, I once had under my observation an insane patient who produced, almost word for word, a long symbolic passage which can be read in a papyrus published by Dieterich a few

[1] Cf. *Studies in Word-Association* (1918 edn.), p. 435.

years later.[2] After I had seen a sufficient number of such cases, my original idea that such things could only happen to people belonging to the same race was shattered, and I accordingly investigated the dreams of pure-bred Negroes living in the southern United States. I found in these dreams, among other things, motifs from Greek mythology, and this dispelled any doubt I had that it might be a question of racial inheritance.

From "The Psychology of the Child Archetype," CW 9 i, par. 262

262   Although tradition and transmission by migration certainly play a part, there are, as we have said, very many cases that cannot be accounted for in this way and drive us to the hypothesis of "autochthonous revival." These cases are so numerous that we are obliged to assume the existence of a collective psychic substratum. I have called this the *collective unconscious*.

(c) Rejection of the Experience of the External World as the Source of Independent Invention

Because the apparent subject matter of most myths is the external world, Jung must argue against the commonplace view that myths are alike worldwide because the experience of natural phenomena is alike worldwide. Jung contends that the experience of merely natural, impersonal, inanimate phenomena, even ones as awesome as the sun, cannot account for the experience of those phenomena as gods and in turn for myths about those gods.

From "General Description of the Types," CW 6, par. 625

625   The archetype is a symbolic formula which always begins to function when there are no conscious ideas present, or when conscious ideas are inhibited for internal or external reasons. The contents of the collective unconscious are represented in consciousness in the form of pronounced preferences and definite ways of looking at things. These subjective tendencies and views are generally regarded by the individual as being determined by the object—incorrectly, since they have their source

[2] [Cf. "The Structure of the Psyche," CW 8, pars. 317ff.—EDITORS.]

in the unconscious structure of the psyche and are merely released by the effect of the object. They are stronger than the object's influence, their psychic value is higher, so that they superimpose themselves on all impressions. Thus, just as it seems incomprehensible to the introvert that the object should always be the decisive factor, it remains an enigma to the extravert how a subjective standpoint can be superior to the objective situation. He inevitably comes to the conclusion that the introvert is either a conceited egoist or crack-brained bigot. Today he would be suspected of harbouring an unconscious power-complex. The introvert certainly lays himself open to these suspicions, for his positive, highly generalizing manner of expression, which appears to rule out every other opinion from the start, lends countenance to all the extravert's prejudices. Moreover the inflexibility of his subjective judgment, setting itself above all objective data, is sufficient in itself to create the impression of marked egocentricity. Faced with this prejudice the introvert is usually at a loss for the right argument, for he is quite unaware of the unconscious but generally quite valid assumptions on which his subjective judgment and his subjective perceptions are based. In the fashion of the times he looks outside for an answer, instead of seeking it behind his own consciousness. Should he become neurotic, it is the sign of an almost complete identity of the ego with the self; the importance of the self is reduced to nil, while the ego is inflated beyond measure. The whole world-creating force of the subjective factor becomes concentrated in the ego, producing a boundless power-complex and a fatuous egocentricity. Every psychology which reduces the essence of man to the unconscious power drive springs from this kind of disposition. Many of Nietzsche's lapses in taste, for example, are due to this subjectivization of consciousness.

From "Definitions," CW 6, par. 748

748   From[1] the scientific, causal standpoint the primordial image can be conceived as a mnemic deposit, an imprint or *engram* (Semon), which has arisen through the condensation of countless processes of a similar kind. In this respect it is a precipitate and, therefore, a typical basic form, of certain ever-recurring

[1] [This paragraph has been somewhat revised in *Gesammelte Werke*, vol. 6, and the translation reproduces the revisions. — EDITORS.]

psychic experiences. As a mythological motif, it is a continually effective and recurrent expression that reawakens certain psychic experiences or else formulates them in an appropriate way. From this standpoint it is a psychic expression of the physiological and anatomical disposition. If one holds the view that a particular anatomical structure is a product of environmental conditions working on living matter, then the primordial image, in its constant and universal distribution, would be the product of equally constant and universal influences from without, which must, therefore, act like a natural law. One could in this way relate myths to nature, as for instance solar myths to the daily rising and setting of the sun, or to the equally obvious change of the seasons, and this has in fact been done by many mythologists, and still is. But that leaves the question unanswered why the sun and its apparent motions do not appear direct and undisguised as a content of the myths. The fact that the sun or the moon or the meteorological processes appear, at the very least, in allegorized form points to an independent collaboration of the psyche, which in that case cannot be merely a product or stereotype of environmental conditions. For whence would it draw the capacity to adopt a standpoint outside sense perception? How, for that matter, could it be at all capable of any performance more or other than the mere corroboration of the evidence of the senses? In view of such questions Semon's naturalistic and causalistic engram theory no longer suffices. We are forced to assume that the given structure of the brain does not owe its peculiar nature merely to the influence of surrounding conditions, but also and just as much to the peculiar and autonomous quality of living matter, i.e., to a law inherent in life itself. The given constitution of the organism, therefore, is on the one hand a product of external conditions, while on the other it is determined by the intrinsic nature of living matter. Accordingly, the primordial image is related just as much to certain palpable, self-perpetuating, and continually operative natural processes as it is to certain inner determinants of psychic life and of life in general. The organism confronts light with a new structure, the eye, and the psyche confronts the natural process with a symbolic image, which apprehends it in the same way as the eye catches the light. And just as the eye bears witness to the peculiar and spontaneous creative activity of living matter, the primordial image expresses the unique and unconditioned creative power of the psyche.

From "**On Psychic Energy**," CW 8, par. 71

71   Many objections have been raised against the view that myths represent psychological facts. People are very loath to give up the idea that the myth is some kind of explanatory allegory of astronomical, meteorological, or vegetative processes. The coexistence of explanatory tendencies is certainly not to be denied, since there is abundant proof that myths also have an explanatory significance, but we are still faced with the question: why should myths explain things in this allegorical way? It is essential to understand where the primitive gets this explanatory material from, for it should not be forgotten that the primitive's need of causal explanations is not nearly so great as it is with us. He is far less interested in explaining things than in weaving fables. We can see almost daily in our patients how mythical fantasies arise: they are not thought up, but present themselves as images or chains of ideas that force their way out of the unconscious, and when they are recounted they often have the character of connected episodes resembling mythical dramas. That is how myths arise, and that is the reason why the fantasies from the unconscious have so much in common with primitive myths. But in so far as the myth is nothing but a projection from the unconscious and not a conscious invention at all, it is quite understandable that we should everywhere come upon the same myth-motifs, and that myths actually represent typical psychic phenomena.

From "**Archetypes of the Collective Unconscious**," CW 9 i, par. 7

7   What the word "archetype" means in the nominal sense is clear enough, then, from its relations with myth, esoteric teaching, and fairytale. But if we try to establish what an archetype is *psychologically*, the matter becomes more complicated. So far mythologists have always helped themselves out with solar, lunar, meteorological, vegetal, and other ideas of the kind. The fact that myths are first and foremost psychic phenomena that reveal the nature of the soul is something they have absolutely refused to see until now. Primitive man is not much interested in objective explanations of the obvious, but he has an imperative need — or rather, his unconscious psyche has an irresistible

urge — to assimilate all outer sense experiences to inner, psychic events. It is not enough for the primitive to see the sun rise and set; this external observation must at the same time be a psychic happening: the sun in its course must represent the fate of a god or hero who, in the last analysis, dwells nowhere except in the soul of man. All the mythologized processes of nature, such as summer and winter, the phases of the moon, the rainy seasons, and so forth, are in no sense allegories[2] of these objective occurrences; rather they are symbolic expressions of the inner, unconscious drama of the psyche which becomes accessible to man's consciousness by way of projection — that is, mirrored in the events of nature. The projection is so fundamental that it has taken several thousand years of civilization to detach it in some measure from its outer object. In the case of astrology, for instance, this age-old "scientia intuitiva" came to be branded as rank heresy because man had not yet succeeded in making the psychological description of character independent of the stars. Even today, people who still believe in astrology fall almost without exception for the old superstitious assumption of the influence of the stars. And yet anyone who can calculate a horoscope should know that, since the days of Hipparchus of Alexandria, the spring-point has been fixed at 0° Aries, and that the zodiac on which every horoscope is based is therefore quite arbitrary, the spring-point having gradually advanced, since then, into the first degrees of Pisces, owing to the precession of the equinoxes.

From "Flying Saucers: A Modern Myth," CW 10, par. 625

625   Nuclear physics has begotten in the layman's head an uncertainty of judgment that far exceeds that of the physicists and makes things appear possible which but a short while ago would have been declared nonsensical. Consequently the Ufos can easily be regarded and believed in as a physicists' miracle. I still remember, with misgivings, the time when I was convinced that something heavier than air could not fly, only to be taught a painful lesson. The apparently physical nature of the Ufos creates such insoluble puzzles for even the best brains, and on the other hand has built up such an impressive

---

[2] An allegory is a paraphrase of a conscious content, whereas a symbol is the best possible expression for an unconscious content whose nature can only be guessed, because it is still unknown.

legend, that one feels tempted to take them as a ninety-nine per cent psychic product and subject them accordingly to the usual psychological interpretation. Should it be that an unknown physical phenomenon is the outward cause of the myth, this would detract nothing from the myth, for many myths have meteorological and other natural phenomena as accompanying causes which by no means explain them. A myth is essentially a product of the unconscious archetype and is therefore a symbol which requires psychological interpretation. For primitive man any object, for instance an old tin that has been thrown away, can suddenly assume the importance of a fetish. This effect is obviously not inherent in the tin, but is a psychic product.

From "Marginalia on Contemporary Events," CW 18, pars. 1362–63

1362   One can scarcely imagine the unspeakable change that was wrought in man's emotional life when he took farewell from that almost wholly antique world. Nevertheless, anyone whose childhood was filled with fantasy can feel his way back to it to a certain extent. Whether one laments or welcomes the inevitable disappearance of that primordial world is irrelevant. The important thing is the question that nobody ever asks: What happens to those figures and phantoms, those gods, demons, magicians, those messengers from heaven and monsters of the abyss, when we see that there is no mercurial serpent in the caverns of the earth, that there are no dryads in the forest and no undines in the water, and that the mysteries of faith have shrunk to articles in a creed? Even when we have corrected an illusion, it by no means follows that the psychic agency which produces illusions, and actually needs them, has been abolished. It is very doubtful whether our way of rectifying such illusions can be regarded as valid. If, for example, one is content to prove that there is no whale that could or would like to swallow a Jonah, and that, even if it did, a man would rapidly suffocate under those conditions and could not possibly be spewed forth alive again — when we criticize in this way we are not doing justice to the myth. Indeed, such an argument is decidedly ridiculous because it takes the myth literally, and today this seems a little bit too naïve. Already we are beginning to see that enlightened correction of this kind is painfully beside the point. For it is one of the typical qualities of a myth to fabulate, to assert the unusual, the extraordinary, and even the impossible. In the face of this tendency, it is quite inappropriate to trot out one's elementary-school knowledge. This sort of criticism does nothing to abolish the mythologizing factor. Only an inauthentic conception of the myth has been corrected. But its real meaning is not touched, even remotely, and the mythologizing psychic factor not at all. One has merely created a new illusion, which consists in the belief that what the myth says is not true. Any elementary-school child can see that. But no one has any idea of what the myth is really saying. It expresses psychic facts and situations, just as a normal dream does or the delusion of a schizophrenic. It describes, in figurative form, psychic facts whose existence can never be dispelled by mere explanation. We have lost our superstitious fear of evil spirits and things that go bump in the night, but, instead, are seized with terror of people who, possessed by demons, perpetrate the frightful deeds of darkness. That the doers of such deeds think of themselves not as possessed, but as "supermen," does not alter the fact of their possession.

1363   The fantastic, mythological world of the Middle Ages has, thanks to our so-called enlightenment, simply changed its place. It is no longer incubi, succubi, wood-nymphs, melusines, and the rest that terrify and tease mankind; man himself has taken over their role without knowing it and does the devilish work of destruction with far more effective tools than the spirits did. In the olden days men were brutal, now they are dehumanized and possessed to a degree that even the blackest Middle Ages did not know. Then a decent and intelligent person could still — within limits — escape the devil's business, but today his very ideals drag him down into the bloody mire of his national existence.

From **Letters**, vol. 1, pp. 208–9

To Baroness Tinti

Dear Baroness,   10 January 1936
    Many thanks for your interesting letter. Indeed, many of the peculiarities of the figures in the unconscious could be explained by a long-lasting primeval matriarchy if only we knew for certain that it ever existed, just as the flood myths could be explained by the myth of Atlantis if only we knew that there

ever was an Atlantis. Equally, the contents of the unconscious could be explained by reincarnation if we knew that there is reincarnation. These hypotheses are at present articles of faith, and science is always in the modest role of a beggar since it has to be content with what it has. If it didn't it would be a fraud. This is the reason why I restrict myself essentially to facts and observations and fight shy of mythological explanations.

The book you very kindly promised me is unfortunately not yet in my hands. All the same I thank you for it.

Yours sincerely, c. g. jung

(d) Independent Invention as the Projection of the Unconscious onto the External World

Rather than arising from the experience of the external world, myth for Jung arises from the projection of the archetypes of the collective unconscious onto the world. Cultures have the same myths worldwide because their members have the same archetypes in their heads. The subject matter of myths is supernatural and personified because archetypes commonly manifest themselves as gods. Jung grants that outward experience can trigger the projection of archetypes, but he denies that outward experience can deify the world. Archetypes are projected not only onto inanimate objects like the sun but also onto plants, animals, and even human beings, who, while already personified, become heroes or demons.

From "Symbols of the Mother and of Rebirth," CW 5, par. 395

395   As the reader will long since have guessed, the dragon represents the negative mother-imago and thus expresses resistance to incest, or the fear of it. Dragon and snake are symbolic representations of the fear of the consequences of breaking the taboo and regressing to incest. It is therefore understandable that we should come over and over again upon the motif of the tree and the snake. Snakes and dragons are especially significant as guardians or defenders of the treasure. The black horse Apaosha also has this meaning in the old Persian *Song of Tishtriya*, where he blocks up the sources of the rain-lake. The white horse, Tishtriya, makes two futile attempts to vanquish

Apaosha; at the third attempt he succeeds with the help of Ahura-Mazda.[1] Whereupon the sluices of heaven are opened and the fertilizing rain pours down upon the earth.[2] In this symbolism we can see very clearly how libido fights against libido, instinct against instinct, how the unconscious is in conflict with itself, and how mythological man perceived the unconscious in all the adversities and contrarieties of external nature without ever suspecting that he was gazing at the paradoxical background of his own consciousness.

From "The Dual Mother," CW 5, par. 612

612   Looked at in this light, the hero myth is an unconscious drama seen only in projection, like the happenings in Plato's parable of the cave. The hero himself appears as a being of more than human stature. He is distinguished from the very beginning by his godlike characteristics. Since he is psychologically an archetype of the self, his divinity only confirms that the self is numinous, a sort of god, or having some share in the divine nature. In this mythologem may lie the root of the argument in favour of "homoousia." For psychology it makes a vast difference whether the self is to be considered "of the same nature" as the Father ($\acute{o}\mu oo\acute{v}\sigma\iota o\varsigma$), or merely "of a similar nature" ($\acute{o}\mu o\iota o\acute{v}\sigma\iota o\varsigma$). The decision in favour of homoousia was of great psychological importance, for it asserted that Christ is of the same nature as God. But Christ, from the point of view of psychology and comparative religion, is a typical manifestation of the self. For psychology the self is an *imago Dei* and cannot be distinguished from it empirically. The two ideas are therefore of the same nature. The hero is the protagonist of God's transformation in man; he corresponds to what I call the "mana personality."[3] The latter has such an immense fascination for the conscious mind that the ego all too easily succumbs to the temptation to identify with the hero, thus bringing on a

---

[1] A variation of the same motif can be found in a legend from Lower Saxony: There was once a young ash-tree that grew unnoticed in a wood. Each New Year's Eve a white knight riding upon a white horse comes to cut down the young shoot. At the same time a black knight arrives and engages him in combat. After a lengthy battle the white knight overcomes the black-knight and cuts down the tree. But one day the white knight will be unsuccessful, then the ash will grow, and when it is big enough for a horse to be tethered under it, a mighty king will come and a tremendous battle will begin: i.e., the end of the world. (Grimm, III, p. 960.)

[2] J.E. Lehmann, in Chantepie de la Saussaye, *Lehrbuch der Religionsgeschichte*, II, p. 185.

[3] See "The Relations between the Ego and the Unconscious," pars. 374ff.

psychic inflation with all its consequences. For this reason the repugnance felt by certain ecclesiastical circles for the "inner Christ" is understandable enough, at least as a preventive measure against the danger of psychic inflation which threatens the Christian European. Although the religion and philosophy of India are largely dominated by the idea of homoousia,[4] there is less danger in this direction because the Indian has an equally homoousian idea of God (Brahman), which is very definitely not the case with the Christian. The latter has far too little introspection to be able to realize what modifications in his present conception of God the homoousia of the self (Atman) would involve. I hope my reader will pardon these reflections, which may seem very remote from our theme. I add them here only to put the numinosity of the hero archetype in the right perspective.[5]

From "The Type Problem in Poetry," CW 6, par. 325

325   *Faust* and *Zarathustra* are of very great assistance in the individual mastery of the problem, while Spitteler's *Prometheus and Epimetheus*, thanks to the wealth of mythological material, affords a more general insight into it and the way it appears in collective life. What, first and foremost, is revealed in Spitteler's portrayal of unconscious religious contents is the *symbol of God's renewal*, which was subsequently treated at greater length in his *Olympian Spring*. This symbol appears to be intimately connected with the opposition between the psychological types and functions, and is obviously an attempt to find a solution in the form of a renewal of the general attitude, which in the language of the unconscious is expressed as a renewal of God. This is a well-known primordial image that is practically universal; I need only mention the whole mythological complex of the dying and resurgent god and its primitive precursors all the way down to the re-charging of fetishes and churingas with magical force. It expresses a transformation of attitude by means of which a new potential, a new manifestation of life, a new fruitfulness, is created. This latter analogy explains the well-attested connection between the renewal of the god and seasonal and vegetational phenomena. One is naturally inclined

---

[4] Identity of the personal and the suprapersonal atman.
[5] Cf. *Psychological Types* (1923 edn., pp. 245ff.), and *Aion*, the chapters on the symbolism of the self.

to assume that seasonal, vegetational, lunar, and solar myths underlie these analogies. But that is to forget that a myth, like everything psychic, cannot be solely conditioned by external events. Anything psychic brings its own internal conditions with it, so that one might assert with equal right that the myth is purely psychological and uses meteorological or astronomical events merely as a means of expression. The whimsicality and absurdity of many primitive myths often makes the latter explanation seem far more appropriate than any other.

From "On the Psychology of the Unconscious," CW 7, par. 109

109   So this idea has been stamped on the human brain for aeons. That is why it lies ready to hand in the unconscious of every man. Only, certain conditions are needed to cause it to appear. These conditions were evidently fulfilled in the case of Robert Mayer. The greatest and best thoughts of man shape themselves upon these primordial images as upon a blueprint. I have often been asked where the archetypes or primordial images come from. It seems to me that their origin can only be explained by assuming them to be deposits of the constantly repeated experiences of humanity. One of the commonest and at the same time most impressive experiences is the apparent movement of the sun every day. We certainly cannot discover anything of the kind in the unconscious, so far as the known physical process is concerned. What we do find, on the other hand, is the myth of the sun-hero in all its countless variations. It is this myth, and not the physical process, that forms the sun archetype. The same can be said of the phases of the moon. The archetype is a kind of readiness to produce over and over again the same or similar mythical ideas. Hence it seems as though what is impressed upon the unconscious were exclusively the subjective fantasy-ideas aroused by the physical process. We may therefore assume that the archetypes are recurrent impressions made by subjective reactions.[6] Naturally this assumption only pushes the problem further back without solving it. There is nothing to prevent us from assuming that certain archetypes exist even in animals, that they are grounded in the peculiarities of the living organism itself and are therefore direct expressions of life whose nature cannot be further explained. Not only are the

6 Cf. "The Structure of the Psyche," pp. 152ff.

archetypes, apparently, impressions of ever-repeated typical experiences, but, at the same time, they behave empirically like agents that tend towards the repetition of these same experiences. For when an archetype appears in a dream, in a fantasy, or in life, it always brings with it a certain influence or power by virtue of which it either exercises a numinous or a fascinating effect, or impels to action.

From "On the Psychology of the Unconscious," CW 7, par. 152

152   On account of their affinity with physical phenomena,[7] the archetypes usually appear in projection; and, because projections are unconscious, they appear on persons in the immediate environment, mostly in the form of abnormal over- or undervaluations which provoke misunderstandings, quarrels, fanaticisms, and follies of every description. Thus we say, "He makes a god of so-and-so," or, "So-and-so is Mr. X's *bête noire.*" In this way, too, there grow up modern myth-formations, i.e., fantastic rumours, suspicions, prejudices. The archetypes are therefore exceedingly important things with a powerful effect, meriting our closest attention. They must not be suppressed out of hand, but must be very carefully weighed and considered, if only because of the danger of psychic infection they carry with them. Since they usually occur as projections, and since these only attach themselves where there is a suitable hook, their evaluation and assessment is no light matter. Thus, when somebody projects the devil upon his neighbour, he does so because this person has something about him which makes the attachment of such an image possible. But this is not to say that the man is on that account a devil; on the contrary, he may be a particularly good fellow, but antipathetic to the maker of the projection, so that a "devilish" (i.e., *dividing*) effect arises between them. Nor need the projector necessarily be a devil, although he has to recognize that he has something just as devilish in himself, and has only stumbled upon it by projecting it. But that does not make him a devil; indeed he may be just as decent as the other man. The appearance of the devil in such a case simply means that the two people are at present incompatible: for which reason the unconscious forces them apart and keeps them away from each other. The devil is a variant of the

---

[7] Cf. "The Structure of the Psyche," pars. 325ff.

"shadow" archetype, i.e., of the dangerous aspect of the unre-
cognized dark half of the personality.

From "The Structure of the Psyche," CW 8, par. 325

325   The collective unconscious — so far as we can say anything
about it at all — appears to consist of mythological motifs or
primordial images, for which reason the myths of all nations
are its real exponents. In fact, the whole of mythology could
be taken as a sort of projection of the collective unconscious.
We can see this most clearly if we look at the heavenly constellations, whose originally chaotic forms were organized
through the projection of images. This explains the influence
of the stars as asserted by astrologers. These influences are
nothing but unconscious, introspective perceptions of the activity of the collective unconscious. Just as the constellations
were projected into the heavens, similar figures were projected
into legends and fairytales or upon historical persons. We can
therefore study the collective unconscious in two ways, either
in mythology or in the analysis of the individual. As I cannot
make the latter material available here, I must confine myself
to mythology. This is such a wide field that we can select
from it only a few types. Similarly, environmental conditions
are endlessly varied, so here too only a few of the more typical can be discussed.

(e) Independent Invention as the Projection of the Collective Rather Than the Personal Unconscious onto the External World

*Having argued that myth originates in the mind rather than in
the world, Jung argues finally that myth originates in the Jungian rather than the Freudian mind. Projections onto the world
emanate from the distinctively Jungian collective unconscious
rather than from the largely Freudian personal unconscious. As
the product of the repression by individuals of unacceptable
impulses, the Freudian unconscious cannot account for the
presence in myth of motifs that have never been experienced by
myth makers and have therefore had no opportunity to be repressed. As the product of individual experience, the Freudian
unconscious cannot account for the presence in myth of motifs
so similar worldwide.*

From "Flying Saucers: A Modern Myth," CW 10, par. 646

646   In dealing with the products of the collective unconscious, all images that show an unmistakably mythological character have to be examined in their symbological context. They are the inborn language of the psyche and its structure, and, as regards their basic form, are in no sense individual acquisitions. Despite its pre-eminent capacity for learning and for consciousness, the human psyche is a natural phenomenon like the psyche of animals, and is rooted in inborn instincts which bring their own specific forms with them and so constitute the heredity of the species. Volition, intention, and all personal differentiations are acquired late and owe their existence to a consciousness that has emancipated itself from mere instinctivity. Wherever it is a question of archetypal formations, personalistic attempts at explanation lead us astray. The method of comparative symbology, on the other hand, not only proves fruitful on scientific grounds but makes a deeper understanding possible in practice. The symbological or "amplificatory" approach produces a result that looks at first like a translation back into primitive language. And so it would be, if understanding with the help of the unconscious were a purely intellectual exercise and not one that brought our total capacities into play. In other words, besides its formal mode of manifestation the archetype possesses a numinous quality, a feeling-value that is highly effective in practice. One can be unconscious of this value, since it can be repressed artificially; but a repression has neurotic consequences, because the repressed affect still exists and simply makes an outlet for itself elsewhere, in some unsuitable place.

From "The Psychology of Eastern Meditation," CW 11, par. 944

944   What has our psychology to say about this Indian assertion of a supra-personal, world-embracing unconscious that appears when the darkness of the personal unconscious grows transparent? Modern psychology knows that the personal unconscious is only the top layer, resting on a foundation of a wholly different nature which we call the collective unconscious. The reason for this designation is the circumstance that, unlike the personal unconscious and its purely personal contents, the images in the deeper unconscious have a distinctly mythological character.

That is to say, in form and content they coincide with those widespread primordial ideas which underlie the myths. They are no longer of a personal but of a purely supra-personal nature and are therefore common to all men. For this reason they are to be found in the myths and legends of all peoples and all times, as well as in individuals who have not the slightest knowledge of mythology.

From "The Philosophical Tree," CW 13, par. 478

478 It goes without saying that all personal affects and resentments participate in the making of a dream and can therefore be read from its imagery. The analyst, especially at the beginning of a treatment, will have to be satisfied with this, since it seems reasonable to the patient that his dreams come from his personal psyche. He would be completely bewildered if the collective aspect of his dreams were pointed out to him. Freud himself, as we know, tried to reduce myth motifs to personal psychology, in defiance of his own insight that dreams contain archaic residues. These are not personal acquisitions, but vestiges of an earlier collective psyche. There are, however, not a few patients who, as if to prove the reversibility of psychological rules, not only understand the universal significance of their dream symbols but also find it therapeutically effective. The great psychic systems of healing, the religions, likewise consist of universal myth motifs whose origin and content are collective and not personal; hence Lévy-Bruhl rightly called such motifs *représentations collectives*. The conscious psyche is certainly of a personal nature, but it is by no means the whole of the psyche. The foundation of consciousness, the psyche *per se*, is unconscious, and its structure, like that of the body, is common to all, its individual features being only insignificant variants. For the same reason it is difficult or almost impossible for the inexperienced eye to recognize individual faces in a crowd of coloured people.

(f) Myths and Archetypes

While the principal contents of myths for Jung are expressions of archetypes, myths are more than archetypes. Myths are stories. Archetypes, or "mythologems," are the motifs, or images, in stories. Myths are consciously created. Archetypes are the unconscious raw material of myths. Myth makers unconsciously appropriate archetypal material in consciously creating myths.

From "Archetypes of the Collective Unconscious," CW 9 i, par. 6

6   Another well-known expression of the archetypes is myth and fairytale. But here too we are dealing with forms that have received a specific stamp and have been handed down through long periods of time. The term "archetype" thus applies only indirectly to the "représentations collectives," since it designates only those psychic contents which have not yet been submitted to conscious elaboration and are therefore an immediate datum of psychic experience. In this sense there is a considerable difference between the archetype and the historical formula that has evolved. Especially on the higher levels of esoteric teaching the archetypes appear in a form that reveals quite unmistakably the critical and evaluating influence of conscious elaboration. Their immediate manifestation, as we encounter it in dreams and visions, is much more individual, less understandable, and more naïve than in myths, for example. The archetype is essentially an unconscious content that is altered by becoming conscious and by being perceived, and it takes its colour from the individual consciousness in which it happens to appear.[1]

From "The Psychology of the Child Archetype," CW 9 i, par. 260

260   These products are never (or at least very seldom) myths with a definite form, but rather mythological components which, because of their typical nature, we can call "motifs," "primordial images," types or—as I have named them—*archetypes*. The child archetype is an excellent example. Today we can hazard the formula that the archetypes appear in myths and fairytales just as they do in dreams and in the products of psychotic fan-

---

[1] One must, for the sake of accuracy, distinguish between "archetype" and "archetypal ideas." The archetype as such is a hypothetical and irrepresentable model, something like the "pattern of behaviour" in biology. Cf. "On the Nature of the Psyche," sec. 7.

tasy. The medium in which they are embedded is, in the former case, an ordered and for the most part immediately understandable context, but in the latter case a generally unintelligible, irrational, not to say delirious sequence of images which nonetheless does not lack a certain hidden coherence. In the individual, the archetypes appear as involuntary manifestations of unconscious processes whose existence and meaning can only be inferred, whereas the myth deals with traditional forms of incalculable age. They hark back to a prehistoric world whose spiritual preconceptions and general conditions we can still observe today among existing primitives. Myths on this level are as a rule tribal history handed down from generation to generation by word of mouth. Primitive mentality differs from the civilized chiefly in that the conscious mind is far less developed in scope and intensity. Functions such as thinking, willing, etc. are not yet differentiated; they are pre-conscious, and in the case of thinking, for instance, this shows itself in the circumstance that the primitive does not think *consciously*, but that thoughts *appear*. The primitive cannot assert that he thinks; it is rather that "something thinks in him." The spontaneity of the act of thinking does not lie, causally, in his conscious mind, but in his unconscious. Moreover, he is incapable of any conscious effort of will; he must put himself beforehand into the "mood of willing," or let himself be put—hence his *rites d'entrée et de sortie*. His consciousness is menaced by an almighty unconscious: hence his fear of magical influences which may cross his path at any moment; and for this reason, too, he is surrounded by unknown forces and must adjust himself as best he can. Owing to the chronic twilight state of his consciousness, it is often next to impossible to find out whether he merely dreamed something or whether he really experienced it. The spontaneous manifestation of the unconscious and its archetypes intrudes everywhere into his conscious mind, and the mythical world of his ancestors—for instance, the *alchera* or *bugari* of the Australian aborigines—is a reality equal if not superior to the material world.[2] It is not the world as we know it that speaks out of his unconscious, but the unknown world of the psyche, of which we know that it mirrors our empirical world only in part, and that, for the other part, it moulds this empirical world in accordance with its own psychic assump-

---

[2] This fact is well known, and the relevant ethnological literature is too extensive to be mentioned here.

tions. The archetype does not proceed from physical facts, but describes how the psyche experiences the physical fact, and in so doing the psyche often behaves so autocratically that it denies tangible reality or makes statements that fly in the face of it.

Chapter 3. The Function of Myth

(a) Revealing the Unconscious

Myth for Jung serves multiple functions. Myth serves, first, to reveal to consciousness the collective unconscious. Because the collective unconscious is inherently unconscious, it can communicate with consciousness only indirectly, through intermediaries like myth. Myth succeeds as an intermediary when the conscious, literal meaning of a myth suggests another, symbolic meaning, which for Jung is the psychological one.

From "The Psychology of the Child Archetype," CW 9 i, par. 262

262   Modern psychology treats the products of unconscious fantasy-activity as self-portraits of what is going on in the unconscious psyche about itself.

From "The Dual Mother," CW 5, par. 466

466   It is in this situation that our author now finds herself. Chiwantopel is the very devil of a fellow: a breaker of hearts by the dozen, all the women rave about him. He knows so many of them that he can pass them under review. Not one of them gets him, for he seeks one who (so she thinks) is known only to our author. That is, she believes in her heart of hearts that he is looking for *her*. In this she is labouring under a delusion, for experience shows that this particular cat jumps quite differently. The animus, a typical "son"-hero, is not after her at all; true to his ancient prototype, he is seeking the mother. This youthful hero is always the son-lover of the mother-goddess and is doomed to an early death. The libido that will not flow into life at the right time regresses to the mythical world of the archetypes, where it activates images which, since the remotest times, have expressed the non-human life of the gods, whether

of the upper world or the lower. If this regression occurs in a young person, his own individual life is supplanted by the divine archetypal drama, which is all the more devastating for him because his conscious education provides him with no means of recognizing what is happening, and thus with no possibility of freeing himself from its fascination. Herein lay the vital importance of myths: they explained to the bewildered human being what was going on in his unconscious and why he was held fast. The myths told him: "This is not you, but the gods. You will never reach them, so turn back to your human avocations, holding the gods in fear and respect." These ingredients can also be found in the Christian myth, but it is too veiled to have enlightened our author. Nor is anything said about these things in the catechism. The "shining heights" are beyond the reach of mere mortals, and the "superhuman word Love" betrays the divine nature of the *dramatis personae*, since even human love presents such a thorny problem to man that he would rather creep into the remotest corner than touch it with his little finger. The words we have quoted show how deeply our author has been drawn into the unconscious drama and how much she is under its spell. Looked at in this light, the pathos rings hollow and the heroics seem hysterical.

From "A Psychological Approach to the Dogma of the Trinity," CW 11, pars. 291–92

291   The Lucifer legend is in no sense an absurd fairytale; like the story of the serpent in the Garden of Eden, it is a "therapeutic" myth. We naturally boggle at the thought that good and evil are both contained in God, and we think God could not possibly want such a thing. We should be careful, though, not to pare down God's omnipotence to the level of our human opinions; but that is just how we do think, despite everything. Even so, it would not do to impute all evil to God: thanks to his moral autonomy, man can put down a sizable portion of it to his own account. Evil is a relative thing, partly avoidable, partly fate — just as virtue is, and often one does not know which is worse. Think of the fate of a woman married to a recognized saint! What sins must not the children commit in order to feel their lives their own under the overwhelming influence of such a father! Life, being an energetic process, needs the opposites, for without opposition there is, as we know, no energy. Good and evil are simply the moral aspects of this natural polarity. The fact that we have to feel this polarity so excruciatingly makes

human existence all the more complicated. Yet the suffering that necessarily attaches to life cannot be evaded. The tension of opposites that makes energy possible is a universal law, fittingly expressed in the *yang* and *yin* of Chinese philosophy. Good and evil are feeling-values of human provenance, and we cannot extend them beyond the human realm. What happens beyond this is beyond our judgment: God is not to be caught with human attributes. Besides, where would the *fear* of God be if only good—i.e., what seems good to us—were to be expected from him? After all, eternal damnation doesn't bear much resemblance to goodness as we understand it! Although good and evil are unshakable as moral values, they still need to be subjected to a bit of psychological revision. Much, that is to say, that proves to be abysmally evil in its ultimate effects does not come from man's wickedness but from his stupidity and unconsciousness. One has only to think of the devastating effects of Prohibition in America or of the hundred thousand autos-da-fé in Spain, which were all caused by a praiseworthy zeal to save people's souls. One of the toughest roots of all evil is unconsciousness, and I could wish that the saying of Jesus, "Man, if thou knowest what thou doest, thou art blessed, but if thou knowest not, thou art accursed, and a transgressor of the law,"[1] were still in the gospels, even though it has only one authentic source. It might well be the motto for a new morality.

292   The individuation process is invariably started off by the patient's becoming conscious of the shadow, a personality component usually with a negative sign. This "inferior" personality is made up of everything that will not fit in with, and adapt to, the laws and regulations of conscious life. It is compounded of "disobedience" and is therefore rejected not on moral grounds only, but also for reasons of expediency. Closer investigation shows that there is at least one function in it which ought to collaborate in orienting consciousness. Or rather, this function does collaborate, not for the benefit of conscious, purposive intentions, but in the interests of unconscious tendencies pursuing a different goal. It is this fourth, "inferior" function which acts autonomously towards consciousness and cannot be harnessed to the latter's intentions. It lurks behind every neurotic dissociation and can only be annexed to consciousness if the corresponding unconscious contents are made conscious at the same time. But this integration cannot take place and be put to a useful purpose unless one can admit the tendencies bound up

[1] Cf. James, *The Apocryphal New Testament*, p. 33.

with the shadow and allow them some measure of realization —
tempered, of course, with the necessary criticism. This leads to
disobedience and self-disgust, but also to self-reliance, without
which individuation is unthinkable. The ability to "will otherwise" must, unfortunately, be real if ethics are to make any
sense at all. Anyone who submits to the law from the start, or
to what is generally expected, acts like the man in the parable
who buried his talent in the earth. Individuation is an exceedingly difficult task: it always involves a conflict of duties, whose
solution requires us to understand that our "counter-will" is
also an aspect of God's will. One cannot individuate with mere
words and convenient self-deceptions, because there are too
many destructive possibilities in the offing. One almost unavoidable danger is that of getting stuck in the conflict and
hence in the neurotic dissociation. Here the therapeutic myth
has a helpful and loosening effect, even when the patient shows
not a trace of conscious understanding. The felt presence of the
archetype is enough; it only fails to work when the possibility
of conscious understanding is there, within the patient's reach.
In those circumstances it is positively deleterious for him to remain unconscious, though this happens frequently enough in
our Christian civilization today. So much of what Christian
symbolism taught has gone by the board for large numbers of
people, without their ever having understood what they have
lost. Civilization does not consist in progress as such and in
mindless destruction of the old values, but in developing and
refining the good that has been won.

(b) Encountering the Unconscious

*Myth for Jung serves not only to disclose the existence of the
unconscious but actually to open up human beings to the unconscious. Myth works when it "grabs" one emotionally. Consciously, one may be stirred by the feats of a hero, but unconsciously it is the heroic side of one's own personality that is
being aroused.*

From "Background to the Psychology of Christian Alchemical
Symbolism," CW 9 ii, par. 280

280   Myths and fairytales give expression to unconscious processes, and their retelling causes these processes to come alive
again and be recollected, thereby re-establishing the connection

between conscious and unconscious. What the separation of the two psychic halves means, the psychiatrist knows only too well. He knows it as dissociation of the personality, the root of all neuroses: the conscious goes to the right and the unconscious to the left. As opposites never unite at their own level (*tertium non datur!*), a supraordinate "third" is always required, in which the two parts can come together. And since the symbol derives as much from the conscious as from the unconscious, it is able to unite them both, reconciling their conceptual polarity through its form and their emotional polarity through its numinosity.

From "**Paracelsus as a Spiritual Phenomenon**," CW 13, par. 199

199   Just as this prayer has come down to us embedded in a mass of magical recipes, so does the *lumen naturae* rise up from a world of kobolds and other creatures of darkness, veiled in magical spells and almost extinguished in a morass of mystification. Nature is certainly equivocal, and one can blame neither Paracelsus nor the alchemists if, anxiously aware of their responsibilities, they cautiously expressed themselves in parables. This procedure is indeed the more appropriate one in the circumstances. What takes place between light and darkness, what unites the opposites, has a share in both sides and can be judged just as well from the left as from the right, without our becoming any the wiser: indeed, we can only open up the opposition again. Here only the symbol helps, for, in accordance with its paradoxical nature, it represents the "tertium" that in logic does not exist, but which in reality is the living truth. So we should not begrudge Paracelsus and the alchemists their secret language: deeper insight into the problems of psychic development soon teaches us how much better it is to reserve judgment instead of prematurely announcing to all and sundry what's what. Of course we all have an understandable desire for crystal clarity, but we are apt to forget that in psychic matters we are dealing with processes of experience, that is, with transformations which should never be given hard and fast names if their living movement is not to petrify into something static. The protean mythologem and the shimmering symbol express the processes of the psyche far more trenchantly and, in the end, far more clearly than the clearest concept; for the symbol not only conveys a visualization of the process but—and this is perhaps just as important—it also brings a re-experienc-

ing of it, of that twilight which we can learn to understand only through inoffensive empathy, but which too much clarity only dispels. Thus the symbolic hints of marriage and exaltation in the "true May," when the heavenly flowers bloom and the secret of the inner man is made manifest, by the very choice and sound of the words convey a vision and experience of a climax whose significance could be amplified only by the finest flights of the poets. But the clear and unambiguous concept would find not the smallest place where it would fit. And yet something deeply significant has been said, for as Paracelsus rightly remarks: "When the heavenly marriage is accomplished, who will deny its superexcellent virtue?"

From "The Conjunction," CW 14, par. 751

751   The analyst who is himself struggling for all those things which he seeks to inculcate into his patients will not get round the problem of the transference so easily. The more he knows how difficult it is for him to solve the problems of his own life, the less he can overlook the fear and uncertainty or the frivolity and dangerously uncritical attitude of his patients. Even Freud regarded the transference as a neurosis at second hand and treated it as such. He could not simply shut the door, but honestly tried to analyze the transference away. This is not so simple as it sounds when technically formulated. Practice often turns out to be rather different from theory. You want, of course, to put a whole man on his feet and not just a part of him. You soon discover that there is nothing for him to stand on and nothing for him to hold on to. Return to the parents has become impossible, so he hangs on to the analyst. He can go neither backwards nor forwards, for he sees nothing before him that could give him a hold. All so-called reasonable possibilities have been tried out and have proved useless. Not a few patients then remember the faith in which they were brought up, and some find their way back to it, but not all. They know, perhaps, what their faith ought to mean to them, but they have found to their cost how little can be achieved with will and good intentions if the unconscious does not lend a hand. In order to secure its co-operation the religions have long turned to myths for help, or rather, the myths always flung out bridges between the helpless consciousness and the effective *idées forces* of the unconscious. But you cannot, artificially and with an effort of will, believe the statements of myth if you have not previously been gripped by them. If you are honest, you will doubt the

truth of the myth because our present-day consciousness has no means of understanding it. Historical and scientific criteria do not lend themselves to a recognition of mythological truth; it can be grasped only by the intuitions of faith or by psychology, and in the latter case although there may be insight it remains ineffective unless it is backed by experience.

From "**Principles of Practical Psychotherapy,**" CW 16, pars. 18–22

18   I cannot, within the compass of a lecture, describe all the motifs that crop up in the process of individuation — when, that is to say, the material is no longer reduced to generalities applicable only to the collective man. There are numerous motifs, and we meet them everywhere in mythology. Hence we can only say that the psychic development of the individual produces something that looks very like the archaic world of fable, and that the individual path looks like a regression to man's prehistory, and that consequently it seems as if something very untoward were happening which the therapist ought to arrest. We can in fact observe similar things in psychotic illnesses, especially in the paranoid forms of schizophrenia, which often swarm with mythological images. The fear instantly arises that we are dealing with some misdevelopment leading to a world of chaotic or morbid fantasy. A development of this kind may be dangerous with a person whose social personality has not found its feet; moreover any psychotherapeutic intervention may occasionally run into a latent psychosis and bring it to full flower. For this reason to dabble in psychotherapy is to play with fire, against which amateurs should be stringently cautioned. It is particularly dangerous when the mythological layer of the psyche is uncovered, for these contents have a fearful fascination for the patient — which explains the tremendous influence mythological ideas have had on mankind.

19   Now, it would seem that the recuperative process mobilizes these powers for its own ends. Mythological ideas with their extraordinary symbolism evidently reach far into the human psyche and touch the historical foundations where reason, will, and good intentions never penetrate; for these ideas are born of the same depths and speak a language which strikes an answering chord in the inner man, although our reason may not understand it. Hence, the process that at first sight looks like an alarming regression is rather a *reculer pour mieux sauter*, an amassing and integration of powers that will develop into a new order.

20   A neurosis at this level is an entirely spiritual form of suffering which cannot be tackled with ordinary rational methods.
For this reason there are not a few psychotherapists who, when
all else fails, have recourse to one of the established religions or
creeds. I am far from wishing to ridicule these efforts. On the
contrary, I must emphasize that they are based on an extremely
sound instinct, for our religions contain the still living remains
of a mythological age. Even a political creed may occasionally
revert to mythology, as is proved very clearly by the swastika,
the German Christians, and the German Faith Movement. Not
only Christianity with its symbols of salvation, but all religions,
including the primitive with their magical rituals, are forms of
psychotherapy which treat and heal the suffering of the soul,
and the suffering of the body caused by the soul. How much in
modern medicine is still suggestion therapy is not for me to say.
To put it mildly, consideration of the psychological factor in
practical therapeutics is by no means a bad thing. The history
of medicine is exceedingly revealing in this respect.

21   Therefore, when certain doctors resort to the mythological
ideas of some religion or other, they are doing something historically justified. But they can only do this with patients for
whom the mythological remains are still alive. For these patients some kind of rational therapy is indicated until such time
as mythological ideas become a necessity. In treating devout
Catholics, I always refer them to the Church's confessional and
its means of grace. It is more difficult in the case of Protestants,
who must do without confession and absolution. The more
modern type of Protestantism has, however, the safety-valve of
the Oxford Group movement, which prescribes lay confession
as a substitute, and group experience instead of absolution. A
number of my patients have joined this movement with my entire approval, just as others have become Catholics, or at least
better Catholics than they were before. In all these cases I refrain from applying the dialectical procedure, since there is no
point in promoting individual development beyond the needs of
the patient. If he can find the meaning of his life and the cure
for his disquiet and disunity within the framework of an existing credo — including a political credo — that should be enough
for the doctor. After all, the doctor's main concern is the sick,
not the cured.

22   There are, however, very many patients who have either no
religious convictions at all or highly unorthodox ones. Such
persons are, on principle, not open to any conviction. All rational therapy leaves them stuck where they were, although on the

face of it their illness is quite curable. In these circumstances nothing is left but the dialectical development of the mythological material which is alive in the sick man himself, regardless of history and tradition. It is here that we come across those mythological dreams whose characteristic sequence of images presents the doctor with an entirely new and unexpected task. He then needs the sort of knowledge for which his professional studies have not equipped him in the least. For the human psyche is neither a psychiatric nor a physiological problem; it is not a biological problem at all but—precisely—a psychological one. It is a field on its own with its own peculiar laws. Its nature cannot be deduced from the principles of other sciences without doing violence to the idiosyncrasy of the psyche. It cannot be identified with the brain, or the hormones, or any known instinct; for better or worse it must be accepted as a phenomenon unique in kind. The phenomenology of the psyche contains more than the measurable facts of the natural sciences: it embraces the problem of mind, the father of all science. The psychotherapist becomes acutely aware of this when he is driven to penetrate below the level of accepted opinion. It is often objected that people have practiced psychotherapy before now and did not find it necessary to go into all these complications. I readily admit that Hippocrates, Galen, and Paracelsus were excellent doctors, but I do not believe that modern medicine should on that account give up serum therapy and radiology. It is no doubt difficult, particularly for the layman, to understand the complicated problems of psychotherapy; but if he will just consider for a moment why certain situations in life or certain experiences are pathogenic, he will discover that human opinion often plays a decisive part. Certain things accordingly seem dangerous, or impossible, or harmful, simply because there are opinions that cause them to appear in that light. For instance, many people regard wealth as the supreme happiness and poverty as man's greatest curse, although in actual fact riches never brought supreme happiness to anybody, nor is poverty a reason for melancholia. But we have these opinions, and these opinions are rooted in certain mental preconceptions—in the *Zeitgeist*, or in certain religious or anti-religious views. These last play an important part in moral conflicts. As soon as the analysis of a patient's psychic situation impinges on the area of his mental preconceptions, we have already entered the realm of general ideas. The fact that dozens of normal people never criticize their mental preconceptions—obviously not, since they are unconscious of them—does not prove that these preconceptions are valid for all men, or indeed unconscious for all men, any more than it proves that they may not become the source of the severest moral conflict. Quite the contrary: in our age of revolutionary change, inherited prejudices of a general nature on the one hand and spiritual and moral disorientation on the other are very often the deeper-lying causes of far-reaching disturbances in psychic equilibrium. To these patients the doctor has absolutely nothing to offer but the possibility of individual development. And for their sake the specialist is compelled to extend his knowledge over the field of the humane sciences, if he is to do justice to the symbolism of psychic contents.

(c) Making Life Meaningful

For all his insistence on the inner, psychological function of myth, Jung maintains that myth also serves to connect human beings to the external world. That connection gives meaning to life. By transforming an indifferent, impersonal world into a world of responsive, divine personalities, myth harmonizes the outer world with the inner one—the gods "out there" with the gods within.

From "The Psychology of the Child Archetype," CW 9 i, par. 261

261   Myths, on the contrary, have a vital meaning. Not merely do they represent, they *are* the psychic life of the primitive tribe, which immediately falls to pieces and decays when it loses its mythological heritage, like a man who has lost his soul. A tribe's mythology is its living religion, whose loss is always and everywhere, even among the civilized, a moral catastrophe.

From "The Archetype in Dream Symbolism," CW 18, pars. 547–48

547   One can perceive the specific energy of the archetypes when one experiences the peculiar feeling of numinosity that accompanies them—the fascination or spell that emanates from them. This is also characteristic of the personal complexes, whose be-

haviour may be compared with the role played by the archetypal *représentations collectives* in the social life of all times. As personal complexes have their individual history, so do social complexes of an archetypal character. But while personal complexes never produce more than a personal bias, archetypes create myths, religions, and philosophical ideas that influence and set their stamp on whole nations and epochs. And just as the products of personal complexes can be understood as compensations of onesided or faulty attitudes of consciousness, so myths of a religious nature can be interpreted as a sort of mental therapy for the sufferings of mankind, such as hunger, war, disease, old age, and death.

548 The universal hero myth, for example, shows the picture of a powerful man or god-man who vanquishes evil in the form of dragons, serpents, monsters, demons, and enemies of all kinds, and who liberates his people from destruction and death. The narration or ritual repetition of sacred texts and ceremonies, and the worship of such a figure with dances, music, hymns, prayers, and sacrifices, grip the audience with numinous emotions and exalt the participants to identification with the hero. If we contemplate such a situation with the eyes of a believer, we can understand how the ordinary man is gripped, freed from his impotence and misery, and raised to an almost superhuman status, at least for the time being, and often enough he is sustained by such a conviction for a long time. An initiation of this kind produces a lasting impression, and may even create an attitude that gives a certain form and style to the life of a society. I would mention as an example the Eleusinian mysteries, which were finally suppressed at the beginning of the seventh century. They formed, together with the Delphic oracle, the essence and spirit of ancient Greece. On a much greater scale the Christian era owes its name and significance to another antique mystery, that of the god-man, which has its roots in the archetypal Osiris-Horus myth of ancient Egypt.

From "The Function of Religious Symbols," CW 18, pars. 566–67

566 One even regrets the loss of such convictions. Since it is a matter of invisible and unknowable things (God is beyond human understanding, and immortality cannot be proved), why should we bother about evidence or truth? Suppose we did not know and understand the need for salt in our food, we would nevertheless profit from its use. Even if we should assume that

salt is an illusion of our taste-buds, or a superstition, it would
still contribute to our wellbeing. Why, then, should we deprive
ourselves of views that prove helpful in crises and give a meaning to our existence? And how do we know that such ideas are
not true? Many people would agree with me if I stated flatly
that such ideas are illusions. What they fail to realize is that this
denial amounts to a "belief" and is just as impossible to prove
as a religious assertion. We are entirely free to choose our
standpoint; it will in any case be an arbitrary decision. There is,
however, a strong empirical reason why we should hold beliefs
that we know can never be proved. It is that they are known to
be useful. Man positively needs general ideas and convictions
that will give a meaning to his life and enable him to find his
place in the universe. He can stand the most incredible hard-
ships when he is convinced that they make sense; but he is
crushed when, on top of all his misfortunes, he has to admit
that he is taking part in a "tale told by an idiot."

567   It is the purpose and endeavor of religious symbols to give a
meaning to the life of man. The Pueblo Indians believe that
they are the sons of Father Sun, and this belief gives their life a
perspective and a goal beyond their individual and limited existence. It leaves ample room for the unfolding of their personality, and is infinitely more satisfactory than the certainty that
one is and will remain the underdog in a department store. If
St. Paul had been convinced that he was nothing but a wandering weaver of carpets, he would certainly not have been himself. His real and meaningful life lay in the certainty that he was
the messenger of the Lord. You can accuse him of megalomania, but your opinion pales before the testimony of history
and the *consensus omnium*. The myth that took possession of
him made him something greater than a mere craftsman.

From **Memories, Dreams, Reflections**, p. 340

The need for mythic statements is satisfied when we frame a
view of the world which adequately explains the meaning of
human existence in the cosmos, a view which springs from our
psychic wholeness, from the co-operation between conscious
and unconscious. Meaninglessness inhibits fullness of life and is
therefore equivalent to illness. Meaning makes a great many
things endurable — perhaps everything. No science will ever replace myth, and a myth cannot be made out of any science.

(d) Abetting Therapy

Clinically, myth "amplifies" the symbols that appear in the dreams and waking lives of patients and analysands by providing parallels from around the world. Myth here means comparative mythology, which, by cataloguing recurrent motifs, helps identify the archetypes expressed by the particular symbols in the lives of patients and analysands.

From "**Schizophrenia**," CW 3, pars. 575–76

575   In general, the patient's degree of intelligence and education is of considerable importance for the prognosis. In cases of passing, acute intervals, or in the early stages of the disease, an explanatory discussion of the symptoms, especially of the psychotic contents, seems to me of the greatest value. Since fascination by archetypal contents is particularly dangerous, an explanation of their universal, impersonal meaning seems to me especially helpful, as opposed to the usual discussion of personal complexes. These complexes are the things that called forth the archaic reactions and compensations in the first place, and can obviously produce the same effects again at any time. Often, therefore, one must help the patient to detach his interest from these personal sources of excitation, at least temporarily, so as to give him a general orientation and a broader view of his confused situation. I have therefore made it a rule to give the intelligent patient as much psychological knowledge as he can stand. The more he knows in this respect, the better his whole prognosis will turn out; for if he is equipped with the necessary knowledge he can meet renewed irruptions of the unconscious with understanding and in this way assimilate the strange contents and integrate them into his conscious life. So in cases where the patients remember the content of their psychosis, I discuss it with them in detail and try to get them to understand it as thoroughly as possible.

576   This procedure naturally demands of the doctor more than merely psychiatric knowledge, for he must know about mythology, primitive psychology, etc. All this is today part of the equipment of the psychotherapist, just as it formed an essential part of medical knowledge up to the Age of Enlightenment. (One thinks, for instance, of the Paracelsist physicians of the Middle Ages.) You cannot handle the human psyche, especially when it is sick, with the ignorance of a layman, whose knowledge of it is confined to his personal complexes. For the same

reason the practice of somatic medicine presupposes a thorough knowledge of anatomy and physiology. For just as there is an objective human body and not merely a subjective and personal one, so also there is an objective psyche with its specific structures and activities of which the psychotherapist should have at any rate adequate knowledge. In this matter little has changed during the last half century. There are some — in my view — premature attempts at theory-building, but they are frustrated by professional prejudice and by insufficient knowledge of the facts. Very many more experiences in all fields of psychic research need to be collected before even such foundations could be laid as would bear comparison, for instance, with the findings of comparative anatomy. Nowadays we know infinitely more about the nature of the body than we do about the structure of the psyche, despite the fact that its biology is becoming more and more important for an understanding of somatic disorders and, finally, of man himself.

From "The Aims of Psychotherapy," CW 16, pars. 95–96

95   But I go still further: Not only do I give the patient an opportunity to find associations to his dreams, I give myself the same opportunity. Further, I present him with my ideas and opinions. If, in so doing, I open the door to "suggestion," I see no occasion for regret; for it is well known that we are susceptible only to those suggestions with which we are already secretly in accord. No harm is done if now and then one goes astray in this riddle-reading: sooner or later the psyche will reject the mistake, much as the organism rejects a foreign body. I do not need to prove that my interpretation of the dream is right (a pretty hopeless undertaking anyway), but must simply try to discover, with the patient, what *acts* for him — I am almost tempted to say, what is actual.

96   For this reason it is particularly important for me to know as much as possible about primitive psychology, mythology, archaeology, and comparative religion, because these fields offer me invaluable analogies with which I can enrich the associations of my patients. Together, we can then find meaning in apparent irrelevancies and thus vastly increase the effectiveness of the dream. For the layman who has done his utmost in the personal and rational sphere of life and yet has found no meaning and no satisfaction there, it is enormously important to be able to enter a sphere of irrational experience. In this way, too, the habitual and the commonplace come to wear an altered

countenance, and can even acquire a new glamour. For it all depends on how we look at things, and not on how they are in themselves. The least of things with a meaning is always worth more in life than the greatest of things without it.

From "Foreword to the First Volume of Studies from the C. G. Jung Institute," CW 18, par. 1164[1]

1164   The forthcoming publications in this series will show the great diversity of psychological interests and needs. Recent developments in psychological research, in particular the psychology of the collective unconscious, have confronted us with problems which require the collaboration of other sciences. The facts and relationships unearthed by the analysis of the unconscious offer so many parallels to the phenomenology of myths, for example, that their psychological elucidation may also shed light on the mythological figures and their symbols. At all events, we must gratefully acknowledge the invaluable support psychology has received from students of myths and fairytales, as well as from comparative religion, even if they on their part have not yet learnt how to make use of its insights. The psychology of the unconscious is still a very young science which must first justify its existence before a critical public. This is the end which the publications of the Institute are designed to serve.

September 1948

(e) Providing Models for Behavior

The lives of heroes described in myths serve as models for members of society to emulate. Myth here abets socialization. Hero myths also reassure one that others have had struggles like one's own. Myth here helps the individual and not just society.

[1] [Vol. I of Studien aus dem C. G. Jung Institut, Zurich, 1949: C. A. Meier, *Antike Inkubation und moderne Psychotherapie*. The foreword was published in a trans. by Ralph Manheim, in the first vol. of Studies in Jungian Thought, James Hillman, General Editor: *Evil: Essays by Carl Kerényi* [and others] (Evanston, Ill., 1967), and (same series, same year), in a trans. of Meier's book: *Ancient Incubation and Modern Psychotherapy*. The present trans. is by R.F.C. Hull.]

From **C. G. Jung Speaking,** pp. 292–93

For instance, the way in which a man should behave is given by an archetype. That is why primitives tell the stories they do. A great deal of education goes through story-telling. They call a palaver of the young men and two older men *perform* before the eyes of the younger all the things they should not do. Then they say, "Now that's exactly the thing you shall not do." Another way is to *tell* them of all the things they should not do, like the decalogue — "Thou shalt not." And that is always supported by mythological tales. Our ancestors have done so and so, and so shall you. Or such and such a hero has done so and so, and this is your model. Again, in the teachings of the Catholic Church there are several thousand saints. They show us what to do, they serve as models. They have their legends and that is Christian mythology. In Greece there was Theseus, there was Heracles, models of fine men, of gentlemen, you know, and they teach us how to behave. They are archetypes of behavior.

Chapter 4. Myths and Dreams/ Fantasies

Like Freud, Jung takes dreams as the analogue to myths. For Jung, both myths and dreams arise from the collective unconscious and serve to spur one to tend to it. Still, myths are not the same as dreams. Whereas many dreams hail from the personal unconscious, all myths emanate from the collective unconscious. Whereas dreams are created unconsciously, myths are in part consciously created, even if their meaning is unconscious. Whereas dreams are private, however recurrent their contents, myths are public, though there are also personal myths.

From "The Theory of Psychoanalysis," CW 4, par. 316

316   Without wishing to enter fully into the question of technique, I must here meet an objection that is constantly heard. It is that the so-called unconscious fantasies are merely suggested to the patient and exist only in the mind of the analyst. This objection is on the same vulgar level as those which impute to us the crude mistakes of beginners. Only people with no psychological experience and no knowledge of the history of psychology are capable of making such accusations. No one with the faintest glimmering of mythology could possibly fail to see the startling parallels between the unconscious fantasies brought to light by the psychoanalytic school and mythological ideas. The objection that our knowledge of mythology has been suggested to the patient is without foundation, because the psychoanalytic school discovered the fantasies first and only then became acquainted with their mythology. Mythology, as we know, is something quite outside the ken of the medical man.

From "The Theory of Psychoanalysis," CW 4, par. 341

341   The fantasies of adults are, in so far as they are conscious, immensely varied and take the most strongly individual forms. It is therefore impossible to give a general description of them. But it is very different when we enter by means of analysis into the world of unconscious fantasies. The diversity of the fantasy-material is indeed very great, but we do not find nearly so many individual peculiarities as in the conscious realm. We meet here with more typical material which is not infrequently repeated in similar form in different individuals. Constantly recurring in these fantasies are ideas which are variations of those found in religion and mythology. This fact is so striking that we may say we have discovered in these fantasies the forerunners of religious and mythological ideas.

From "The Role of the Unconscious," CW 10, pars. 11-13

11   The concept of a personal unconscious does not, however, enable us fully to grasp the nature of the unconscious. If the unconscious were only personal, it would in theory be possible to trace all the fantasies of an insane person back to individual experiences and impressions. No doubt a large proportion of the fantasy-material could be reduced to his personal history, but there are certain fantasies whose roots in the individual's previous history one would seek for in vain. What sort of fantasies are these? They are, in a word, *mythological fantasies.* They are elements which do not correspond to any events or experiences of personal life, but only to myths.

12   Where do these mythological fantasies come from, if they do not spring from the personal unconscious and hence from the experiences of personal life? Indubitably they come from the brain — indeed, precisely from the brain and not from personal memory-traces, but from the inherited brain-structure itself. Such fantasies always have a highly original and "creative" character. They are like new creations; obviously they derive from the creative activity of the brain and not simply from its mnemonic activity. We receive along with our body a highly differentiated brain which brings with it its entire history, and when it becomes creative it creates out of this history — out of the history of mankind. By "history" we usually mean the history which we "make," and we call this "objective history." The truly creative fantasy activity of the brain has nothing to do with this kind of history, but solely with

that age-old natural history which has been transmitted in living form since the remotest times, namely, the history of the brain-structure. And this structure tells its own story, which is the story of mankind: the unending myth of death and rebirth, and of the multitudinous figures who weave in and out of this mystery.

13   This unconscious, buried in the structure of the brain and disclosing its living presence only through the medium of creative fantasy, is the *suprapersonal unconscious*. It comes alive in the creative man, it reveals itself in the vision of the artist, in the inspiration of the thinker, in the inner experience of the mystic. The suprapersonal unconscious, being distributed throughout the brain-structure, is like an all-pervading, omnipresent, omniscient spirit. It knows man as he always was, and not as he is at this moment; it knows him as myth. For this reason, also, the connection with the suprapersonal or *collective* unconscious means an extension of man beyond himself; it means death for his personal being and a rebirth in a new dimension, as was literally enacted in certain of the ancient mysteries. It is certainly true that without the sacrifice of man as he is, man as he was — and always will be — cannot be attained. And it is the artist who can tell us most about this sacrifice of the personal man, if we are not satisfied with the message of the Gospels.

From "**Analytical Psychology and Education**," CW 17, pars. 208–10

208   Our individual consciousness is a superstructure based on the collective unconscious, of whose existence it is normally quite unaware. The collective unconscious influences our dreams only occasionally, and whenever this happens, it produces strange and marvellous dreams remarkable for their beauty, or their demoniacal horror, or for their enigmatic wisdom — "big dreams," as certain primitives call them. People often hide such dreams as though they were precious secrets, and they are quite right to think them so. Dreams of this kind are enormously important for the individual's psychic balance. Often they go far beyond the limits of his mental horizon and stand out for years like spiritual landmarks, even though they may never be quite understood. It is a hopeless undertaking to interpret such dreams reductively, as their real value and meaning lie in themselves. They are spiritual experiences that defy any attempt at rationalization. In order to illustrate what I mean, I should like

to tell you the dream of a young theological student.[1] I do not know the dreamer myself, so my personal influence is ruled out. He dreamed *he was standing in the presence of a sublime hieratic figure called the "white magician," who was nevertheless clad in a long black robe. This magician had just ended a lengthy discourse with the words "And for that we require the help of the black magician." Then the door suddenly opened and another old man came in, the "black magician," who however was dressed in a white robe. He too looked noble and sublime. The black magician evidently wanted to speak with the white, but hesitated to do so in the presence of the dreamer. At that the white magician said, pointing to the dreamer, "Speak, he is an innocent." So the black magician began to relate a strange story of how he had found the lost keys of paradise and did not know how to use them. He had, he said, come to the white magician for an explanation of the secret of the keys. He told him that the king of the country in which he lived was looking for a suitable monument for himself. His subjects had chanced to dig up an old sarcophagus containing the mortal remains of a virgin. The king opened the sarcophagus, threw away the bones and had the sarcophagus buried again for later use. But no sooner had the bones seen the light of day, than the being to whom they had once belonged — the virgin — changed into a black horse that galloped off into the desert. The black magician pursued it across the sandy wastes and beyond, and there after many vicissitudes and difficulties he found the lost keys of paradise.* That was the end of his story and also, unfortunately, of the dream.

209   I think a dream like this will help to make clear the difference between an ordinary, personal dream and the "big" dream. Anybody with an open mind can at once feel the significance of the dream and will agree with me that such dreams come from a "different level" from that of the dreams we dream every night. We touch here upon problems of vast import, and it is tempting to dwell on this subject for a while. Our dream should serve to illustrate the activity of the layers that lie below the personal unconscious. The manifest meaning of the dream takes on a quite special aspect when we consider that the dreamer was a young theologian. It is evident that the relativity of good and evil is being presented to him in a most impressive manner. It would therefore be advisable to probe him on this point, and it

[1] [This case is also discussed in *Two Essays on Analytical Psychology*, CW 7, par. 287. — EDITORS.]

would be exceedingly interesting to learn what a theologian has to say about this eminently psychological question. Also the psychologist would be in the highest degree interested to see how a theologian would reconcile himself to the fact that the unconscious, while clearly distinguishing between the opposites, nevertheless recognizes their identity. It is hardly likely that a youthful theologian would consciously have thought of anything so heretical. Who, then, is the thinker of such thoughts? If we further consider that there are not a few dreams in which mythological motifs appear, and that these motifs are absolutely unknown to the dreamer, then the question arises of where such material comes from, since he has never encountered it anywhere in his conscious life, and who or what it is that thinks such thoughts and clothes them in such imagery—thoughts which, moreover, go beyond the dreamer's own mental horizon.[2] In many dreams and in certain psychoses we frequently come across archetypal material, i.e., ideas and associations whose exact equivalents can be found in mythology. From these parallels I have drawn the conclusion that there is a layer of the unconscious which functions in exactly the same way as the archaic psyche that produced the myths.

210   Although dreams in which these mythological parallels appear are not uncommon, the emergence of the collective unconscious, as I have called this myth-like layer, is an unusual event which only takes place under special conditions. It appears in the dreams dreamt at important junctures in life. The earliest dreams of childhood, if we can still remember them, often contain the most astonishing mythologems; we also find the primordial images in poetry and in art generally, while religious experience and dogma are a mine of archetypal lore.

From "The Tavistock Lectures: Lecture II," CW 18, pars. 85–86

85   The idea of the collective unconscious is really very simple. If it were not so, then one could speak of a miracle, and I am not a miracle-monger at all. I simply go by experience. If I could tell you the experiences you would draw the same conclusions about these archaic motifs. By chance, I stumbled somehow into mythology and have read more books perhaps than you. I have not always been a student of mythology. One day, when I

[2] I do not wish to give offense to the dreamer of the dream under discussion, whom I do not know personally; but I hardly think that a young man of twenty-two would be conscious of the problem broached by this dream, at least not of its full extent.

was still at the clinic, I saw a patient with schizophrenia who had a peculiar vision, and he told me about it. He wanted me to see it and, being very dull, I could not see it. I thought, "This man is crazy and I am normal and his vision should not bother me." But it did. I asked myself: What does it mean? I was not satisfied that it was just crazy, and later I came on a book by a German scholar, Dieterich,³ who had published part of a magic papyrus. I studied it with great interest, and on page 7 I found the vision of my lunatic "word for word." That gave me a shock. I said: "How on earth is it possible that this fellow came into possession of that vision?" It was not just one image, but a series of images and a literal repetition of them. I do not want to go into it now because it would lead us too far. It is a highly interesting case; as a matter of fact, I published it.⁴

86   This astonishing parallelism set me going. You probably have not come across the book of the learned professor Dieterich, but if you had read the same books and observed such cases you would have discovered the idea of the collective unconscious.

From "Foreword to Perry: *The Self in Psychotic Progress*," CW 18, pars. 833–34

833   Dr. Perry, in this book, gives an excellent picture of the psychic contents with which I found myself confronted. At the beginning, I felt completely at a loss in understanding the association of ideas which I could observe daily with my patients. I did not know then that all the time I had the key to the mystery in my pocket, inasmuch as I could not help seeing the often striking parallelism between the patients' delusions and mythological motifs. But for a long time I did not dare to assume any relationship between mythological formations and individual morbid delusions. Moreover, my knowledge of folklore, mythology, and primitive psychology was regrettably deficient, so that I was slow in discovering how common these parallels were. Our clinical approach to the human mind was only medical, which was about as helpful as the approach of the mineralogist to Chartres Cathedral. Our training as alienists was much concerned with the anatomy of the brain but not at all with the human psyche. One could not expect very much more

---

³ [Albrecht Dieterich, *Eine Mithrasliturgie*.]
⁴ [*Symbols of Transformation*, pars. 151ff.; *The Archetypes and the Collective Unconscious*, par. 105; *The Structure and Dynamics of the Psyche* (CW 8), pars. 228 and 318f.]

in those days, when even neuroses, with their overflow of psychological material, were a psychological *terra incognita*. The main art the students of psychiatry had to learn in those days was how not to listen to their patients.

834 Well, I had begun to listen, and so had Freud. He was impressed with certain facts of neurotic psychology, which he even named after a famous mythological model, but I was overwhelmed with "historical" material while studying the psychotic mind. From 1906 until 1912 I acquired as much knowledge of mythology, primitive psychology, and comparative religion as possible. This study gave me the key to an understanding of the deeper layers of the psyche and I was thus enabled to write my book[5] with the English title *Psychology of the Unconscious*. This title is slightly misleading, for the book represents the analysis of a prodromal schizophrenic condition. It appeared forty years ago, and last year I published a fourth, revised edition under the title *Symbols of Transformation*. One could not say that it had any noticeable influence on psychiatry. The alienist's lack of psychological interest is by no means peculiar to him. He shares it with a number of other schools of thought, such as theology, philosophy, political economy, history, and medicine, which all stand in need of psychological understanding and yet allow themselves to be prejudiced against it and remain ignorant of it. It is only within the last years, for instance, that medicine has recognized "psychosomatics."

From **C. G. Jung Speaking,** pp. 370–71

AT THE BASEL PSYCHOLOGY CLUB

QUESTION 2: *Can myth be equated with a collective dream? If so, are we to assume that a historical event either precedes or follows it?*

Here you must define more precisely what you mean by myth. Strictly speaking, a myth is a historical document. It is told, it is recorded, but it is not in itself a dream. It is the product of an unconscious process in a particular social group, at a particular time, at a particular place. This unconscious process can naturally be equated with a dream. Hence anyone who "mythologizes," that is, tells myths, is speaking out of this dream, and what is then retold or actually recorded is the myth. But you cannot, strictly speaking, properly take the myth as a unique historical event like a dream, an individual dream which

[5] [*Wandlungen und Symbole der Libido* (1911–12).]

has its place in a time sequence; you can do that only *grosso modo*. You can say that at a particular place, at a particular time, a particular social group was caught up in such a process, and perhaps you can so to speak condense this process, covering it may be several thousand years, and say this epoch historically precedes such and such, and historically follows such and such.

Chapter 5. Myth as a Way of Thinking.

Myth for Jung is not only a set of thoughts but also a way of thinking. In contrast to "directed," or "logical," thinking, which is deliberate, organized, and purposeful, mythic, or "fantasy," thinking is spontaneous, associative, and directionless. Directed thinking, which moderns equate with thinking per se, is subject to proof and evaluation. It develops slowly and is to be found above all in modern science. Fantasy thinking is unfettered. It is evinced above all in dreams and myths, in both of which anything can happen. Fantasy thinking is primitive thinking and is only gradually supplanted by directed thinking. Yet fantasy thinking continues to exist, especially in the dreams and myths of moderns. Myths carry fantasy thinking beyond dreams to the external world. Mythic thinking is thinking about the world, which is transformed into a dream-like reality.

From "Two Kinds of Thinking," CW 5, pars. 11–28

11   How is it that dreams are symbolical at all? In other words, whence comes this capacity for symbolic representation, of which we can discover no trace in our conscious thinking? Let us examine the matter a little more closely. If we analyse a train of thought, we find that we begin with an "initial" idea, or a "leading" idea, and then, without thinking back to it each time, but merely guided by a sense of direction, we pass on to a series of separate ideas that all hang together. There is nothing symbolical in this, and our whole conscious thinking proceeds along these lines.[1] If we scrutinize our thinking more closely still and follow out an intensive train of thought—the solution

---

[1] Cf. Liepmann, *Über Ideenflucht*; also my "Studies in Word Association" (1918/19 edn., p. 124). For thinking as subordination to a ruling idea, cf. Ebbinghaus, in *Kultur der Gegenwart*, pp. 221ff. Kuelpe (*Outlines of Psychology*, p. 447) expresses himself in a similar manner: in thinking "we find an anticipatory apperception, which covers a more or less extensive circle of individual reproductions, and differs from a group of accidental incentives to reproduction only in the consistency with which all ideas outside the circle are checked or suppressed."

of a difficult problem, for instance—we suddenly notice that we are *thinking in words*, that in very intensive thinking we begin talking to ourselves, or that we occasionally write down the problem or make a drawing of it, so as to be absolutely clear. Anyone who has lived for some time in a foreign country will certainly have noticed that after a while he begins to think in the language of that country. Any very intensive train of thought works itself out more or less in verbal form—if, that is to say, one wants to express it, or teach it, or convince someone of it. It is evidently directed *outwards*, to the outside world. To that extent, directed or logical thinking is reality-thinking,[2] a thinking that is adapted to reality,[3] by means of which we imitate the successiveness of objectively real things, so that the images inside our mind follow one another in the same strictly causal sequence as the events taking place outside it.[4] We also call this "thinking with directed attention." It has in addition the peculiarity of causing fatigue, and is for that reason brought into play for short periods only. The whole laborious achievement of our lives is adaptation to reality, part of which consists in directed thinking. In biological terms it is simply a process of psychic assimilation that leaves behind a corresponding state of exhaustion, like any other vital achievement.

12   The material with which we think is *language* and *verbal concepts*—something which from time immemorial has been directed outwards and used as a bridge, and which has but a single purpose, namely that of communication. So long as we think directedly, we think *for* others and speak *to* others.[5] Language was originally a system of emotive and imitative sounds—sounds which express terror, fear, anger, love, etc., and sounds which imitate the noises of the elements: the rush-

---

[2] In his *Psychologia empirica*, ch. II, § 23, p. 16, Christian Wolff says simply and precisely: "Cogitatio est actus animae quo sibi sui rerumque aliarum extra se conscia est" (Thinking is an act of the soul whereby it becomes conscious of itself and of other things outside itself).

[3] The element of adaptation is particularly stressed by William James in his definition of logical thinking (*Principles of Psychology*, II, p. 330): "Let us make this ability to deal with *novel* data the technical differentia of reasoning. This will sufficiently mark it out from common associative thinking."

[4] "Thoughts are shadows of our feelings, always darker, emptier, and simpler than these," says Nietzsche. Lotze (*Logik*, p. 552) remarks in this connection: "Thinking, if left to the logical laws of its own movement, coincides once more at the end of its correct trajectory with the behaviour of objectively real things."

[5] Cf. Baldwin's remarks quoted below. The eccentric philosopher Johann Georg Hamann (1730–88) actually equates reason with language. (See Hamann's writings, pub. 1821–43.) With Nietzsche reason fares even worse as "linguistic metaphysics." Friedrich Mauthner goes the furthest in this direction (*Sprache und Psychologie*); for him there is absolutely no thought without speech, and only speaking is thinking. His idea of the "word fetishism" that dominates science is worth noting.

ing and gurgling of water, the rolling of thunder, the roaring of the wind, the cries of the animal world, and so on; and lastly, those which represent a combination of the sound perceived and the emotional reaction to it.[6] A large number of onomatopoeic vestiges remain even in the more modern languages; note, for instance, the sounds for running water: *rauschen, rieseln, rûschen, rinnen, rennen, rush, river, ruscello, ruisseau, Rhein.* And note *Wasser, wissen, wissern, pissen, piscis, Fisch.*

13   Thus, language, in its origin and essence, is simply a system of signs or symbols that denote real occurrences or their echo in the human soul.[7] We must emphatically agree with Anatole France when he says:

What is thinking? And how does one think? We think with words; that in itself is sensual and brings us back to nature. Think of it! a metaphysician has nothing with which to build his world system except the perfected cries of monkeys and dogs. What he calls profound speculation and transcendental method is merely the stringing together, in an arbitrary order, of onomatopoeic cries of hunger, fear, and love from the primeval forests, to which have become attached, little by little, meanings that are believed to be abstract merely because they are loosely used. Have no fear that the succession of little cries, extinct or enfeebled, that composes a book of philosophy will teach us so much about the universe that we can no longer go on living in it.[8]

14   So our directed thinking, even though we be the loneliest thinkers in the world, is nothing but the first stirrings of a cry to our companions that water has been found, or the bear been killed, or that a storm is approaching, or that wolves are prowling round the camp. There is a striking paradox of Abelard's which intuitively expresses the human limitations of our complicated thought-process: "Speech is generated by the intellect and in turn generates intellect." The most abstract system of philosophy is, in its method and purpose, nothing more than an extremely ingenious combination of natural sounds.[9] Hence the

---

[6] Cf. Kleinpaul, *Das Leben der Sprache.*
[7] My small son gave me an explicit example of the subjectivity of such symbols, which originally seem to belong entirely to the subject: He described everything he wanted to take or eat with an energetic "stô lô!" (Swiss-German for "leave it!").
[8] *Le Jardin d'Epicure*, p. 80.
[9] It is difficult to estimate how great is the seductive influence of primitive word meanings on our thinking. "Everything that has ever been in consciousness remains as an active element in the unconscious," says Hermann Paul (*Prinzipien der Sprach-*

craving of a Schopenhauer or a Nietzsche for recognition and understanding, and the despair and bitterness of their loneliness. One might expect, perhaps, that a man of genius would luxuriate in the greatness of his own thoughts and renounce the cheap approbation of the rabble he despises; yet he succumbs to the more powerful impulse of the herd instinct. His seeking and his finding, his heart's cry, are meant for the herd and must be heeded by them. When I said just now that directed thinking is really thinking in words, and quoted that amusing testimony of Anatole France as drastic proof, this might easily give rise to the misunderstanding that directed thinking is after all "only a matter of words." That would certainly be going too far. Language must be taken in a wider sense than speech, for speech is only the outward flow of thoughts formulated for communication. Were it otherwise, the deaf-mute would be extremely limited in his thinking capacity, which is not the case at all. Without any knowledge of the spoken word, he too has his "language." Historically speaking, this ideal language, this directed thinking, is derived from primitive words, as Wundt has explained:

A further important consequence of the interaction of sound and meaning is that many words come to lose their original concrete significance altogether, and turn into signs for general ideas expressive of the apperceptive functions of relating and comparing, and their products. In this way abstract thought develops, which, because it would not be possible without the underlying changes of meaning, is itself the product of those psychic and psychophysical interchanges in which the development of language consists.[10]

15   Jodl[11] rejects the identity of language and thought on the ground that the same psychic fact can be expressed in different ways in different languages. From this he infers the existence of a "supra-linguistic" type of thinking. No doubt there is such a thing, whether one elects to call it "supra-linguistic" with Jodl

---

geschichte, p. 25). The old word-meanings continue to have an effect which is imperceptible at first and proceeds "from that dark chamber of the unconscious in the soul" (ibid.). Hamann states emphatically (Schriften, VII, p. 8): "Metaphysics misuses all the verbal signs and figures of speech based on empirical knowledge and reduces them to empty hieroglyphs and types of ideal relationships." Kant is supposed to have learnt a thing or two from Hamann.

[10] Grundriss der Psychologie, pp. 363–64.
[11] Lehrbuch aer Psychologie, II, ch. 10, par. 26, p. 260.

or "hypological" with Erdmann. Only, it is not logical thinking. My views coincide with those of Baldwin, who says:

> The transition from pre-judgmental to judgmental meaning is just that from knowledge which has social confirmation to that which gets along without it. The meanings utilized for judgment are those already developed in their presuppositions and implications through the confirmations of social intercourse. Thus the personal judgment, trained in the methods of social rendering, and disciplined by the interaction of its social world, projects its content into that world again. In other words, the platform for all movement into the assertion of individual judgment — the level from which new experience is utilized — is *already and always socialized*; and it is just this movement that we find reflected in the actual result as the sense of the "appropriateness" or synnomic character of the meaning rendered. . . .
>
> Now the development of thought, as we are to see in more detail, is by a method essentially of trial and error, of experimentation, of *the use of meanings as worth more than they are as yet recognized to be worth*. The individual must use his old thoughts, his established knowledge, his grounded judgments, for the embodiment of his new inventive constructions. He erects his thought as we say "schematically" — in logical terms, problematically, conditionally, disjunctively — projecting into the world an opinion still personal to himself, as if it were true. *Thus all discovery proceeds*. But this is, from the linguistic point of view, still to use the current language, still to work by meanings already embodied in social and conventional usage.
>
> By this experimentation both thought and language are together advanced. . . .
>
> Language grows, therefore, just as thought does, *by never losing its synnomic* or dual reference; its meaning is both personal and social. . . .
>
> Language is the register of tradition, the record of racial conquest, the deposit of all the gains made by the genius of individuals. . . . The social "copy-system" thus established reflects the judgmental processes of the race, and in turn becomes the training-school of the judgment of new generations. . . .
>
> Most of the training of the self, whereby the vagaries of personal reaction to fact and image are reduced to the funded basis of sound judgment, comes through the use of speech.

When the child speaks, he lays before the world his suggestion for a general or common meaning; the reception it gets confirms or refutes him. In either case he is instructed. His next venture is from a platform of knowledge on which the newer item is more nearly convertible into the common coin of effective intercourse. The point to notice here is not so much the exact mechanism of the exchange — secondary conversion — by which this gain is made, as the training in judgment that the constant use of it affords. In each case, effective judgment is the common judgment. . . . Here the object is to point out that it is secured by the development of a function *whose rise is directly* ad hoc . . . *— the function of speech.*

In language, therefore, to sum up the foregoing, we have the tangible — the actual and historical — instrument of the development and conservation of psychic meaning. It is the material evidence and proof of *the concurrence of social and personal judgment.* In it synnomic meaning, judged as "appropriate," becomes "social" meaning, held as socially generalized and acknowledged.[12]

16   Baldwin's argument lays ample stress on the limitations imposed on thought by language,[13] which are of the greatest importance both subjectively and objectively, i.e., psychologically and socially — so great, indeed, that we must ask ourselves whether the sceptical Mauthner[14] was not right in his view that thinking is speech and nothing more. Baldwin is more cautious and reserved, but at bottom he is plainly in favour of the primacy of speech.

17   Directed thinking or, as we might also call it, *thinking in words*, is manifestly an instrument of culture, and we shall not be wrong in saying that the tremendous work of education which past centuries have devoted to directed thinking, thereby forcing it to develop from the subjective, individual sphere to the objective, social sphere, has produced a readjustment of the human mind to which we owe our modern empiricism and technics. These are absolutely new developments in the history of the world and were unknown to earlier ages. Inquiring

---

[12] Baldwin, *Thought and Things*, II pp. 145ff.
[13] In this connection I would mention the experimental "investigations into the linguistic components of association" (1908) made by Eberschweiler [q.v., Bibliography] at my request, which disclose the remarkable fact that during an association experiment the intrapsychic association is influenced by phonetic considerations.
[14] See n. 5, above.

minds have often wrestled with the question of why the first-rate knowledge which the ancients undoubtedly had of mathematics, mechanics, and physics, coupled with their matchless craftsmanship, was never applied to developing the rudimentary techniques already known to them (e.g., the principles of simple machines) into a real technology in the modern sense of the word, and why they never got beyond the stage of inventing amusing curiosities. There is only one answer to this: the ancients, with a few illustrious exceptions, entirely lacked the capacity to concentrate their interest on the transformations of inanimate matter and to reproduce the natural process artificially, by which means alone they could have gained control of the forces of nature. What they lacked was training in directed thinking.[15] The secret of cultural development is the *mobility and disposability of psychic energy*. Directed thinking, as we know it today, is a more or less modern acquisition which earlier ages lacked.

18   This brings us to a further question: What happens when we do not think directedly? Well, our thinking then lacks all leading ideas and the sense of direction emanating from them.[16] We no longer compel our thoughts along a definite track, but let them float, sink or rise according to their specific gravity. In Kuelpe's view,[17] thinking is a sort of "inner act of the will," and its absence necessarily leads to an "automatic play of ideas." William James regards non-directed thinking, or "merely associative" thinking, as the ordinary kind. He expresses himself as follows:

Much of our thinking consists of trains of images suggested one by another, of a sort of spontaneous revery of which it seems likely enough that the higher brutes should be

[15] There was as a matter of fact no external compulsion which would have made technical thinking necessary. The labour question was solved by an endless supply of cheap slaves, so that efforts to save labour were superfluous. We must also remember that the interest of the man of antiquity was turned in quite another direction: he reverenced the divine cosmos, a quality which is entirely lacking in our technological age.

[16] So at least it appears to the conscious mind. Freud (*The Interpretation of Dreams*, II, p. 528) says in this connection: "For it is demonstrably untrue that we are being carried along a purposeless stream of ideas when, in the process of interpreting a dream, we abandon reflection and allow involuntary ideas to emerge. It can be shown that all we can ever get rid of are purposive ideas that are *known* to us; as soon as we have done this, *unknown*—or, as we inaccurately say, 'unconscious'—purposive ideas take charge and thereafter determine the course of the involuntary ideas. No influence that we can bring to bear upon our mental processes can ever enable us to think without purposive ideas; nor am I aware of any states of psychical confusion which can do so."

[17] *Outlines*, p. 448.

capable. This sort of thinking leads nevertheless to rational conclusions both practical and theoretical.

As a rule, in this sort of irresponsible thinking the terms which come to be coupled together are empirical concretes, not abstractions.[18]

19   We can supplement James's definitions by saying that this sort of thinking does not tire us, that it leads away from reality into fantasies of the past or future. At this point thinking in verbal form ceases, image piles on image, feeling on feeling,[19] and there is an ever-increasing tendency to shuffle things about and arrange them not as they are in reality but as one would like them to be. Naturally enough, the stuff of this thinking which shies away from reality can only be the past with its thousand and-one memory images. Common speech calls this kind of thinking "dreaming."

20   Anyone who observes himself attentively will find that the idioms of common speech are very much to the point, for almost every day we can see for ourselves, when falling asleep, how our fantasies get woven into our dreams, so that between day-dreaming and night-dreaming there is not much difference. We have, therefore, two kinds of thinking: directed thinking, and dreaming or fantasy-thinking. The former operates with speech elements for the purpose of communication, and is difficult and exhausting; the latter is effortless, working as it were spontaneously, with the contents ready to hand, and guided by

---

[18] *Principles*, II, p. 325.

[19] This statement is based primarily on experiences derived from the field of normal psychology. Indefinite thinking is very far removed from "reflection," particularly where readiness of speech is concerned. In psychological experiments I have frequently found that subjects—I am speaking only of cultivated and intelligent people—whom I allowed to indulge in reveries, as though unintentionally and without previous instruction, exhibited affects which could be registered experimentally, but that with the best will in the world they could express the underlying thought only very imperfectly or not at all. More instructive are experiences of a pathological nature, not so much those arising in the field of hysteria and the various neuroses, which are characterized by an overwhelming transference tendency, as experiences connected with introversion neurosis or psychosis, which must be regarded as constituting by far the greater number of mental disturbances, at any rate the whole of Bleuler's schizophrenic group. As already indicated by the term "introversion" (which I cursorily introduced in 1910, in my "Psychic Conflicts in a Child," pp. 13 and 16 [*Coll. Works*, Vol. 17]), this type of neurosis leads to an isolated inner life. And here we meet with that "supralinguistic" or pure "fantasy thinking" which moves in "inexpressible" images and feelings. You get some idea of this when you try to find out the meaning of the pitiful and muddled expressions used by these people. As I have often observed, it costs these patients endless trouble and effort to put their fantasies into ordinary human speech. A highly intelligent patient, who "translated" such a fantasy system for me piecemeal, used to say to me: "I know quite well what it's all about, I can see and feel everything, but it is quite impossible for me to find the right words for it."

unconscious motives. The one produces innovations and adaptation, copies reality, and tries to act upon it; the other turns away from reality, sets free subjective tendencies, and, as regards adaptation, is unproductive.[20]

21   As I have indicated above, history shows that directed thinking was not always as developed as it is today. The clearest expression of modern directed thinking is science and the techniques fostered by it. Both owe their existence simply and solely to energetic training in directed thinking. Yet at the time when the forerunners of our present-day culture, such as the poet Petrarch, were just beginning to approach nature in a spirit of understanding,[21] an equivalent of our science already existed in scholasticism.[22] This took its subjects from fantasies of the past, but it gave the mind a dialectical training in directed thinking. The one goal of success that shone before the thinker was rhetorical victory in disputation, and not the visible transformation of reality. The subjects he thought about were often unbelievably fantastic; for instance, it was debated how many angels could stand on the point of a needle, whether Christ could have performed his work of redemption had he come into the world in the shape of a pea, etc., etc. The fact that these problems could be posed at all—and the stock metaphysical problem of how to know the unknowable comes into this category—

[20] Similarly James, *Principles*, II, pp. 325–26. Reasoning is productive, whereas "empirical" (merely associative) thinking is only reproductive. This opinion, however, is not altogether satisfying. It is no doubt true that fantasy-thinking is not immediately productive, i.e., is unadapted and therefore useless for all practical purposes. But in the long run the play of fantasy uncovers creative forces and contents, just as dreams do. Such contents cannot as a rule be realized except through passive, associative, and fantasy-thinking.

[21] Cf. the impressive description of Petrarch's ascent of Mt. Ventoux, in Burckhardt, *The Civilization of the Renaissance in Italy*, pp. 180–81: "A description of the view from the summit would be looked for in vain, not because the poet was insensible to it, but, on the contrary, because the impression was too overwhelming. His whole past life, with all its follies, rose before his mind; he remembered that ten years ago that day he had quitted Bologna a young man, and turned a longing gaze towards his native country; he opened a book which was then his constant companion, the 'Confessions of St. Augustine,' and his eye fell on the passage in the tenth chapter: 'and men go forth, and admire lofty mountains and broad seas, and roaring torrents, and the ocean, and the course of the stars, and turn away from themselves while doing so.' His brother, to whom he read these words, could not understand why he closed the book and said no more."

[22] Wundt gives a short account of the scholastic method in his *Philosophische Studien* (XIII, p. 345). The method consisted "firstly, in regarding as the chief aim of scientific investigation the discovery of a firmly established conceptual scheme capable of being applied in a uniform manner to the most varied problems; secondly, in laying an inordinate value upon certain general concepts, and consequently upon the verbal symbols designating these concepts, as a result of which an analysis of the meanings of words or, in extreme cases, a vapid intellectual subtlety and splitting of hairs comes to replace an investigation of the real facts from which the concepts are abstracted."

proves how peculiar the medieval mind must have been, that it could contrive questions which for us are the height of absurdity. Nietzsche glimpsed something of the background of this phenomenon when he spoke of the "glorious tension of mind" which the Middle Ages produced.

22   On a historical view, the scholastic spirit in which men of the intellectual calibre of St. Thomas Aquinas, Duns Scotus, Abelard, William of Ockham, and others worked is the mother of our modern scientific method, and future generations will see clearly how far scholasticism still nourishes the science of today with living undercurrents. It consisted essentially in a dialectical gymnastics which gave the symbol of speech, the word, an absolute meaning, so that words came in the end to have a substantiality with which the ancients could invest their Logos only by attributing to it a mystical value. The great achievement of scholasticism was that it laid the foundations of a solidly built intellectual function, the *sine qua non* of modern science and technology.

23   If we go still further back into history, we find what we call science dissolving in an indistinct mist. The culture-creating mind is ceaselessly employed in stripping experience of everything subjective, and in devising formulas to harness the forces of nature and express them in the best way possible. It would be a ridiculous and unwarranted presumption on our part if we imagined that we were more energetic or more intelligent than the men of the past — our material knowledge has increased, but not our intelligence. This means that we are just as bigoted in regard to new ideas, and just as impervious to them, as people were in the darkest days of antiquity. We have become rich in knowledge, but poor in wisdom. The centre of gravity of our interest has switched over to the materialistic side, whereas the ancients preferred a mode of thought nearer to the fantastic type. To the classical mind everything was still saturated with mythology, even though classical philosophy and the beginnings of natural science undeniably prepared the way for the work of "enlightenment."

24   Unfortunately, we get at school only a very feeble idea of the richness and tremendous vitality of Greek mythology. All the creative power that modern man pours into science and technics the man of antiquity devoted to his myths. This creative urge explains the bewildering confusion, the kaleidoscopic changes and syncretistic regroupings, the continual rejuvenation, of myths in Greek culture. We move in a world of fantasies which, untroubled by the outward course of things, well up

from an inner source to produce an ever-changing succession of plastic or phantasmal forms. This activity of the early classical mind was in the highest degree artistic: the goal of its interest does not seem to have been how to understand the real world as objectively and accurately as possible, but how to adapt it aesthetically to subjective fantasies and expectations. There was very little room among the ancients for that coldness and disillusionment which Giordano Bruno's vision of infinite worlds and Kepler's discoveries brought to mankind. The naïve man of antiquity saw the sun as the great Father of heaven and earth, and the moon as the fruitful Mother. Everything had its demon, was animated like a human being, or like his brothers the animals. Everything was conceived anthropomorphically or theriomorphically, in the likeness of man or beast. Even the sun's disc was given wings or little feet to illustrate its motion. Thus there arose a picture of the universe which was completely removed from reality, but which corresponded exactly to man's subjective fantasies. It needs no very elaborate proof to show that children think in much the same way. They too animate their dolls and toys, and with imaginative children it is easy to see that they inhabit a world of marvels.

25   We also know that the same kind of thinking is exhibited in dreams. The most heterogeneous things are brought together regardless of the actual conditions, and a world of impossibilities takes the place of reality. Freud finds that the hallmark of waking thought is *progression*: the advance of the thought stimulus from the systems of inner or outer perception through the endopsychic work of association to its motor end, i.e., innervation. In dreams he finds the reverse: regression of the thought stimulus from the pre-conscious or unconscious sphere to the perceptual system, which gives the dream its peculiar atmosphere of sensuous clarity, rising at times to almost hallucinatory vividness. Dream-thinking thus regresses back to the raw material of memory. As Freud says: "In regression the fabric of the dream-thoughts is resolved into its raw material."[23] The reactivation of original perceptions is, however, only one side of regression. The other side is regression to infantile memories, and though this might equally well be called regression to the original perceptions, it nevertheless deserves special mention because it has an importance of its own. It might even be considered as an "historical" regression. In this sense the dream can, with Freud, be described as a modified memory — modified

---

[23] *The Interpretation of Dreams*, II, p. 543.

through being projected into the present. The original scene of the memory is unable to effect its own revival, so has to be content with returning as a dream.[24] In Freud's view it is an essential characteristic of dreams to "elaborate" memories that mostly go back to early childhood, that is, to bring them nearer to the present and recast them in its language. But, in so far as infantile psychic life cannot deny its archaic character, the latter quality is the especial peculiarity of dreams. Freud expressly draws attention to this:

Dreams, which fulfil their wishes along the short path of regression, have merely preserved for us in that respect a sample of the psychical apparatus's primary method of working, a method which was abandoned as being inefficient. What once dominated waking life, while the mind was still young and incompetent, seems now to have been banished into the night — just as the primitive weapons, the bows and arrows, that have been abandoned by adult men, turn up once more in the nursery.[25]

26   These considerations[26] tempt us to draw a parallel between the mythological thinking of ancient man and the similar thinking found in children,[27] primitives, and in dreams. This idea is

---

[24] Ibid., p. 546.

[25] Ibid., p. 567.

[26] The passage in *The Interpretation of Dreams* that follows immediately afterwards has since been confirmed through investigation of the psychoses. "These methods of working on the part of the psychical apparatus, which are normally suppressed in waking hours, become current once more in psychosis and then reveal their incapacity for satisfying our needs in relation to the external world" (ibid., p. 567). The importance of this sentence is borne out by the views of Pierre Janet, which were developed independently of Freud and deserve mention here because they confirm it from an entirely different angle, namely the biological side. Janet distinguishes in the function a firmly organized "inferior" part and a "superior" part that is in a state of continuous transformation: "It is precisely on this 'superior' part of the functions, on their adaptation to existing circumstances, that the neuroses depend. . . . Neuroses are disturbances or checks in the evolution of the functions. . . . Neuroses are maladies dependent on the various functions of the organism and are characterized by an alteration in the superior parts of these functions, which are checked in their evolution, in their adaptation to the present moment and the existing state of the external world and of the individual, while there is no deterioration in the older parts of these same functions. . . . In place of these superior operations some degree of physical and mental disturbance develops — above all, emotionality. This is nothing but the tendency to replace the superior operations by an exaggeration of certain inferior operations, and particularly by gross visceral disturbances." (*Les Névroses*, pp. 386ff.) The "older parts" are the same as the "inferior parts" of the functions, and they replace the abortive attempts at adaptation. Similar views concerning the nature of neurotic symptoms are expressed by Claparède (p. 169). He regards the hysterogenic mechanism as a "tendance à la reversion," a kind of atavistic reaction.

[27] I am indebted to Dr. Abraham for the following story: "A small girl of three and a

not at all strange; we know it quite well from comparative anatomy and from evolution, which show that the structure and function of the human body are the result of a series of embryonic mutations corresponding to similar mutations in our racial history. The supposition that there may also be in psychology a correspondence between ontogenesis and phylogenesis therefore seems justified. If this is so, it would mean that infantile thinking[28] and dream-thinking are simply a recapitulation of earlier evolutionary stages.

27   In this regard, Nietzsche takes up an attitude well worth noting:

In sleep and in dreams we pass through the whole thought of earlier humanity. . . . What I mean is this: as man now reasons in dreams, so humanity also reasoned for many thousands of years when awake; the first cause which occurred to the mind as an explanation of anything that required explanation was sufficient and passed for truth. . . . This atavistic element in man's nature still manifests itself in our dreams, for it is the foundation upon which the higher reason has developed and still develops in every individual. Dreams carry us back to remote conditions of human culture and give us a ready means of understanding them better. Dream thinking comes so easily to us now because this form of fantastic and facile explanation in terms of the first random idea has been drilled into us for immense periods of time. To that extent dreaming is a recreation for the brain, which by day has to satisfy the stern demands of thought imposed by a higher culture. . . .

From this we can see how *lately* the more acute logical thinking, the strict discrimination of cause and effect, has been developed, since our rational and intellectual faculties still involuntarily hark back to those primitive forms of reasoning, and we pass about half our lives in this condition.[29]

---

half had been presented with a baby brother, who soon became the object of well-known childish jealousy. One day she said to her mother: 'You are two Mamas. You are my Mama, and your breast is little brother's Mama.' " She had just been observing with great interest the act of suckling. It is characteristic of the archaic thinking of the child to call the breast "Mama" [so in the original—EDITORS]. *Mamma* is Latin for 'breast.'

[28] Cf. particularly Freud's "Analysis of a Phobia in a Five-year-old Boy" and my "Psychic Conflicts in a Child."

[29] *Human, All-Too Human,* trans. by Zimmern and Cohn, I, pp. 24–27, modified.

28   Freud, as we have seen, reached similar conclusions regarding the archaic nature of dream-thinking on the basis of dream-analysis. It is therefore not such a great step to the view that myths are dreamlike structures. Freud himself puts it as follows: "The study of constructions of folk-psychology such as these is far from being complete, but it is extremely probable that myths, for instance, are distorted vestiges of the wishful phantasies of whole nations, the [age-long] dreams of youthful humanity."[30] In the same way Rank[31] regards myth as the collective dream of a whole people.[32]

[30] "Creative Writers and Day-Dreaming," p. 152, mod.
[31] *Der Künstler*, p. 36.
[32] Cf. also Rank, *The Birth of the Hero*.

Chapter 6. Kinds of Myths

(a) Myths of the Child

Jung's key essay on myth is "The Psychology of the Child Archetype." The following selection contains all but the first few pages of the essay. Scattered in other sections of this book are portions of those first few pages. Using the case of myths of the child to advance his theory of myth generally, Jung asserts that the figure of the child in mythology represents not, as for Freud, the actual child but the archetypal child, who symbolizes life's possibilities. The biography of the child in myth symbolizes both the range and the course of human psychological development. At birth, the child symbolizes the ego, but ultimately the child comes to symbolize the self, the archetype of psychological life as a whole. The course of the life of the child, who on the literal level remains a child all life long, symbolizes the course that an individual must follow to attain full psychological development.[1]

[1] "The Psychology of the Child Archetype" and the companion essay, "The Psychological Aspect of the Kore" (*The Archetypes and the Collective Unconscious*, pp. 151–81 and 182–203), were originally published separately in German (in 1940 and 1941). Each was accompanied by an essay by the Hungarian classicist and mythographer Carl (or Karl) Kerényi (1897–1973). In 1941 the two volumes were combined, with an added "prolegomena" by Kerényi, in a volume entitled *Einführung in das Wesen der Mythologie*, which was translated into English in 1949 as *Essays on a Science of Mythology* (or, in the 1950 British edition, as *Introduction to a Science of Mythology*). Despite their collaboration, Kerényi and Jung hold different, even opposing, views of myth. Kerényi does, like Jung, espouse the universality of archetypes, for which Kerényi prefers the term "mythologems," and Kerényi does allow for the origin of mythologems in the unconscious. But his interpretation of mythologems and therefore of myths themselves is far more spiritual than psychological. While he, like Jung, dismisses the reduction of myth to the allegorizing of natural phenomena, he dismisses as well the reduction of myth to anything else either, including psychology. He stresses the link of myth to cosmic, even if not physical, reality. Like Jung, Kerényi urges moderns to rediscover myths, but the fulfillment myths provide is for him more religious than psychological. Kerényi's theory is much closer to that of Mircea Eliade or of fellow classicist Walter Otto, whom he regularly cites, than to that of Jung. For his part, Jung uses Kerényi primarily as a data gatherer, whose cross-cultural examples of mythologems/archetypes serve to support Jung's claim that they are universal. For Kerényi's theory, see, in addition to the collaborative essays with Jung, *The Gods of the Greeks*, trans. Norman Cameron, esp. chap. 1; *Archetypal Images in Greek Religion*, 5 vols., trans. Ralph Manheim and Christopher Holme (New York: Pantheon, 1959–63; Princeton, N.J.: Princeton University Press, 1967–76), esp. *Asklepios*, vol. 3, preface.

From "The Psychology of the Child Archetype," CW 9 i, pars. 268–305

268   This archetype of the "child god" is extremely widespread and intimately bound up with all the other mythological aspects of the child motif. It is hardly necessary to allude to the still living "Christ-child," who, in the legend of Saint Christopher, also has the typical feature of being "smaller than small and bigger than big." In folklore the child motif appears in the guise of the *dwarf* or the *elf* as personifications of the hidden forces of nature. To this sphere also belongs the little metal man of late antiquity, the ἀνθρωπάριον,[2] who, till far into the Middle Ages, on the one hand inhabited the mine-shafts,[3] and on the other represented the alchemical metals,[4] above all Mercurius reborn in perfect form (as the hermaphrodite, *filius sapientiae*, or *infans noster*).[5] Thanks to the religious interpretation of the "child," a fair amount of evidence has come down to us from the Middle Ages showing that the "child" was not merely a traditional figure, but a vision spontaneously experienced (as a so-called "irruption of the unconscious"). I would mention Meister Eckhart's vision of the "naked boy" and the dream of Brother Eustachius.[6] Interesting accounts of these spontaneous experiences are also to be found in English ghost-stories, where we read of the vision of a "Radiant Boy" said to have been seen in a place where there are Roman remains.[7] This apparition was supposed to be of evil omen. It almost looks as though we were dealing with the figure of a *puer aeternus* who had become inauspicious through "metamorphosis," or in other words had shared the fate of the classical and the Germanic gods, who have all become bugbears. The mystical character of the experience is also confirmed in Part II of Goethe's *Faust*, where Faust himself is transformed into a boy and admitted into the "choir of blessed youths," this being the "larval stage" of Doctor Marianus.[8]

---

[2] Berthelot, *Alchimistes grecs*, III, xxv.

[3] Agricola, *De animantibus subterraneis* (1549); Kircher, *Mundus subterraneus* (1678), VIII, 4.

[4] Mylius, *Philosophia reformata* (1622).

[5] "Allegoria super librum Turbae" in *Artis auriferae*, I (1572), p. 161.

[6] *Texte aus der deutschen Mystik des 14. und 15. Jahrhunderts*, ed. Spamer, pp. 143, 150.

[7] Ingram, *The Haunted Homes and Family Traditions of Great Britain*, pp. 43ff.

[8] An old alchemical authority variously named Morienes, Morienus, Marianus ("De compositione alchemiae," Manget, *Bibliotheca chemica curiosa*, I, pp. 509ff.). In view of the explicitly alchemical character of *Faust*, Part II, such a connection would not be surprising.

269   In the strange tale called *Das Reich ohne Raum*, by Bruno Goetz, a *puer aeternus* named Fo (= Buddha) appears with whole troops of "unholy" boys of evil significance. (Contemporary parallels are better let alone.) I mention this instance only to demonstrate the enduring vitality of the child archetype.

270   The child motif not infrequently occurs in the field of psychopathology. The "imaginary" child is common among women with mental disorders and is usually interpreted in a Christian sense. Homunculi also appear, as in the famous Schreber case,[9] where they come in swarms and plague the sufferer. But the clearest and most significant manifestation of the child motif in the therapy of neuroses is in the maturation process of personality induced by the analysis of the unconscious, which I have termed the process of *individuation*.[10] Here we are confronted with preconscious processes which, in the form of more or less well-formed fantasies, gradually pass over into the conscious mind, or become conscious as dreams, or, lastly, are made conscious through the method of active imagination.[11] This material is rich in archetypal motifs, among them frequently that of the child. Often the child is formed after the Christian model; more often, though, it develops from earlier, altogether non-Christian levels — that is to say, out of chthonic animals such as crocodiles, dragons, serpents, or monkeys. Sometimes the child appears in the cup of a flower, or out of a golden egg, or as the centre of a mandala. In dreams it often appears as the dreamer's son or daughter or as a boy, youth, or young girl; occasionally it seems to be of exotic origin, Indian or Chinese, with a dusky skin, or, appearing more cosmically, surrounded by stars or with a starry coronet; or as the king's son or the witch's child with daemonic attributes. Seen as a special instance of "the treasure hard to attain" motif,[12] the child motif is extremely variable and assumes all manner of shapes, such as the jewel, the pearl, the flower, the chalice, the golden egg, the quaternity, the golden ball, and so on. It can be interchanged with these and similar images almost without limit.

---

[9] Schreber, *Memoirs of My Nervous Illness.*
[10] For a general presentation see infra, "Conscious, Unconscious, and Individuation." Special phenomena in the following text, also in *Psychology and Alchemy*, Part II.
[11] "The Relations between the Ego and the Unconscious," Part II, ch. 3 [also "The Transcendent Function" — EDITORS].
[12] *Symbols of Transformation*, index, s.v.

II. THE PSYCHOLOGY OF THE CHILD ARCHETYPE

1. *The Archetype as a Link with the Past*

271   As to the *psychology* of our theme I must point out that every statement going beyond the purely phenomenal aspects of an archetype lays itself open to the criticism we have expressed above. Not for a moment dare we succumb to the illusion that an archetype can be finally explained and disposed of. Even the best attempts at explanation are only more or less successful translations into another metaphorical language. (Indeed, language itself is only an image.) The most we can do is to *dream the myth onwards* and give it a modern dress. And whatever explanation or interpretation does to it, we do to our own souls as well, with corresponding results for our own well-being. The archetype — let us never forget this — is a psychic organ present in all of us. A bad explanation means a correspondingly bad attitude to this organ, which may thus be injured. But the ultimate sufferer is the bad interpreter himself. Hence the "explanation" should always be such that the functional significance of the archetype remains unimpaired, so that an adequate and meaningful connection between the conscious mind and the archetypes is assured. For the archetype is an element of our psychic structure and thus a vital and necessary component in our psychic economy. It represents or personifies certain instinctive data of the dark, primitive psyche, the real but invisible roots of consciousness. Of what elementary importance the connection with these roots is, we see from the preoccupation of the primitive mentality with certain "magic" factors, which are nothing less than what we would call archetypes. This original form of *religio* ("linking back") is the essence, the working basis of all religious life even today, and always will be, whatever future form this life may take.

272   There is no "rational" substitute for the archetype any more than there is for the cerebellum or the kidneys. We can examine the physical organs anatomically, histologically, and embryologically. This would correspond to an outline of archetypal phenomenology and its presentation in terms of comparative history. But we only arrive at the *meaning* of a physical organ when we begin to ask teleological questions. Hence the query arises: What is the biological purpose of the archetype? Just as physiology answers such a question for the body, so it is the business of psychology to answer it for the archetype.

273   Statements like "The child motif is a vestigial memory of one's own childhood" and similar explanations merely beg the

question. But if, giving this proposition a slight twist, we were to say, "The child motif is a picture of certain *forgotten* things in our childhood," we are getting closer to the truth. Since, however, the archetype is always an image belonging to the whole human race and not merely to the individual, we might put it better this way: "The child motif represents the pre-conscious, childhood aspect of the collective psyche."[13]

274 We shall not go wrong if we take this statement for the time being *historically*, on the analogy of certain psychological experiences which show that certain phases in an individual's life can become autonomous, can personify themselves to the extent that they result in a *vision of oneself*—for instance, one sees oneself as a child. Visionary experiences of this kind, whether they occur in dreams or in the waking state, are, as we know, conditional on a dissociation having previously taken place between past and present. Such dissociations come about because of various incompatibilities; for instance, a man's present state may have come into conflict with his childhood state, or he may have violently sundered himself from his original character in the interests of some arbitrary persona[14] more in keeping with his ambitions. He has thus become unchildlike and artificial, and has lost his roots. All this presents a favourable opportunity for an equally vehement confrontation with the primary truth.

275 In view of the fact that men have not yet ceased to make statements about the child god, we may perhaps extend the individual analogy to the life of mankind and say in conclusion that humanity, too, probably always comes into conflict with its childhood conditions, that is, with its original, unconscious, and instinctive state, and that the danger of the kind of conflict which induces the vision of the "child" actually exists. Reli-

[13] It may not be superfluous to point out that lay prejudice is always inclined to identify the child motif with the concrete experience "child," as though the real child were the cause and pre-condition of the existence of the child motif. In psychological reality, however, the empirical idea "child" is only the means (and not the only one) by which to express a psychic fact that cannot be formulated more exactly. Hence by the same token the mythological idea of the child is emphatically not a copy of the empirical child but a *symbol* clearly recognizable as such: it is a wonder-child, a divine child, begotten, born, and brought up in quite extraordinary circumstances, and not—this is the point—a human child. Its deeds are as miraculous or monstrous as its nature and physical constitution. Only on account of these highly unempirical properties is it necessary to speak of a "child motif" at all. Moreover, the mythological "child" has various forms: now a god, giant, Tom Thumb, animal, etc., and this points to a causality that is anything but rational or concretely human. The same is true of the "father" and "mother" archetypes which, mythologically speaking, are equally irrational symbols.
[14] *Psychological Types*, Def. 48; and *Two Essays on Analytical Psychology*, index, s.v. "persona."

gious observances, i.e., the retelling and ritual repetition of the mythical event, consequently serve the purpose of bringing the image of childhood, and everything connected with it, again and again before the eyes of the conscious mind so that the link with the original condition may not be broken.

2. The Function of the Archetype

276   The child motif represents not only something that existed in the distant past but also something that exists *now*; that is to say, it is not just a vestige but a system functioning in the present whose purpose is to compensate or correct, in a meaningful manner, the inevitable one-sidednesses and extravagances of the conscious mind. It is in the nature of the conscious mind to concentrate on relatively few contents and to raise them to the highest pitch of clarity. A necessary result and precondition is the exclusion of other potential contents of consciousness. The exclusion is bound to bring about a certain one-sidedness of the conscious contents. Since the differentiated consciousness of civilized man has been granted an effective instrument for the practical realization of its contents through the dynamics of his will, there is all the more danger, the more he trains his will, of his getting lost in one-sidedness and deviating further and further from the laws and roots of his being. This means, on the one hand, the possibility of human freedom, but on the other it is a source of endless transgressions against one's instincts. Accordingly, primitive man, being closer to his instincts, like the animal, is characterized by fear of novelty and adherence to tradition. To our way of thinking he is painfully backward, whereas we exalt progress. But our progressiveness, though it may result in a great many delightful wish-fulfillments, piles up an equally gigantic Promethean debt which has to be paid off from time to time in the form of hideous catastrophes. For ages man has dreamed of flying, and all we have got for it is saturation bombing! We smile today at the Christian hope of a life beyond the grave, and yet we often fall into chiliasms a hundred times more ridiculous than the notion of a happy Hereafter. Our differentiated consciousness is in continual danger of being uprooted; hence it needs compensation through the still existing state of childhood.

277   The symptoms of compensation are described, from the progressive point of view, in scarcely flattering terms. Since, to the superficial eye, it looks like a retarding operation, people speak of inertia, backwardness, scepticism, fault-finding, con-

servatism, timidity, pettiness, and so on. But inasmuch as man has, in high degree, the capacity for cutting himself off from his own roots, he may also be swept uncritically to catastrophe by his dangerous one-sidedness. The retarding ideal is always more primitive, more natural (in the good sense as in the bad), and more "moral" in that it keeps faith with law and tradition. The progressive ideal is always more abstract, more unnatural, and less "moral" in that it demands disloyalty to tradition. Progress enforced by will is always *convulsive*. Backwardness may be closer to naturalness, but in its turn it is always menaced by painful awakenings. The older view of things realized that progress is only possible *Deo concedente*, thus proving itself conscious of the opposites and repeating the age-old *rites d'entrée et de sortie* on a higher plane. The more differentiated consciousness becomes, the greater the danger of severance from the root-condition. Complete severance comes when the *Deo concedente* is forgotten. Now it is an axiom of psychology that when a part of the psyche is split off from consciousness it is only *apparently* inactivated; in actual fact it brings about a possession of the personality, with the result that the individual's aims are falsified in the interests of the split-off part. If, then, the childhood state of the collective psyche is repressed to the point of total exclusion, the unconscious content overwhelms the conscious aim and inhibits, falsifies, even destroys its realization. Viable progress only comes from the co-operation of both.

3. The Futurity of the Archetype

278   One of the essential features of the child motif is its futurity. The child is potential future. Hence the occurrence of the child motif in the psychology of the individual signifies as a rule an anticipation of future developments, even though at first sight it may seem like a retrospective configuration. Life is a flux, a flowing into the future, and not a stoppage or a backwash. It is therefore not surprising that so many of the mythological saviours are child gods. This agrees exactly with our experience of the psychology of the individual, which shows that the "child" paves the way for a future change of personality. In the individuation process, it anticipates the figure that comes from the synthesis of conscious and unconscious elements in the personality. It is therefore a symbol which unites the opposites;[15] a mediator, bringer of healing, that is, one who makes whole.

---

[15] *Psychological Types*, ch. V, 3: "The Significance of the Uniting Symbol."

Because it has this meaning, the child motif is capable of the numerous transformations mentioned above: it can be expressed by roundness, the circle or sphere, or else by the quaternity as another form of wholeness.[16] I have called this wholeness that transcends consciousness the "self."[17] The goal of the individuation process is the synthesis of the self. From another point of view the term "entelechy" might be preferable to "synthesis." There is an empirical reason why "entelechy" is, in certain conditions, more fitting: the symbols of wholeness frequently occur at the beginning of the individuation process, indeed they can often be observed in the first dreams of early infancy. This observation says much for the *a priori* existence of potential wholeness,[18] and on this account the idea of *entelechy* instantly recommends itself. But in so far as the individuation process occurs, empirically speaking, as a synthesis, it looks, paradoxically enough, as if something already existent were being put together. From this point of view, the term "synthesis" is also applicable.

4. Unity and Plurality of the Child Motif

279   In the manifold phenomenology of the "child" we have to distinguish between the *unity* and *plurality* of its respective manifestations. Where, for instance, numerous homunculi, dwarfs, boys, etc., appear, having no individual characteristics at all, there is the probability of a *dissociation*. Such forms are therefore found especially in schizophrenia, which is essentially a fragmentation of personality. The many children then represent the products of its dissolution. But if the plurality occurs in normal people, then it is the representation of an as yet incomplete synthesis of personality. The personality (viz., the "self") is still in the *plural stage*, i.e., an ego may be present, but it cannot experience its wholeness within the framework of its own personality, only within the community of the family, tribe, or nation; it is still in the stage of unconscious identification with the plurality of the group. The Church takes due account of this widespread condition in her doctrine of the *corpus mysticum*, of which the individual is by nature a member.

280   If, however, the child motif appears in the form of a unity, we are dealing with an unconscious and provisionally complete

---

[16] *Psychology and Alchemy*, pars. 327ff.; "Psychology and Religion," pars. 108ff.
[17] *Two Essays on Analytical Psychology*, pars. 399ff. [Cf. also *Aion*, ch. 4. — EDITORS.]
[18] *Psychology and Alchemy*, pars. 328ff.

synthesis of the personality, which in practice, like everything unconscious, signifies no more than a possibility.

5. Child God and Child Hero

281   Sometimes the "child" looks more like a *child god*, sometimes more like a young *hero*. Common to both types is the miraculous birth and the adversities of early childhood—abandonment and danger through persecution. The god is by nature wholly supernatural; the hero's nature is human but raised to the limit of the supernatural—he is "semi-divine." While the god, especially in his close affinity with the symbolic animal, personifies the collective unconscious which is not yet integrated into a human being, the hero's supernaturalness includes human nature and thus represents a synthesis of the ("divine," i.e., not yet humanized) unconscious and human consciousness. Consequently he signifies the potential anticipation of an individuation process which is approaching wholeness.

282   For this reason the various "child"-fates may be regarded as illustrating the kind of psychic events that occur in the entelechy or genesis of the "self." The "miraculous birth" tries to depict the way in which this genesis is experienced. Since it is a psychic genesis, everything must happen non-empirically, e.g., by means of a virgin birth, or by miraculous conception, or by birth from unnatural organs. The motifs of "insignificance," exposure, abandonment, danger, etc. try to show how precarious is the psychic possibility of wholeness, that is, the enormous difficulties to be met with in attaining this "highest good." They also signify the powerlessness and helplessness of the life-urge which subjects every growing thing to the law of maximum self-fulfillment, while at the same time the environmental influences place all sorts of insuperable obstacles in the way of individuation. More especially the threat to one's inmost self from dragons and serpents points to the danger of the newly acquired consciousness being swallowed up again by the instinctive psyche, the unconscious. The lower vertebrates have from earliest times been favourite symbols of the collective psychic substratum,[19] which is localized anatomically in the subcortical centres, the cerebellum and the spinal cord. These organs constitute the snake.[20] Snake-dreams usually occur, therefore, when the conscious mind is deviating from its instinctual basis.

---

[19] Higher vertebrates symbolize mainly affects.
[20] This interpretation of the snake is found as early as Hippolytus, *Elenchos*, IV, 49–51 (Legge trans., I, p. 117). Cf. also Leisegang, *Die Gnosis*, p. 146.

283   The motif of "smaller than small yet bigger than big" complements the impotence of the child by means of its equally miraculous deeds. This paradox is the essence of the hero and runs through his whole destiny like a red thread. He can cope with the greatest perils, yet, in the end, something quite insignificant is his undoing: Baldur perishes because of the mistletoe, Maui because of the laughter of a little bird, Siegfried because of his one vulnerable spot, Heracles because of his wife's gift, others because of common treachery, and so on.

284   The hero's main feat is to overcome the monster of darkness: it is the long-hoped-for and expected triumph of consciousness over the unconscious. Day and light are synonyms for consciousness, night and dark for the unconscious. The coming of consciousness was probably the most tremendous experience of primeval times, for with it a world came into being whose existence no one had suspected before. "And God said: 'Let there be light!'" is the projection of that immemorial experience of the separation of the conscious from the unconscious. Even among primitives today the possession of a soul is a precarious thing, and the "loss of soul" a typical psychic malady which drives primitive medicine to all sorts of psychotherapeutic measures. Hence the "child" distinguishes itself by deeds which point to the conquest of the dark.

III. THE SPECIAL PHENOMENOLOGY OF THE CHILD ARCHETYPE

1. The Abandonment of the Child

285   Abandonment, exposure, danger, etc. are all elaborations of the "child's" insignificant beginnings and of its mysterious and miraculous birth. This statement describes a certain psychic experience of a creative nature, whose object is the emergence of a new and as yet unknown content. In the psychology of the individual there is always, at such moments, an agonizing situation of conflict from which there seems to be no way out — at least for the conscious mind, since as far as this is concerned, *tertium non datur*. But out of this collision of opposites the unconscious psyche always creates a third thing of an irrational nature,[21] which the conscious mind neither expects nor understands. It presents itself in a form that is neither a straight "yes" nor a straight "no," and is consequently rejected by both. For the conscious mind knows nothing beyond the opposites

---

[21] *Psychological Types*, Def. 51.

and, as a result, has no knowledge of the thing that unites them. Since, however, the solution of the conflict through the union of opposites is of vital importance, and is moreover the very thing that the conscious mind is longing for, some inkling of the creative act, and of the significance of it, nevertheless gets through. From this comes the numinous character of the "child." A meaningful but unknown content always has a secret fascination for the conscious mind. The new configuration is a nascent whole; it is on the way to wholeness, at least in so far as it excels in "wholeness" the conscious mind when torn by opposites and surpasses it in completeness. For this reason all uniting symbols have a redemptive significance.

286   Out of this situation the "child" emerges as a symbolic content, manifestly separated or even isolated from its background (the mother), but sometimes including the mother in its perilous situation, threatened on the one hand by the negative attitude of the conscious mind and on the other by the *horror vacui* of the unconscious, which is quite ready to swallow up all its progeny, since it produces them only in play, and destruction is an inescapable part of its play. Nothing in all the world welcomes this new birth, although it is the most precious fruit of Mother Nature herself, the most pregnant with the future, signifying a higher stage of self-realization. That is why Nature, the world of the instincts, takes the "child" under its wing: it is nourished or protected by animals.

287   "Child" means something evolving towards independence. This it cannot do without detaching itself from its origins: abandonment is therefore a necessary condition, not just a concomitant symptom. The conflict is not to be overcome by the conscious mind remaining caught between the opposites, and for this very reason it needs a symbol to point out the necessity of detaching itself from its origins. Because the symbol of the "child" fascinates and grips the conscious mind, its redemptive effect passes over into consciousness and brings about that separation from the conflict-situation which the conscious mind by itself was unable to achieve. The symbol anticipates a nascent state of consciousness. So long as this is not actually in being, the "child" remains a mythological projection which requires religious repetition and renewal by ritual. The Christ Child, for instance, is a religious necessity only so long as the majority of men are incapable of giving psychological reality to the saying: "Except ye become as little children. . . ." Since all such developments and transitions are extraordinarily difficult and dangerous, it is no wonder that figures of this kind persist for hun-

dreds or even thousands of years. Everything that man should, and yet cannot, be or do — be it in a positive or negative sense — lives on as a mythological figure and anticipation alongside his consciousness, either as a religious projection or — what is still more dangerous — as unconscious contents which then project themselves spontaneously into incongruous objects, e.g., hygienic and other "salvationist" doctrines or practices. All these are so many rationalized substitutes for mythology, and their unnaturalness does more harm than good.

288   The conflict-situation that offers no way out, the sort of situation that produces the "child" as the irrational third, is of course a formula appropriate only to a psychological, that is, modern stage of development. It is not strictly applicable to the psychic life of primitives, if only because primitive man's childlike range of consciousness still excludes a whole world of possible psychic experiences. Seen on the nature-level of the primitive, our modern *moral* conflict is still an *objective* calamity that threatens life itself. Hence not a few child-figures are culture-heroes and thus identified with things that promote culture, e.g., fire,[22] metal, corn, maize, etc. As bringers of light, that is, enlargers of consciousness, they overcome darkness, which is to say that they overcome the earlier unconscious state. Higher consciousness, or knowledge going beyond our present-day consciousness, is equivalent to being *all alone in the world*. This loneliness expresses the conflict between the bearer or symbol of higher consciousness and his surroundings. The conquerors of darkness go far back into primeval times, and, together with many other legends, prove that there once existed a state of *original psychic distress*, namely *unconsciousness*. Hence in all probability the "irrational" fear which primitive man has of the dark even today. I found a form of religion among a tribe living on Mount Elgon that corresponded to pantheistic optimism. Their optimistic mood was, however, always in abeyance between six o'clock in the evening and six o'clock in the morning, during which time it was replaced by fear, for in the night the dark being Ayik has his dominion — the "Maker of Fear." During the daytime there were no monster snakes anywhere in the vicinity, but at night they were lurking on every path. At night the whole of mythology was let loose.

---

[22] Even Christ is of a fiery nature ("he that is near to me is near to the fire" — Origen, *In Jeremiam Homiliae*, XX, 3); likewise the Holy Ghost.

2. The Invincibility of the Child

289   It is a striking paradox in all child myths that the "child" is on the one hand delivered helpless into the power of terrible enemies and in continual danger of extinction, while on the other he possesses powers far exceeding those of ordinary humanity. This is closely related to the psychological fact that though the child may be "insignificant," unknown, "a mere child," he is also divine. From the conscious standpoint we seem to be dealing with an insignificant content that has no releasing, let alone redeeming, character. The conscious mind is caught in its conflict-situation, and the combatant forces seem so overwhelming that the "child" as an isolated content bears no relation to the conscious factors. It is therefore easily overlooked and falls back into the unconscious. At least, this is what we should have to fear if things turned out according to our conscious expectations. Myth, however, emphasizes that it is not so, but that the "child" is endowed with superior powers and, despite all dangers, will unexpectedly pull through. The "child" is born out of the womb of the unconscious, begotten out of the depths of human nature, or rather out of living Nature herself. It is a personification of vital forces quite outside the limited range of our conscious mind; of ways and possibilities of which our one-sided conscious mind knows nothing; a wholeness which embraces the very depths of Nature. It represents the strongest, the most ineluctable urge in every being, namely the urge to realize itself. It is, as it were, an incarnation of *the inability to do otherwise*, equipped with all the powers of nature and instinct, whereas the conscious mind is always getting caught up in its supposed ability to do otherwise. The urge and compulsion to self-realization is a law of nature and thus of invincible power, even though its effect, at the start, is insignificant and improbable. Its power is revealed in the miraculous deeds of the child hero, and later in the *athla* ('works') of the bondsman or thrall (of the Heracles type), where, although the hero has outgrown the impotence of the "child," he is still in a menial position. The figure of the thrall generally leads up to the real epiphany of the semi-divine hero. Oddly enough, we have a similar modulation of themes in alchemy — in the synonyms for the *lapis*. As the *materia prima*, it is the *lapis exilis et vilis*. As a substance in process of transmutation, it is *servus rubeus* or *fugitivus*; and finally, in its true apotheosis, it attains

the dignity of a *filius sapientiae* or *deus terrenus*, a "light above all lights," a power that contains in itself all the powers of the upper and nether regions. It becomes a *corpus glorificatum* which enjoys everlasting incorruptibility and is therefore a panacea ("bringer of healing").[23] The size and invincibility of the "child" are bound up in Hindu speculation with the nature of the atman, which corresponds to the "smaller than small yet bigger than big" motif. As an individual phenomenon, the self is "smaller than small"; as the equivalent of the cosmos, it is "bigger than big." The self, regarded as the counter-pole of the world, its "absolutely other," is the *sine qua non* of all empirical knowledge and consciousness of subject and object. Only because of this psychic "otherness" is consciousness possible at all. Identity does not make consciousness possible; it is only separation, detachment, and agonizing confrontation through opposition that produce consciousness and insight. Hindu introspection recognized this psychological fact very early and consequently equated the subject of cognition with the subject of ontology in general. In accordance with the predominantly introverted attitude of Indian thinking, the object lost the attribute of absolute reality and, in some systems, became a mere illusion. The Greek-Occidental type of mind could not free itself from the conviction of the world's absolute existence — at the cost, however, of the cosmic significance of the self. Even today Western man finds it hard to see the psychological necessity for a transcendental subject of cognition as the counterpole of the empirical universe, although the postulate of a world-confronting self, at least as a *point of reflection*, is a logical necessity. Regardless of philosophy's perpetual attitude of dissent or only half-hearted assent, there is always a compensating tendency in our unconscious psyche to produce a symbol of the self in its cosmic significance. These efforts take on the archetypal forms of the hero myth such as can be observed in almost any individuation process.

290   The phenomenology of the "child's" birth always points back to an original psychological state of non-recognition, i.e., of darkness or twilight, of non-differentiation between subject and object, of unconscious identity of man and the universe. This phase of non-differentiation produces the *golden egg*, which is both man and universe and yet neither, but an irrational third. To the twilight consciousness of primitive man it seems as if the

---

[23] The material is collected in *Psychology and Alchemy*, Parts II and III. For Mercurius as a servant, see the parable of Eirenaeus Philalethes, *Ripley Reviv'd: or, An Exposition upon Sir George Ripley's Hermetico-Poetical Works* (1678).

egg came out of the womb of the wide world and were, accordingly, a cosmic, objective, external occurrence. To a differentiated consciousness, on the other hand, it seems evident that this egg is nothing but a symbol thrown up by the psyche or — what is even worse — a fanciful speculation and therefore "nothing but" a primitive phantasm to which no "reality" of any kind attaches. Present-day medical psychology, however, thinks somewhat differently about these "phantasms." It knows only too well what dire disturbances of the bodily functions and what devastating psychic consequences can flow from "mere" fantasies. "Fantasies" are the natural expressions of the life of the unconscious. But since the unconscious is the psyche of all the body's autonomous functional complexes, its "fantasies" have an aetiological significance that is not to be despised. From the psychopathology of the individuation process we know that the formation of symbols is frequently associated with physical disorders of a psychic origin, which in some cases are felt as decidedly "real." In medicine, fantasies are *real things* with which the psychotherapist has to reckon very seriously indeed. He cannot therefore deprive of all justification those primitive phantasms whose content is so real that it is projected upon the external world. In the last analysis the human body, too, is built of the stuff of the world, the very stuff wherein fantasies become visible; indeed, without it they could not be experienced at all. Without this stuff they would be like a sort of abstract crystalline lattice in a solution where the crystallization process had not yet started.

291   The symbols of the self arise in the depths of the body and they express its materiality every bit as much as the structure of the perceiving consciousness. The symbol is thus a living body, *corpus et anima*; hence the "child" is such an apt formula for the symbol. The uniqueness of the psyche can never enter wholly into reality, it can only be realized approximately, though it still remains the absolute basis of all consciousness. The deeper "layers" of the psyche lose their individual uniqueness as they retreat farther and farther into darkness. "Lower down," that is to say as they approach the autonomous functional systems, they become increasingly collective until they are universalized and extinguished in the body's materiality, i.e., in chemical substances. The body's carbon is simply carbon. Hence "at bottom" the psyche is simply "world." In this sense I hold Kerényi to be absolutely right when he says that in the symbol the *world itself* is speaking. The more archaic and "deeper," that is the more *physiological*, the symbol is, the

more collective and universal, the more "material" it is. The more abstract, differentiated, and specific it is, and the more its nature approximates to conscious uniqueness and individuality, the more it sloughs off its universal character. Having finally attained full consciousness, it runs the risk of becoming a mere allegory which nowhere oversteps the bounds of conscious comprehension, and is then exposed to all sorts of attempts at rationalistic and therefore inadequate explanation.

3. The Hermaphroditism of the Child

292   It is a remarkable fact that perhaps the majority of cosmogonic gods are of a bisexual nature. The hermaphrodite means nothing less than a union of the strongest and most striking opposites. In the first place this union refers back to a primitive state of mind, a twilight where differences and contrasts were either barely separated or completely merged. With increasing clarity of consciousness, however, the opposites draw more and more distinctly and irreconcilably apart. If, therefore, the hermaphrodite were only a product of primitive non-differentiation, we would have to expect that it would soon be eliminated with increasing civilization. This is by no means the case; on the contrary, man's imagination has been preoccupied with this idea over and over again on the high and even the highest levels of culture, as we can see from the late Greek and syncretic philosophy of Gnosticism. The hermaphroditic *rebis* has an important part to play in the natural philosophy of the Middle Ages. And in our own day we hear of Christ's androgyny in Catholic mysticism.[24]

293   We can no longer be dealing, then, with the continued existence of a primitive phantasm, or with an original contamination of opposites. Rather, as we can see from medieval writings,[25] the primordial idea has become a *symbol of the creative union of opposites*, a "uniting symbol" in the literal sense. In its functional significance the symbol no longer points back, but forward to a goal not yet reached. Notwithstanding its monstrosity, the hermaphrodite has gradually turned into a subduer of conflicts and a bringer of healing, and it acquired this meaning in relatively early phases of civilization. This vital meaning explains why the image of the hermaphrodite did not fade out in primeval times but, on the contrary, was able to assert itself

---

[24] Koepgen, *Die Gnosis des Christentums*, pp. 315ff.
[25] For the *lapis* as mediator and medium, cf. *Tractatus aureus*, in Manget, *Bibliotheca chemica curiosa*, I, p. 408b, and *Artis auriferae* (1572), p. 641.

with increasing profundity of symbolic content for thousands of years. The fact that an idea so utterly archaic could rise to such exalted heights of meaning not only points to the vitality of archetypal ideas, it also demonstrates the rightness of the principle that the archetype, because of its power to unite opposites, mediates between the unconscious substratum and the conscious mind. It throws a bridge between present-day consciousness, always in danger of losing its roots, and the natural, unconscious, instinctive wholeness of primeval times. Through this mediation the uniqueness, peculiarity, and one-sidedness of our present individual consciousness are linked up again with its natural, racial roots. Progress and development are ideals not lightly to be rejected, but they lose all meaning if man only arrives at his new state as a fragment of himself, having left his essential hinterland behind him in the shadow of the unconscious, in a state of primitivity or, indeed, barbarism. The conscious mind, split off from its origins, incapable of realizing the meaning of the new state, then relapses all too easily into a situation far worse than the one from which the innovation was intended to free it—*exempla sunt odiosa!* It was Friedrich Schiller who first had an inkling of this problem; but neither his contemporaries nor his successors were capable of drawing any conclusions. Instead, people incline more than ever to educate *children* and nothing more. I therefore suspect that the *furor paedogogicus* is a god-sent method of by-passing the central problem touched on by Schiller, namely the *education of the educator.* Children are educated by what the grown-up *is* and not by what he *says.* The popular faith in words is a veritable disease of the mind, for a superstition of this sort always leads farther and farther away from man's foundations and seduces people into a disastrous identification of the personality with whatever slogan may be in vogue. Meanwhile everything that has been overcome and left behind by so-called "progress" sinks deeper and deeper into the unconscious, from which there re-emerges in the end the primitive condition of *identity with the mass.* Instead of the expected progress, this condition now becomes reality.

294   As civilization develops, the bisexual primordial being turns into a symbol of the unity of personality, a symbol of the self, where the war of opposites finds peace. In this way the primordial being becomes the distant goal of man's self-development, having been from the very beginning a projection of his unconscious wholeness. Wholeness consists in the union of the conscious and the unconscious personality. Just as every individual

derives from masculine and feminine genes, and the sex is determined by the predominance of the corresponding genes, so in
the psyche it is only the conscious mind, in a man, that has the
masculine sign, while the unconscious is by nature feminine.
The reverse is true in the case of a woman. All I have done in
my anima theory is to rediscover and reformulate this fact.[26] It
had long been known.

295   The idea of the *coniunctio* of male and female, which became
almost a technical term in Hermetic philosophy, appears in
Gnosticism as the *mysterium iniquitatis*, probably not uninfluenced by the Old Testament "divine marriage" as performed,
for instance, by Hosea.[27] Such things are hinted at not only by
certain traditional customs,[28] but by the quotation from the
Gospel according to the Egyptians in the second epistle of
Clement: "When the two shall be one, the outside as the inside,
and the male with the female neither male nor female."[29] Clement of Alexandria introduces this logion with the words:
"When ye have trampled on the garment of shame (with thy
feet) . . . ,"[30] which probably refers to the body; for Clement as
well as Cassian (from whom the quotation was taken over),
and the pseudo-Clement, too, interpreted the words in a spiritual sense, in contrast to the Gnostics, who would seem to have
taken the *coniunctio* all too literally. They took care, however,
through the practice of abortion and other restrictions, that the
biological meaning of their acts did not swamp the religious
significance of the rite. While, in Church mysticism, the primordial image of the *hieros gamos* was sublimated on a lofty plane
and only occasionally — as for instance with Mechthild of Mag-
deburg[31] — approached the physical sphere in emotional intensity, for the rest of the world it remained very much alive and
continued to be the object of especial psychic preoccupation. In
this respect the symbolical drawings of Opicinus de Canistris[32]
afford us an interesting glimpse of the way in which this primordial image was instrumental in uniting opposites, even in a
pathological state. On the other hand, in the Hermetic philosophy that throve in the Middle Ages the *coniunctio* was performed wholly in the physical realm in the admittedly abstract

---

[26] *Psychological Types*, Def. 48; and "Relations between the Ego and the Unconscious," pars. 296ff.
[27] Hosea 1 : 2ff.
[28] Cf. Fendt, *Gnostische Mysterien*.
[29] James, *The Apocryphal New Testament*, p. 11.
[30] Clement, *Stromata*, III, 13, 92, 2.
[31] *The Flowing Light of the Godhead*.
[32] Salomon, *Opicinus de Canistris*.

theory of the *coniugium solis et lunae*, which despite this drawback gave the creative imagination much occasion for anthropomorphic flights.

296   Such being the state of affairs, it is readily understandable that the primordial image of the hermaphrodite should reappear in modern psychology in the guise of the male-female antithesis, in other words as *male* consciousness and personified *female* unconscious. But the psychological process of bringing things to consciousness has complicated the picture considerably. Whereas the old science was almost exclusively a field in which only the man's unconscious could project itself, the new psychology had to acknowledge the existence of an autonomous female psyche as well. Here the case is reversed, and a feminine consciousness confronts a masculine personification of the unconscious, which can no longer be called *anima* but *animus*. This discovery also complicates the problem of the *coniunctio*.

297   Originally this archetype played its part entirely in the field of fertility magic and thus remained for a very long time a purely biological phenomenon with no other purpose than that of fecundation. But even in early antiquity the symbolical meaning of the act seems to have increased. Thus, for example, the physical performance of the *hieros gamos* as a sacred rite not only became a mystery — it faded to a mere conjecture.[33] As we have seen, Gnosticism, too, endeavoured in all seriousness to subordinate the physiological to the metaphysical. Finally, the Church severed the *coniunctio* from the physical realm altogether, and natural philosophy turned it into an abstract *theoria*. These developments meant the gradual transformation of the archetype into a psychological process which, in theory, we can call a combination of conscious and unconscious processes. In practice, however, it is not so simple, because as a rule the feminine unconscious of a man is projected upon a feminine partner, and the masculine unconscious of a woman is projected upon a man. The elucidation of these problems is a special branch of psychology and has no part in a discussion of the mythological hermaphrodite.

4. The Child as Beginning and End

298   Faust, after his death, is received as a boy into the "choir of blessed youths." I do not know whether Goethe was referring,

---

[33] Cf. the diatribe by Bishop Asterius (Foucart, *Mystères of d'Eleusis*, pp. 477ff.). According to Hippolytus' account the hierophant actually made himself impotent by a draught of hemlock. The self-castration of priests in the worship of the Mother Goddess is of similar import.

with this peculiar idea, to the *cupids* on antique grave-stones. It is not unthinkable. The figure of the *cucullatus* points to the hooded, that is, the *invisible* one, the genius of the departed, who reappears in the child-like frolics of a new life, surrounded by the sea-forms of dolphins and tritons. The sea is the favourite symbol for the unconscious, the mother of all that lives. Just as the "child" is, in certain circumstances (e.g., in the case of Hermes and the Dactyls), closely related to the phallus, symbol of the begetter, so it comes up again in the sepulchral phallus, symbol of a renewed begetting.

299   The "child" is therefore *renatus in novam infantiam.* It is thus both beginning and end, an initial and a terminal creature. The initial creature existed before man was, and the terminal creature will be when man is not. Psychologically speaking, this means that the "child" symbolizes the pre-conscious and the post-conscious essence of man. His pre-conscious essence is the unconscious state of earliest childhood; his post-conscious essence is an anticipation by analogy of life after death. In this idea the all-embracing nature of psychic wholeness is expressed. Wholeness is never comprised within the compass of the conscious mind — it includes the indefinite and indefinable extent of the unconscious as well. Wholeness, empirically speaking, is therefore of immeasurable extent, older and younger than consciousness and enfolding it in time and space. This is no speculation, but an immediate psychic experience. Not only is the conscious process continually accompanied, it is often guided, helped, or interrupted, by unconscious happenings. The child had a psychic life before it had consciousness. Even the adult still says and does things whose significance he realizes only later, if ever. And yet he said them and did them as if he knew what they meant. Our dreams are continually saying things beyond our conscious comprehension (which is why they are so useful in the therapy of neuroses). We have intimations and intuitions from unknown sources. Fears, moods, plans, and hopes come to us with no visible causation. These concrete experiences are at the bottom of our feeling that we know ourselves very little; at the bottom, too, of the painful conjecture that we might have surprises in store for ourselves.

300   Primitive man is no puzzle to himself. The question "What is man?" is the question that man has always kept until last. Primitive man has so much psyche outside his conscious mind that the experience of something psychic outside him is far more familiar to him than to us. Consciousness hedged about by psychic powers, sustained or threatened or deluded by them,

is the age-old experience of mankind. This experience has projected itself into the archetype of the child, which expresses man's wholeness. The "child" is all that is abandoned and exposed and at the same time divinely powerful; the insignificant, dubious beginning, and the triumphal end. The "eternal child" in man is an indescribable experience, an incongruity, a handicap, and a divine prerogative; an imponderable that determines the ultimate worth or worthlessness of a personality.

IV. CONCLUSION

301   I am aware that a psychological commentary on the child archetype without detailed documentation must remain a mere sketch. But since this is virgin territory for the psychologist, my main endeavour has been to stake out the possible extent of the problems raised by our archetype and to describe, at least cursorily, its different aspects. Clear-cut distinctions arid strict formulations are quite impossible in this field, seeing that a kind of fluid interpenetration belongs to the very nature of all archetypes. They can only be roughly circumscribed at best. Their living meaning comes out more from their presentation as a whole than from a single formulation. Every attempt to focus them more sharply is immediately punished by the intangible core of meaning losing its luminosity. No archetype can be reduced to a simple formula. It is a vessel which we can never empty, and never fill. It has a potential existence only, and when it takes shape in matter it is no longer what it was. It persists throughout the ages and requires interpreting ever anew. The archetypes are the imperishable elements of the unconscious, but they change their shape continually.

302   It is a well-nigh hopeless undertaking to tear a single archetype out of the living tissue of the psyche: but despite their interwovenness they do form units of meaning that can be apprehended intuitively. Psychology, as one of the many expressions of psychic life, operates with ideas which in their turn are derived from archetypal structures and thus generate a somewhat more abstract kind of myth. Psychology therefore translates the archaic speech of myth into a modern mythologem—not yet, of course, recognized as such—which constitutes one element of the myth "science." This seemingly hopeless undertaking is a *living and lived myth*, satisfying to a person of a corresponding temperament, indeed beneficial in so far as they have been cut off from their psychic origins by neurotic dissociation.

303   As a matter of experience, we meet the child archetype in spontaneous and in therapeutically induced individuation processes. The first manifestation of the "child" is as a rule a totally unconscious phenomenon. Here the patient identifies himself with his personal infantilism. Then, under the influence of therapy, we get a more or less gradual separation from and objectification of the "child," that is, the identity breaks down and is accompanied by an intensification (sometimes technically induced) of fantasy, with the result that archaic or mythological features become increasingly apparent. Further transformations run true to the hero myth. The theme of "mighty feats" is generally absent, but on the other hand the mythical dangers play all the greater part. At this stage there is usually another identification, this time with the hero, whose role is attractive for a variety of reasons. The identification is often extremely stubborn and dangerous to the psychic equilibrium. If it can be broken down and if consciousness can be reduced to human proportions, the figure of the hero can gradually be differentiated into a symbol of the self.

304   In practical reality, however, it is of course not enough for the patient merely to *know about* such developments; what counts is his experience of the various transformations. The initial stage of personal infantilism presents the picture of an "abandoned" or "misunderstood" and unjustly treated child with overweening pretensions. The epiphany of the hero (the second identification) shows itself in a corresponding inflation: the colossal pretension grows into a conviction that one is something extraordinary, or else the impossibility of the pretension ever being fulfilled only proves one's own inferiority, which is favourable to the role of the heroic sufferer (a negative inflation). In spite of their contradictoriness, both forms are identical, because conscious megalomania is balanced by unconscious compensatory inferiority and conscious inferiority by unconscious megalomania (you never get one without the other). Once the reef of the second identification has been successfully circumnavigated, conscious processes can be cleanly separated from the unconscious, and the latter observed objectively. This leads to the possibility of an accommodation with the unconscious, and thus to a possible synthesis of the conscious and unconscious elements of knowledge and action. This in turn leads to a shifting of the centre of personality from the ego to the self.[34]

---

[34] A more detailed account of these developments is to be found in "The Relations between the Ego and the Unconscious."

305   In this psychological framework the motifs of abandonment, invincibility, hermaphroditism, and beginning and end take their place as distinct categories of experience and understanding.

(b) Myths of the Hero

Myths of the hero most readily fit Jung's theory. In contrast to creation myths, hero myths already come packaged as myths about personalities rather than about the impersonal world. Yet Jung's psychological interpretation of hero myths makes the symbolized not persons but parts of the mind. Like the myth of the child, the myth of the hero symbolizes at once an archetype and, even more, the psychological life cycle. The birth, childhood, and adolescence of the hero symbolize the emergence and development of the ego and of ego consciousness, which is consciousness of the difference between oneself and the external world. The adulthood and death of the hero symbolize the return of the ego to the unconscious and its reintegration with the unconscious to form the self.

From "The Origin of the Hero," CW 5, par. 251

251   The finest of all symbols of the libido is the human figure, conceived as a demon or hero. Here the symbolism leaves the objective, material realm of astral and meteorological images and takes on human form, changing into a figure who passes from joy to sorrow, from sorrow to joy, and, like the sun, now stands high at the zenith and now is plunged into darkest night, only to rise again in new splendour.[1] Just as the sun, by its own motion and in accordance with its own inner law, climbs from morn till noon, crosses the meridian and goes its downward way towards evening, leaving its radiance behind it, and finally plunges into all-enveloping night, so man sets his course by immutable laws and, his journey over, sinks into darkness, to rise again in his children and begin the cycle anew. The symbolic transition from sun to man is easily made, and the third and last creation of Miss Miller's follows this pattern. She calls it "Chiwantopel, A hypnagogic drama," and gives us the following information concerning its origin:

[1] Hence the beautiful name of the sun-hero Gilgamesh, "The Man of Joy and Sorrow," in Jensen, *Das Gilgamesch-Epos*.

After an evening of trouble and anxiety, I had gone to bed at half past eleven. I felt restless; unable to sleep although very tired. I had the impression of being in a receptive mood. There was no light in the room. I closed my eyes, and had the feeling of waiting for something that was about to happen. Then I felt a great relaxation come over me, and I remained as completely passive as possible. Lines, sparks, and spirals of fire passed before my eyes, symptoms of nervousness and ocular fatigue, followed by a kaleidoscopic and fragmentary review of recent trivial events.

From "The Origin of the Hero," CW 5, par. 297–99

297   The psychic life-force, the libido, symbolizes itself in the sun[2] or personifies itself in figures of heroes with solar attributes. At the same time it expresses itself through phallic symbols. Both possibilities are found on a late Babylonian gem from Lajard's collection (fig. 1). In the middle stands an androgynous deity. On the masculine side there is a snake with a sun halo round its head; on the feminine side another snake with a sickle moon above it. This picture has a symbolic sexual nuance: on the masculine side there is a lozenge, a favourite symbol of the female genitals, and on the feminine side a wheel without its rim. The spokes are thickened at the ends into knobs, which, like the fingers we mentioned earlier, have a phallic meaning. It seems to be a phallic wheel such as was not unknown in antiquity. There are obscene gems on which Cupid is shown turning a wheel consisting entirely of phalli.[3] As to what the sun signifies, I discovered in the collection of antiquities at Verona a late Roman inscription with the following symbols:[4]

298   The symbolism is plain: sun = phallus, moon = vessel (uterus). This interpretation is confirmed by another monument

---

[2] Among the elements composing man, the Mithraic liturgy lays particular stress on fire as the divine element, describing it as τὸ εἰς ἐμὴν κρᾶσιν θεοδώρητον (the divine gift in my composition). Dieterich, *Mithrasliturgie*, p. 58.
[3] An illustration of the periodicity or rhythm expressed in sexuality.
[4] Reproduced not from a photograph, but from a drawing I myself made.

from the same collection. The symbols are the same, except that the vessel[5] has been replaced by the figure of a woman. Certain symbols on coins can probably be interpreted in a similar manner. In Lajard's *Recherches sur la culte de Vénus* there is a coin from Perga, showing Artemis as a conical stone flanked by a masculine figure (alleged to be the deity Men) and a female figure (alleged to be Artemis). Men (otherwise called Lunus) appears on an Attic bas-relief with a spear, flanked by Pan with a club, and a female figure.[6] From this it is clear that sexuality as well as the sun can be used to symbolize the libido.

299   One further point deserves mention here. The dadophor Cautopates is often represented with a cock[7] and pine-cones. These are the attributes of the Phrygian god Men, whose cult was very widespread. He was shown with the pileus[8] (or "Phrygian cap") and pine-cones, riding on the cock, and also in the form of a boy, just as the dadophors were boyish figures. (This latter characteristic relates both them and Men to the Cabiri and Dactyls.) Now Men has affinities with Attis, the son and lover of Cybele. In Imperial times Men and Attis merged into one. Attis also wears the pileus like Men, Mithras, and the dadophors. As the son and lover of his mother he raises the incest problem. Incest leads logically to ritual castration in the Attis-Cybele cult; for according to legend the hero, driven mad by his mother, mutilates himself. I must refrain from going into this question more deeply at present, as I would prefer to discuss the incest problem at the end of this book. Here I would only point out that the incest motif is bound to arise, because when the regressing libido is introverted for internal or external reasons it always reactivates the parental imagos and thus apparently re-establishes the infantile relationship. But this relationship cannot be re-established, because the libido is an adult libido which is already bound to sexuality and inevitably imports an incompatible, incestuous character into the reactivated relationship to the parents.[9] It is this sexual character that now gives rise to the incest symbolism. Since incest must be avoided

---

[5] In a myth of the Bakairi Indians, of Brazil, a woman appears who sprang from a corn mortar. A Zulu myth tells a woman to catch a drop of blood in a pot, then close the pot, put it aside for eight months, and open it again in the ninth month. She follows this advice, opens the pot in the ninth month, and finds a child inside it. (Frobenius, I, p. 237.)

[6] Roscher, *Lexikon* II, 2733/4, s.v. "Men."

[7] A well-known sun-animal.

[8] Like Mithras and the dadophors.

[9] This explanation is not satisfactory, because I found it impossible to go into the archetypal incest problem and all its complications here. I have dealt with it at some length in my "Psychology of the Transference."

Fig. 1. Androgynous divinity   Fig. 2. Cybele and her son-lover
    Late Babylonian gem   Attis *Roman coin*

at all costs, the result is either the death of the son-lover or his self-castration as punishment for the incest he has committed, or else the sacrifice of instinctuality, and especially of sexuality, as a means of preventing or expiating the incestuous longing. (Cf. fig. 2.) Sex being one of the most obvious examples of instinctuality, it is sex which is liable to be most affected by these sacrificial measures, i.e., through abstinence. The heroes are usually wanderers,[10] and wandering is a symbol of longing,[11] of the restless urge which never finds its object, of nostalgia for the lost mother. The sun comparison can easily be taken in this sense: the heroes are like the wandering sun, from which it is concluded that the myth of the hero is a solar myth. It seems to us, rather, that he is first and foremost a self-representation of the longing of the unconscious, of its unquenched and unquenchable desire for the light of consciousness. But consciousness, continually in danger of being led astray by its own light and of becoming a rootless will o' the wisp, longs for the healing power of nature, for the deep wells of being and for unconscious communion with life in all its countless forms. Here I must make way for the master, who has plumbed to the root of these Faustian longings:

MEPHISTOPHELES: This lofty mystery I must now unfold.
Goddesses throned in solitude, sublime,
Set in no place, still less in any time,
At the mere thought of them my blood runs cold.

[10] Like Gilgamesh, Dionysus, Heracles, Mithras, etc.
[11] Cf. Graf, *Richard Wagner im Fliegenden Holländer*.

They are the Mothers!

. . . .

    Goddesses, unknown to mortal mind,
And named indeed with dread among our kind.
To reach them you must plumb earth's deepest vault;
That we have need of them is your own fault.

FAUST: Where leads the way?

MEPHISTOPHELES: There's none! To the untrodden,
Untreadable regions — the unforgotten
And unforgettable — for which prepare!
There are no bolts, no hatches to be lifted,
Through endless solitudes you shall be drifted.
Can you imagine Nothing everywhere?

. . . .

Supposing you had swum across the ocean
And gazed upon the immensity of space,
Still you would see wave after wave in motion,
And even though you feared the world should cease,
You'd still see something — in the limpid green
Of the calm deep are gliding dolphins seen,
The flying clouds above, sun, moon, and star.
But blank is that eternal Void afar.
You do not hear your footfall, and you meet
No solid ground on which to set your feet.

. . . .

Here, take this key.

. . . .

The key will smell the right place from all others:
Follow it down, it leads you to the Mothers.

. . . .

Then to the depths! — I could as well say height:
It's all the same. From the Existent fleeing,
Take the free world of forms for your delight,
Rejoice in things that long have ceased from being.
The busy brood will weave like coiling cloud,
But swing your key to keep away the crowd!

. . . .

A fiery tripod warns you to beware,
This is the nethermost place where now you are.
You shall behold the Mothers by its light,
Some of them sit, some walk, some stand upright,
Just as they please. Formation, transformation,

Eternal blind's eternal recreation.
Thronged round with images of things to be,
They see you not, shadows are all they see.
Then pluck up heart, the danger here is great,
Approach the tripod, do not hesitate,
And touch it with the key.[12]

From "Symbols of the Mother and of Rebirth," CW 5, pars. 309–12

309   Instead of using numerous separate examples, I shall content myself with reproducing the diagram which Frobenius constructed from numberless myths of this sort:

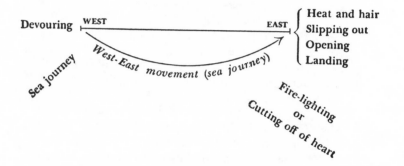

310   Frobenius gives the following legend by way of illustration:

A hero is devoured by a water-monster in the West (*devouring*). The animal travels with him to the East (*sea journey*). Meanwhile, the hero lights a fire in the belly of the monster (*fire-lighting*), and feeling hungry, cuts himself a piece of the heart (*cutting off of heart*). Soon afterwards, he notices that the fish has glided on to dry land (*landing*); he immediately begins to cut open the animal from within (*opening*); then he slips out (*slipping out*). It was so hot in the fish's belly that all his hair has fallen out (*heat and hair*). The hero may at the same time free all those who were previously devoured by the monster, and who now slip out too.[13]

311   A very close parallel is Noah's journey over the Flood that killed all living things; only he and his animals lived to experi-

---

[12] Trans. based on MacNeice, pp. 175ff. Cf. also trans. by Wayne, part II, pp. 76ff.
[13] Frobenius, *Das Zeitalter des Sonnengottes*, p. 421.

ence a new Creation. A Polynesian myth[14] tells how the hero, in the belly of Kombili, the King Fish, seized his obsidian knife and cut open the fish's belly. "He slipped out and beheld a splendour. Then he sat down and began to think. 'I wonder where I am?' he said to himself. Then the sun rose up with a bound and threw itself from one side to the other." The sun had again slipped out. Frobenius cites from the Ramayana the story of the ape Hanuman, who represents the sun-hero:

The sun, travelling through the air with Hanuman in it, cast a shadow on the sea, a sea monster seized hold of it and drew Hanuman down from the sky. But when Hanuman saw that the monster was about to devour him, he stretched himself out to enormous size, and the monster followed suit. Then Hanuman shrank to the size of a thumb, slipped into the huge body of the monster, and came out on the other side.[15] Hanuman thereupon resumed his flight, and encountered a new obstacle in another sea monster, who was the mother of Rahu, the sun-devouring demon. She also drew Hanuman down to her by his shadow.[16] Once more he had recourse to his earlier stratagem, made himself small, and slipped into her body; but scarcely was he inside than he swelled up to gigantic size, burst her, and killed her, and so made his escape.[17]

We now understand why the Indian fire-bringer Matarisvan is called "he who swells in the mother." The ark (fig. 3), chest, casket, barrel, ship, etc. is an analogy of the womb, like the sea into which the sun sinks for rebirth. That which swells in the mother can also signify her conquest and death. Fire-making is a pre-eminently conscious act and therefore "kills" the dark state of union with the mother.

312   In the light of these ideas we can understand the mythological statements about Ogyges: it is he who possesses the mother, the city, and is thus united with the mother, therefore under him came the great flood, for it is typical of the sun myth that the hero, once he is united with the woman "hard to attain," is exposed in a cask and thrown out to sea, and then lands on a distant shore to begin a new life. The middle section, the night sea journey in the ark, is lacking in the Ogyges tradition. But

[14] Ibid., pp. 60f.
[15] Elsewhere in the poem we are told that he came out of the monster's right ear (like Rabelais' Gargantua, who was born from the ear of his mother).
[16] This probably means simply his soul. No moral considerations are implied.
[17] Frobenius, pp. 173f.

Fig. 3. Noah in the Ark *Enamelled altar of Nicholas of Verdun, 1186, Klosterneuburg, near Vienna*

the rule in mythology is that the typical parts of a myth can be fitted together in every conceivable variation, which makes it extraordinarily difficult to interpret one myth without a knowledge of all the others. The meaning of this cycle of myths is clear enough: it is the longing to attain rebirth through a return to the womb, and to become immortal like the sun. This longing for the mother is amply expressed in the literature of the Bible. I cite first the passage in Galatians 4:26ff. and 5:1:

But Jerusalem which is above is free, which is the mother of us all.

For it is written, Rejoice, thou barren that bearest not; break forth and cry, thou that travailest not: for the desolate hath many more children than she which hath an husband.

Now we, brethren, as Isaac was, are the children of promise.

But as then he that was born after the flesh persecuted him that was born after the Spirit, even so it is now.

Nevertheless what saith the scripture? Cast out the bondwoman and her son: for the son of the bondwoman shall not be heir with the son of the freewoman.

So then, brethren, we are not children of the bondwoman, but of the free.

Stand fast therefore in the liberty wherewith Christ hath made us free . . .

From "Symbols of the Mother and of Rebirth," CW 5, pars. 351–52

351   The wicked Set lured Osiris into the chest by a ruse, in other words the original evil in man wants to get back into the mother again, and the illicit, incestuous longing for the mother is the ruse supposedly invented by Set. It is significant that it is "evil" which lures Osiris into the chest; for, in the light of teleology, the motif of containment signifies the latent state that precedes regeneration. Thus evil, as though cognizant of its imperfection, strives to be made perfect through rebirth — "Part of that power which would / Ever work evil, but engenders good!"[18] The ruse, too, is significant: man tries to sneak into rebirth by a subterfuge in order to become a child again. That is how it appears to the "rational" mind. An Egyptian hymn[19] even charges Isis with having struck down the sun god Ra by treachery: it was because of her ill will towards her son that she banished and betrayed him. The hymn describes how Isis fashioned a poisonous snake and set it in his path, and how the snake wounded the sun-god with its bite. From this wound he never recovered, so that he finally had to retire on the back of the heavenly cow. But the cow was the cow-headed mother-goddess, just as Osiris was the bull Apis. The mother is accused as though *she* were the cause of his having to fly to her in order to be cured of the wound she herself had inflicted. But the real cause of the wound is the incest-taboo,[20] which cuts a man off

---

[18] *Faust*, Part I, trans. by Wayne, p. 75, modified.
[19] Erman, *Life in Ancient Egypt*, p. 265.
[20] Here I must again remind the reader that I give the word "incest" a different meaning from that which properly belongs to it. Incest is the urge to act back to childhood. For the child, of course, this cannot be called incest; it is only for an adult with a fully developed sexuality that this backward striving becomes incest, because he is no longer a child but possesses a sexuality which cannot be allowed a regressive outlet.

from the security of childhood and early youth, from all those unconscious, instinctive happenings that allow the child to live without responsibility as an appendage of his parents. There must be contained in this feeling many dim memories of the animal age, when there was as yet no "thou shalt" and "thou shalt not," and everything just happened of itself. Even now a deep resentment seems to dwell in man's breast against the brutal law that once separated him from instinctive surrender to his desires and from the beautiful harmony of animal nature. This separation manifested itself in the incest prohibition and its correlates (marriage laws, food-taboos, etc.). So long as the child is in that state of unconscious identity with the mother, he is still one with the animal psyche and is just as unconscious as it. The development of consciousness inevitably leads not only to separation from the mother, but to separation from the parents and the whole family circle and thus to a relative degree of detachment from the unconscious and the world of instinct. Yet the longing for this lost world continues and, when difficult adaptations are demanded, is forever tempting one to make evasions and retreats, to regress to the infantile past, which then starts throwing up the incestuous symbolism. If only this temptation were perfectly clear, it would be possible, with a great effort of will, to free oneself from it. But it is far from clear, because a new adaptation or orientation of vital importance can only be achieved in accordance with the instincts. Lacking this, nothing durable results, only a convulsively willed, artificial product which proves in the long run to be incapable of life. No man can change himself into anything from sheer reason; he can only change into what he potentially is. When such a change becomes necessary, the previous mode of adaptation, already in a state of decay, is unconsciously compensated by the archetype of another mode. If the conscious mind now succeeds in interpreting the constellated archetype in a meaningful and appropriate manner, then a viable transformation can take place. Thus the most important relationship of childhood, the relation to the mother, will be compensated by the mother archetype as soon as detachment from the childhood state is indicated. One such successful interpretation has been, for instance, Mother Church, but once this form begins to show signs of age and decay a new interpretation becomes inevitable.

352   Even if a change does occur, the old form loses none of its attractions; for whoever sunders himself from the mother longs to get back to the mother. This longing can easily turn into a

consuming passion which threatens all that has been won. The mother then appears on the one hand as the supreme goal, and on the other as the most frightful danger — the "Terrible Mother."[21]

From "The Dual Mother," CW 5, pars. 493–96

493   At this point we might ask ourselves why the birth of a hero always has to take place under such extraordinary circumstances. One would think it possible for a hero to be born in the normal manner, and then gradually to grow out of his humble and homely surroundings, perhaps with a great effort and in face of many dangers. (This motif is by no means uncommon in the hero-myths.) As a general rule, however, the story of his origins is miraculous. The singular circumstances of his procreation and birth are part and parcel of the hero-myth. What is the reason for these beliefs?

494   The answer to this question is that the hero is not born like an ordinary mortal because his birth is a rebirth from the mother-wife. That is why the hero so often has two mothers. As Rank[22] has shown with a wealth of examples, the hero is frequently exposed and then reared by foster-parents. In this way he gets two mothers. An excellent example of this is the relation of Heracles to Hera. In the Hiawatha epic, Wenonah dies after giving birth, and her place is taken by Nokomis.[23] Buddha, too, was brought up by a foster-mother. The foster-mother is sometimes an animal, e.g., the she-wolf of Romulus and Remus, etc. The dual mother may be replaced by the motif of dual birth, which has attained a lofty significance in various religions. In Christianity, for example, baptism represents a rebirth, as we have already seen. Man is not merely born in the commonplace sense, but is born again in a mysterious manner, and so partakes of divinity. Anyone who is reborn in this way becomes a hero, a semi-divine being. Thus Christ's redemptive death on the cross was understood as a "baptism," that is to say, as rebirth through the second mother, symbolized by the tree of death. Christ himself said (Luke 12:50): "But I have a baptism to be baptized with; and how am I straitened till it be

---

[21] Frobenius, *Zeitalter*.
[22] *The Myth of the Birth of the Hero*.
[23] The rapid death of the mother, or separation from the mother, is an essential part of the hero-myth. The same idea is expressed in the myth of the swan-maiden, who flies away again after the birth of the child, her purpose fulfilled.

accomplished!" He therefore interprets his own death-agony symbolically as the pangs of rebirth.

495　　The dual-mother motif suggests the idea of a dual birth. One of the mothers is the real, human mother, the other is the symbolical mother; in other words, she is distinguished as being divine, supernatural, or in some way extraordinary. She can also be represented theriomorphically. In certain cases she has more human proportions, and here we are dealing with projections of archetypal ideas upon persons in the immediate environment, which generally brings about complications. For instance the rebirth symbol is liable to be projected upon the step-mother or mother-in-law (unconsciously, of course), just as, for her part, the mother-in-law often finds it difficult not to make her son-in-law her son-lover in the old mythological manner. There are innumerable variations on this motif, especially when we add individual elements to the collective mythological ones.

496　　He who stems from two mothers is the hero: the first birth makes him a mortal man, the second an immortal half-god. That is what all the hints in the story of the hero's procreation are getting at. Hiawatha's father first conquers the mother under the terrifying symbol of the bear;[24] then, having become a god himself, he begets the hero. What the hero Hiawatha then has to do is suggested to him by Nokomis, when she tells him the story of the origin of the moon: he is to throw his mother up into the sky, whereupon she will become pregnant and give birth to a daughter. This rejuvenated mother would, according to the Egyptian fantasy, be given as a daughter-wife to the sun god, the "father of his mother," for purposes of self-reproduction. What Hiawatha does in this respect we shall see presently. We have already examined the behaviour of the dying and resurgent gods of the Near East. In regard to the pre-existence of Christ, the gospel of St. John is, as we know, the crowning witness to this idea. One has only to think of the words of the Baptist (John 1:30): "After me cometh a man which is preferred before me: for he was before me." The opening words are equally significant: "In the beginning was the Word, and the Word was with God, and the Word was God. The same was in the beginning with God. All things were made by him; and without him was not any thing made that was made." Then follows the annunciation of the Light, of the rising sun — the

[24] The bear is associated with Artemis and is thus a "feminine" animal. Cf. also the Gallo-Roman Dea Artio, and my "Psychological Aspects of the Koree," pars. 340ff.

Sol mysticus which was before and will be afterwards. In the baptistry at Pisa, Christ is shown bringing the tree of life to mankind, his head surrounded by a sun-wheel. Over this relief stand the words "INTROITUS SOLIS."

From "The Dual Mother," CW 5, pars. 508–11

508   As against this, therapy must support the regression, and continue to do so until the "prenatal" stage is reached. It must be remembered that the "mother" is really an imago, a psychic image merely, which has in it a number of different but very important unconscious contents. The "mother," as the first incarnation of the anima archetype, personifies in fact the whole unconscious. Hence the regression leads back only apparently to the mother; in reality she is the gateway into the unconscious, into the "realm of the Mothers." Whoever sets foot in this realm submits his conscious ego-personality to the controlling influence of the unconscious, or if he feels that he has got caught by mistake, or that somebody has tricked him into it, he will defend himself desperately, though his resistance will not turn out to his advantage. For regression, if left undisturbed, does not stop short at the "mother" but goes back beyond her to the prenatal realm of the "Eternal Feminine," to the immemorial world of archetypal possibilities where, "thronged round with images of all creation," slumbers the "divine child," patiently awaiting his conscious realization. This son is the germ of wholeness, and he is characterized as such by his specific symbols.

509   When Jonah was swallowed by the whale, he was not simply imprisoned in the belly of the monster, but, as Paracelsus tells us,[25] he saw "mighty mysteries" there. This view probably derives from the *Pirkê de Rabbi Elieser*, which says:

Jonah entered its mouth just as a man enters the great synagogue, and he stood there. The two eyes of the fish were like windows of glass giving light to Jonah. R. Meir said: One pearl was suspended inside the belly of the fish and it gave illumination to Jonah, like this sun which shines with all its might at noon; and it showed to Jonah all that was in the sea and in the depths.[26]

[25] *Liber Azoth*, ed. by Sudhoff, XIV, p. 576.
[26] Trans. by Friedlander, ch. 10, p. 69.

510   In the darkness of the unconscious a treasure lies hidden, the same "treasure hard to attain" which in our text, and in many other places too, is described as the shining pearl, or, to quote Paracelsus, as the "mystery," by which is meant a *fascinosum* par excellence. It is these inherent possibilities of "spiritual" or "symbolic" life and of progress which form the ultimate, though unconscious, goal of regression. By serving as a means of expression, as bridges and pointers, symbols help to prevent the libido from getting stuck in the material corporeality of the mother. Never has the dilemma been more acutely formulated than in the Nicodemus dialogue: on the one hand the impossibility of entering again into the mother's womb; on the other, the need for rebirth from "water and spirit." The hero is a hero just because he sees resistance to the forbidden goal in all life's difficulties and yet fights that resistance with the whole-hearted yearning that strives towards the treasure hard to attain, and perhaps unattainable—a yearning that paralyses and kills the ordinary man.

511   Hiawatha's father is Mudjekeewis, the West Wind: the battle therefore is fought in the West. From that quarter came life (fertilization of Wenonah) and death (Wenonah's). Hence Hiawatha is fighting the typical battle of the hero for rebirth in the Western Sea. The fight is with the father, who is the obstacle barring the way to the goal. In other cases the fight in the West is a battle with the devouring mother. As we have seen, the danger comes from both parents: from the father, because he apparently makes regression impossible, and from the mother, because she absorbs the regressing libido and keeps it to herself, so that he who sought rebirth finds only death. Mudjekeewis, who had acquired his godlike nature by overcoming the maternal bear, is himself overcome by his son:

> Back retreated Mudjekeewis,
> Rushing westward o'er the mountains,
> Stumbling westward down the mountains,
> Three whole days retreated fighting,
> Still pursued by Hiawatha
> To the doorways of the West Wind,
> To the portals of the Sunset,
> To the earth's remotest border,
> Where into the empty spaces
> Sinks the sun, as a flamingo
> Drops into her nest at nightfall.

From "The Dual Mother," CW 5, pars. 538–40

538   This is the almost worldwide myth of the typical deed of the hero. He journeys by ship, fights the sea monster, is swallowed, struggles against being bitten and crushed to death (kicking or stamping motif), and having arrived inside the "whale-dragon," seeks the vital organ, which he proceeds to cut off or otherwise destroy. Often the monster is killed by the hero lighting a fire inside him—that is to say, in the very womb of death he secretly creates life, the rising sun. Thus the fish dies and drifts to land, where with the help of a bird the hero once more sees the light of day.[27] The bird probably signifies the renewed ascent of the sun, the rebirth of the phoenix, and is at the same time one of those "helpful animals" who render supernatural aid during the birth: birds, as aerial beings, symbolize spirits or angels. Divine messengers frequently appear at these mythological

---

[27] As an example, I will quote here the Polynesian myth of Rata (Frobenius, *Zeitalter,* pp. 64–66): "The boat was sailing along merrily over the ocean under a favourable wind, when one day Nganaoa called out: 'O Rata! A fearful enemy is rising up from the sea!' It was a giant clam, wide open. One of its shells was in front of the boat, the other behind, and the vessel lay in between. The next moment the horrible clam would have snapped shut and ground the boat and all its occupants to pulp. But Nganaoa was prepared for this possibility. Seizing his long spear, he thrust it quickly into the creature's belly, so that instead of snapping shut it sank instantly to the bottom of the sea. After escaping from this danger they continued on their way. Yet soon the voice of the ever watchful Nganaoa was heard again: 'O Rata! Another fearful enemy is rising up from the sea!' This time it was a mighty octopus, whose giant tentacles were already wrapped round the boat to destroy it. At this critical moment Nganaoa seized his spear and plunged it into the head of the octopus. The tentacles sank down limply, and the dead monster floated away on the surface of the ocean. Once more they continued on their journey, but a still greater danger awaited them. One day the valiant Nganaoa cried out: 'O Rata! Here is a great whale!' Its huge jaws were wide open, the lower jaw was already under the boat, the upper one was over it. Another moment and the whale would have swallowed them. Then Nganaoa, the 'slayer of monsters,' broke his spear in two, and just as the whale was about to crush them he stuck the two pieces in his enemy's gullet, so that he could not close his jaws. Then Nganaoa leapt into the maw of the great whale (devouring of the hero) and peered down into his belly, and what did he see? There sat his two parents, his father Tairitokerau and his mother Vaiaroa, who had been swallowed by this monster of the deep when out fishing. The oracle had come true. The voyage had reached its goal. Great was the joy of the parents of Nganaoa when they beheld their son, for they were now persuaded that their liberation was at hand. And Nganaoa, too, was bent upon vengeance. Taking one of the two sticks from the animal's gullet—the other was enough to prevent the whale from closing his jaws and to keep the passage clear for Nganaoa and his parents—he broke it into two pieces for use as fire-sticks. He told his father to hold one piece firmly below, while he himself manipulated the upper one until the fire began to glimmer (fire-lighting). Then, blowing it into a flame, he hastened to heat the fatty parts inside the belly (i.e., the heart) with the fire. The monster, writhing with pain, sought relief by swimming to land (sea journey). As soon as it reached the sandbank (landing), father, mother and son stepped ashore through the open gullet of the dying whale (slipping out of the hero)."

births, as can be seen from the use we still make of *god-parents*.
The sun-symbol of the bird rising from the water is preserved
etymologically in the idea of the singing swan. "Swan" derives
from the root *sven*, like "sun" and "sound."²⁸ This ascent signifies rebirth, the bringing forth of life from the mother,²⁹ and the
ultimate conquest of death, which, according to an African Ne-
gro myth, came into the world through the carelessness of one
old woman: when the season of universal skin-casting came
round again (for in those days people renewed themselves by
casting their skins like snakes), she was absent-minded enough
to put on her old skin instead of the new one, and in consequence died.

539   It is easy to see what the battle with the sea monster means:
it is the attempt to free the ego-consciousness from the deadly
grip of the unconscious. The making of a fire in the monster's
belly suggests as much, for it is a piece of apotropaic magic
aimed at dispelling the darkness of unconsciousness. The rescue
of the hero is at the same time a sunrise, the triumph of consciousness. (Cf. fig. 4.)

540   Unfortunately, however, this heroic deed has no lasting effects. Again and again the hero must renew the struggle, and
always under the symbol of deliverance from the mother. Just
as Hera, in her role of the pursuing mother, is the real source of
the mighty deeds performed by Heracles, so Nokomis allows
Hiawatha no rest, but piles up new difficulties in his path, haz-
ardous adventures in which the hero may be victorious, but
may also meet with his death. Man with his consciousness is
always a long way behind the goals of the unconscious; unless
his libido calls him forth to new dangers he sinks into slothful
inactivity, or in the prime of life he is overcome with longing
for the past and is paralysed. But if he rouses himself and follows the dangerous urge to do the forbidden and apparently
impossible thing, then he must either go under or become a
hero. The mother is thus the daemon who challenges the hero
to his deeds and lays in his path the poisonous serpent that will
strike him. Accordingly Nokomis, in the ninth canto, calls Hiawatha, points with her hand to the West, where the sun sets in
purple splendour, and says to him:

²⁸ [Cf. par. 235.]
²⁹ In the Maori myth of Maui (Frobenius, pp. 66ff.) the monster to be overcome is
Grandmother Hine-nui-te po. Maui, the hero, says to the birds who help him: "My
little friends, when I creep into the jaws of the old woman, you must not laugh, but
once I have been in and have come out of her mouth again, you may welcome me
with shouts of laughter." Then Maui creeps into the mouth of the old woman as she
sleeps.

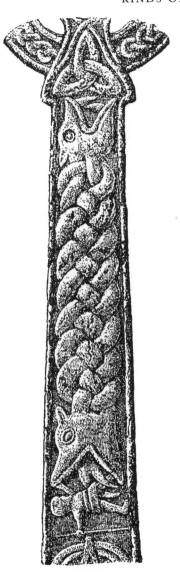

Fig. 4. Vidarr's fight with the
Fenris-Wolf *Relief from a cross,
Churchyard of Gosforth,
Cumberland*

Yonder dwells the great Pearl-Feather,
Megissogwon, the Magician,
Manito of Wealth and Wampum,
Guarded by his fiery serpents,
Guarded by the black pitch-water.

You can see his fiery serpents . . .
Coiling, playing in the water.

From "The Dual Mother," CW 5, par. 553

553   The sun, rising triumphant, tears himself from the enveloping
womb of the sea, and leaving, behind him the noonday zenith
and all its glorious works, sinks down again into the maternal
depths, into all-enfolding and all-regenerating night. This image
is undoubtedly a primordial one, and there was profound justification for its becoming a symbolical expression of human
fate: in the morning of life the son tears himself loose from the
mother, from the domestic hearth, to rise through battle to his
destined heights. Always he imagines his worst enemy in front
of him, yet he carries the enemy within himself — a deadly longing for the abyss, a longing to drown in his own source, to be
sucked down to the realm of the Mothers. His life is a constant
struggle against extinction, a violent yet fleeting deliverance
from ever-lurking night. This death is no external enemy, it is
his own inner longing for the stillness and profound peace of
all-knowing non-existence, for all-seeing sleep in the ocean of
coming-to-be and passing away. Even in his highest strivings for
harmony and balance, for the profundities of philosophy and
the raptures of the artist, he seeks death, immobility, satiety,
rest. If, like Peirithous, he tarries too long in this abode of rest
and peace, he is overcome by apathy, and the poison of the
serpent paralyses him for all time. If he is to live, he must fight
and sacrifice his longing for the past in order to rise to his own
heights. And having reached the noonday heights, he must sacrifice his love for his own achievement, for he may not loiter.
The sun, too, sacrifices its greatest strength in order to hasten
onward to the fruits of autumn, which are the seeds of rebirth.
The natural course of life demands that the young person
should sacrifice his childhood and his childish dependence on
the physical parents, lest he remain caught body and soul in the
bonds of unconscious incest. This regressive tendency has been
consistently opposed from the most primitive times by the great
psychotherapeutic systems which we know as the religions.
They seek to create an autonomous consciousness by weaning
mankind away from the sleep of childhood. The sun breaks
from the mists of the horizon and climbs to undimmed brightness at the meridian.[30] Once this goal is reached, it sinks down

---

[30] Cf. the Μεσουράνισμα ἡλίου, position of the sun at midday as symbol of the
initiate's illumination, in "The Visions of Zosimos," pars. 86 and 95.

again towards night. This process can be allegorized as a gradual seeping away of the water of life: one has to bend ever deeper to reach the source. When we are feeling on top of the world we find this exceedingly disagreeable; we resist the sunset tendency, especially when we suspect that there is something in ourselves which would like to follow this movement, for behind it we sense nothing good, only an obscure, hateful threat. So, as soon as we feel ourselves slipping, we begin to combat this tendency and erect barriers against the dark, rising flood of the unconscious and its enticements to regression, which all too easily takes on the deceptive guise of sacrosanct ideals, principles, beliefs, etc. If we wish to stay on the heights we have reached, we must struggle all the time to consolidate our consciousness and its attitude. But we soon discover that this praiseworthy and apparently unavoidable battle with the years leads to stagnation and desiccation of soul. Our convictions become platitudes ground out on a barrel-organ, our ideals become starchy habits, enthusiasm stiffens into automatic gestures. The source of the water of life seeps away. We ourselves may not notice it, but everybody else does, and that is even more painful. If we should risk a little introspection, coupled perhaps with an energetic attempt to be honest for once with ourselves, we may get a dim idea of all the wants, longings, and fears that have accumulated down there — a repulsive and sinister sight. The mind shies away, but life wants to flow down into the depths. Fate itself seems to preserve us from this, because each of us has a tendency to become an immovable pillar of the past. Nevertheless, the daemon throws us down, makes us traitors to our ideals and cherished convictions — traitors to the selves we thought we were. That is an unmitigated catastrophe, because it is an *unwilling* sacrifice. Things go very differently when the sacrifice is a voluntary one. Then it is no longer an overthrow, a "transvaluation of values," the destruction of all that we held sacred, but transformation and conservation. Everything young grows old, all beauty fades, all heat cools, all brightness dims, and every truth becomes stale and trite. For all these things have taken on shape, and all shapes are worn thin by the working of time; they age, sicken, crumble to dust — unless they change. But change they can, for the invisible spark that generated them is potent enough for infinite generation. No one should deny the danger of the descent, but it *can* be risked. No one *need* risk it, but it is certain that someone will. And let those who go down the sunset way do so with open eyes, for it is a sacrifice which daunts even the gods. Yet every descent is followed by an ascent; the vanishing shapes are shaped anew, and a truth is valid in the end only if it suffers change and bears new witness in new images, in new tongues, like a new wine that is put into new bottles.

From "On the Psychology of the Unconscious," CW 7, par. 160

160   The parallel with the hero-myth is very striking. More often than not the typical struggle of the hero with the monster (the unconscious content) takes place beside the water, perhaps at a ford. This is the case particularly in the Redskin myths with which Longfellow's *Hiawatha* has made us familiar. In the decisive battle the hero is, like Jonah, invariably swallowed by the monster, as Frobenius has shown[31] with a wealth of detail. But, once inside the monster, the hero begins to settle accounts with the creature in his own way, while it swims eastwards with him towards the rising sun. He cuts off a portion of the viscera, the heart for instance, or some essential organ by virtue of which the monster lives (i.e., the valuable energy that activates the unconscious). Thus he kills the monster, which then drifts to land, where the hero, new-born through the transcendent function (the "night sea journey," as Frobenius calls it [fig. 5]), steps forth, sometimes in the company of all those whom the monster has previously devoured. In this manner the normal state of things is restored, since the unconscious, robbed of its energy, no longer occupies the dominant position. Thus the myth graphically describes the problem which also engages our patient.[32]

From "Religious Ideas in Alchemy," CW 12, pars. 437–41

V. THE MYTH OF THE HERO

437   Resulting as it did from the advice of the philosophers, the death of the King's Son is naturally a delicate and dangerous matter. By descending into the unconscious, the conscious mind puts itself in a perilous position, for it is apparently extinguishing itself. It is in the situation of the primitive hero who is devoured by the dragon. Since all this means a diminution or extinction of consciousness, an *abaissement du niveau mental* equivalent to that "peril of the soul" which is primitive man's

---

[31] Frobenius, *Das Zeitalter des Sonnengottes.*

[32] Those of my readers who have a deeper interest in the problem of opposites and its solution, as well as in the mythological activity of the unconscious, are referred to *Symbols of Transformation, Psychological Types,* and *The Archetypes and the Collective Unconscious.* [Cf. also *Mysterium Coniunctionis.* — EDITORS.]

Fig. 5. The night sea journey. Joseph in the cistern, Christ in the sepulchre, Jonah swallowed by the whale *Biblia pauperum (1471)*

greatest dread (i.e., the fear of ghosts[33]), the deliberate and indeed wanton provocation of this state is a sacrilege or breach of taboo attended by the severest punishments. Accordingly the King imprisons Arisleus and his companions in a triple glass house together with the corpse of the King's Son. The heroes are held captive in the underworld at the bottom of the sea, where, exposed to every kind of terror, they languish for eighty days in an intense heat. At the request of Arisleus, Beya is imprisoned with them. (The *Rosarium* version of the "Visio" interprets the prison as Beya's womb.[34]) Clearly, they have been overpowered by the unconscious and are helplessly abandoned, which means that they have volunteered to die in order to beget a new and fruitful life in that region of the psyche which has hitherto lain fallow in darkest unconsciousness, and under the shadow of death (fig. 6).

438   Although the possibility of life is hinted at by the brother-sister pair, these unconscious opposites must be activated by the intervention of the conscious mind, otherwise they will merely remain dormant. But this is a dangerous undertaking. We can understand the anxious plea in *Aurora consurgens*: "Horridas nostrae mentis purge tenebras, accende lumen sensibus!"[35] We can also understand why Michael Maier found few that were

---

[33] The fear of ghosts means, psychologically speaking, the overpowering of consciousness by the autonomous contents of the unconscious. This is equivalent to mental derangement.

[34] *Art. aurif.*, II, pp. 246ff.

[35] I, ch. IX. par. IV. [Originally from a sequence of Notker Balbulus (*c.* 840–912). — EDITORS.] The passage is apparently derived from the first *oratio* of the third Sunday in Advent: "et mentis nostrae tenebras gratia tuae visitationis illustra."

Fig. 6. Hercules on the night sea journey in the vessel of the sun *Base of an Attic vase (5th cent. B.C.)*

willing to plunge into the sea.[36] Arisleus is in danger of succumbing to the fate of Theseus and Peirithous, who descended into Hades and grew fast to the rocks of the underworld, which is to say that the conscious mind, advancing into the unknown regions of the psyche, is overpowered by the archaic forces of the unconscious: a repetition of the cosmic embrace of Nous and Physis. The purpose of the descent as universally exemplified in the myth of the hero is to show that only in the region of danger (watery abyss, cavern, forest, island, castle, etc.) can one find the "treasure hard to attain" (jewel, virgin, life-potion, victory over death) (fig. 7).

[36] "Nonnulli perierunt in opere nostro" (Not a few have perished in our work), the *Rosarium* says. The element of torture is also emphasized in "Allegoriae super librum Turbae," *Art. aurif.*, I, pp. 139ff.: "Accipe hominem, tonde eum, et trahe super lapidem . . . donec corpus eius moriatur . . ." (Take a man, shave him, and drag him over a stone . . . until his body dies . . .).

Fig. 7. Jonah emerging from the belly of the whale. The goal of the night sea journey is equivalent to the *lapis angularis* or cornerstone *"Speculum humanae salvationis"* (*Cod. Lat. 512, Paris, 15th cent.*)

439   The dread and resistance which every natural human being experiences when it comes to delving too deeply into himself is, at bottom, the fear of the journey to Hades. If it were only resistance that he felt, it would not be so bad. In actual fact, however, the psychic substratum, that dark realm of the unknown,[37] exercises a fascinating attraction that threatens to become the more overpowering the further he penetrates into it.[38] The psychological danger that arises here is the disintegration of personality into its functional components, i.e., the separate functions of consciousness, the complexes, hereditary units, etc. Disintegration—which may be functional or occasionally a real schizophrenia—is the fate which overtakes Gabricus (in the *Rosarium* version): he is dissolved into atoms in the body of Beya,[39] this being equivalent to a form of *mortificatio* (fig. 8).

[37] For the quadratic enclosure as the domain of the psyche, cf. the motif of the square in Part II, supra. According to Pythagoras the soul is a square (Zeller, *Die Philosophie der Griechen*, III, p. 120).
[38] Symbolized by a sorceress or by wanton girls, as in *Poliphilo*. Cf. Béroalde de Verville, *Le Songe de Poliphile*. Similar themes in Part II of this volume.
[39] *Art. aurif.*, II, p. 246: "Nam Beya ascendit super Gabricum, et includit eum in suo utero, quod nil penitus videri potest de eo. Tantoque amore amplexata est Gabricum, quod ipsum totum in sui naturam concepit, et in partes indivisibiles divisit. Unde Merculinus ait: . . .

Fig. 8. The slaying of the king (*mortificatio*) Stolcius de Stolcenberg,
Viridarium chymicum (1624)

440   Here again we have a repetition of the *coniunctio* of Nous
and Physis.[40] But the latter is a cosmogonic event, whereas this
is a catastrophe brought about by the intervention of the phi-

---

"Per se solvuntur, per se quoque conficiunter,
    Ut duo qui fuerant, unum quasi corpore fiant."
(Then Beya mounted upon Gabricus and enclosed him in her womb, so that nothing
at all could be seen of him any more. And she embraced Gabricus with so much love
that she absorbed him completely into her own nature, and divided him into indivis-
ible parts. Wherefore Merculinus says: Through themselves they are dissolved,
through themselves they are put together, so that they who were two are made one,
as though of one body.) (NOTE: "Merculinus" is a correction of the text's "Mas-
culinus.") The King, like the King's Son, is killed in a variety of ways. He may be
struck down, or else he drinks so much water that he sickens and dissolves in it.
(Merlinus, "Allegoria de arcano lapidis," *Art. aurif.*, I, pp. 392ff.).
[40] Valentinus, "Practica," *Mus. herm.*, p. 394. In another version of the incorporation
motif, Mars feeds the body of the King to the famished wolf (*fame acerrima occu-
patus*), the son of Saturn (lead). The wolf symbolizes the *prima materia's* appetite for
the King, who often takes the place of the Son (fig. 9).

Fig. 9. The wolf as *prima materia*, devouring the dead king. In the
background, sublimation of the *prima materia* and rebirth of the king
Maier, Scrutinium chymicum (1687)

losophers. So long as consciousness refrains from acting, the
opposites will remain dormant in the unconscious. Once they
have been activated, the *regius filius* — spirit, Logos, Nous — is
swallowed up by Physis; that is to say, the body and the psychic
representatives of the organs gain mastery over the conscious
mind. In the hero myth[41] this state is known as being swallowed
up in the belly of the whale or dragon[42] (fig. 10). The heat there
is usually so intense that the hero loses his hair,[43] i.e., he is
reborn bald as a babe (fig. 11). The heat is *ignis gehennalis*, the
hell into which Christ descended in order to conquer death as
part of his *opus*.

441   The philosopher makes the journey to hell as a "redeemer."
The "hidden fire" forms the inner antithesis to the cold wetness
of the sea.[44] In the "Visio" this heat is undoubtedly the warmth

[41] Cf. *Symbols of Transformation*, passim.
[42] Espagnet, "Arcanum hermeticae philosophiae," *Bibl. chem. curiosa*, II, p. 655,
§LXVIII: "This first digestion takes place as if in a belly."
[43] Frobenius, *Das Zeitalter des Sonnengottes*.
[44] *Turba philosophorum* (Sermo LXVIII): "Our work . . . results from a generation in
the sea."

Fig. 10. Jonah in the whale
*Early   Christian   earthenware
lamp*

of incubation,[45] equivalent to the self-incubating or "brooding"
state of meditation. In Indian yoga we find the kindred idea of
tapas, self-incubation.[46] The aim of *tapas* is the same as in the
"Visio": transformation and resurrection.

From "The Conjunction," CW 14, par. 756

756   Naturally there is an enormous difference between an anticipated psychosis and a real one, but the difference is not always
clearly perceived and this gives rise to uncertainty or even a fit
of panic. Unlike a real psychosis, which comes on you and in-
undates you with uncontrollable fantasies irrupting from the
unconscious, the judging attitude implies a voluntary involvement in those fantasy-processes which compensate the individual and — in particular — the collective situation of consciousness. The avowed purpose of this involvement is to integrate

[45] Cf. the king's sweat-bath, fig. XIV of the Lambspringk, "Figurae," *Mus. herm.*, p.
369, among others. We find exactly the same idea in the hatching of the egg in
goldmaking, as described by Nikephorus Blemmides: περι τῆς ᾠοκρυσοποιίας
(Berthelot, *Alch. grecs*, VI, xx).
[46] Cf. Jung, *Symbols of Transformation*, p. 380.

Fig. 11. Jonah in the belly of the
whale *Khludov Psalter (Byzantine,
9th cent.)*

the statements of the unconscious, to assimilate their compensatory content, and thereby produce a whole meaning which
alone makes life worth living and, for not a few people, possible at all. The reason why the involvement looks very like a
psychosis is that the patient is integrating the same fantasy-
material to which the insane person falls victim because he cannot integrate it but is swallowed up by it. In myths the hero is
the one who conquers the dragon, not the one who is devoured
by it. And yet both have to deal with the same dragon. Also, he
is no hero who never met the dragon, or who, if he once saw it,
declared afterwards that he saw nothing. Equally, only one who
has risked the fight with the dragon and is not overcome by it
wins the hoard, the "treasure hard to attain." He alone has a
genuine claim to self-confidence, for he has faced the dark
ground of his self and thereby has gained himself. This experience gives him faith and trust, the *pistis* in the ability of the self
to sustain him, for everything that menaced him from inside he
has made his own. He has acquired the right to believe that he
will be able to overcome all future threats by the same means.
He has arrived at an inner certainty which makes him capable
of self-reliance, and attained what the alchemists called the
unio mentalis.

From "The Tavistock Lectures: Lecture III," CW 18, pars.
191–97

191   I point out to him that the hero motif appears throughout the
dreams. He has a hero fantasy about himself which comes to
the surface in the last dream. He is the hero as the great man
with the long coat and with the great plan; he is the hero who
dies on the field of honour at St. Jacob; he is going to show the
world who he is; and he is quite obviously the hero who overcomes the monster. The hero motif is invariably accompanied

by the dragon motif; the dragon and the hero who fights him are two figures of the same myth.

192   The dragon appears in his dream as the crab-lizard. This statement does not, of course, explain what the dragon represents as an image of his psychological situation. So the next associations are directed round the monster. When it moves first to the left and then to the right the dreamer has the feeling that he is standing in an angle which could shut on him like open scissors. That would be fatal. He has read Freud, and accordingly he interprets the situation as an incest wish, the monster being the mother, the angle of the open scissors the legs of the mother, and he himself, standing in between, being just born or just going back into the mother.

193   Strangely enough, in mythology, the dragon *is* the mother. You meet that motif all over the world, and the monster is called the mother dragon.[47] The mother dragon eats the child again, she sucks him in after having given birth to him. The "terrible mother," as she is also called, is waiting with wide-open mouth on the Western Seas, and when a man approaches that mouth it closes on him and he is finished. That monstrous figure is the mother sarcophaga, the flesh-eater; it is, in another form, Matuta, the mother of the dead. It is the goddess of death.

194   But these parallels still do not explain why the dream chooses the particular image of the crab. I hold — and when I say I hold I have certain reasons for saying so — that representations of psychic facts in images like the snake or the lizard or the crab or the mastodon or analogous animals also represent organic facts. For instance, the serpent very often represents the cerebro-spinal system, especially the lower centres of the brain, and particularly the medulla oblongata and spinal cord. The crab, on the other hand, having a sympathetic system only, represents chiefly the sympathicus and para-sympathicus of the abdomen; it is an abdominal thing. So if you translate the text of the dream it would read: if you go on like this your cerebro-spinal system and your sympathetic system will come up against you and snap you up. That is in fact what is happening. The symptoms of his neurosis express the rebellion of the sympathetic functions and of the cerebro-spinal system against his conscious attitude.

195   The crab-lizard brings up the archetypal idea of the hero and the dragon as deadly enemies. But in certain myths you find the interesting fact that the hero is not connected with the dragon only by his fight. There are, on the contrary, indications that the hero is himself the dragon. In Scandinavian mythology the

---

[47] [E.g., *Symbols of Transformation*, Part II, ch. V, especially par. 395.]

hero is recognized by the fact that he has snake's eyes. He has snake's eyes because he is a snake. There are many other myths and legends which contain the same idea. Cecrops, the founder of Athens, was a man above and a serpent below. The souls of heroes often appear after death in the form of serpents.

196   Now in our dream the monstrous crab-lizard moves first to the left, and I ask him about this left side. He says, "The crab apparently does not know the way. Left is the unfavourable side, left is sinister." Sinister does indeed mean left and unfavourable. But the right side is also not good for the monster, because when it goes to the right it is touched by the wand and is killed. Now we come to his standing in between the angle of the monster's movement, a situation which at first glance he interpreted as incest. He says, "As a matter of fact, I felt surrounded on either side like a hero who is going to fight a dragon." So he himself realizes the hero motif.

197   But unlike the mythical hero he does not fight the dragon with a weapon, but with a wand. He says, "From its effect on the monster it seems that it is a magical wand." He certainly does dispose of the crab in a magical way. The wand is another mythological symbol. It often contains a sexual allusion, and sexual magic is a means of protection against danger. You may remember, too, how during the earthquake at Messina[48] nature produced certain instinctive reactions against the overwhelming destruction.

(c) Personal Myths

While myths for Jung are usually groupwide rather than, like dreams, individual, he recognizes the existence of individual myths. Indeed, he characterizes the subject of his autobiography, Memories, Dreams, Reflections, *as his personal myth. Personal myths arise by default, when group myths, such as religious myths for moderns, no longer work. Yet personal myths, like custom-made pants, better fit the unique contour of the individual than group myths.*

From **Memories, Dreams, Reflections**, p. 3

My life is a story of the self-realization of the unconscious. Everything in the unconscious seeks outward manifestation, and the personality too desires to evolve out of its unconscious

---

[48] [The reference is to the disaster of 1908, when 90 per cent of the Sicilian city was destroyed, with a loss of 60,000 lives.]

conditions and to experience itself as a whole. I cannot employ the language of science to trace this process of growth in myself, for I cannot experience myself as a scientific problem.

What we are to our inward vision, and what man appears to be *sub specie aeternitatis*, can only be expressed by way of myth. Myth is more individual and expresses life more precisely than does science. Science works with concepts of averages which are far too general to do justice to the subjective variety of an individual life.

Thus it is that I have now undertaken, in my eighty-third year, to tell my personal myth. I can only make direct statements, only "tell stories." Whether or not the stories are "true" is not the problem. The only question is whether what I tell is *my* fable, *my* truth.

From **Memories, Dreams, Reflections**, p. 171

About this time I experienced a moment of unusual clarity in which I looked back over the way I had traveled so far. I thought, "Now you possess a key to mythology and are free to unlock all the gates of the unconscious psyche." But then something whispered within me, "Why open all gates?" And promptly the question arose of what, after all, I had accomplished. I had explained the myths of peoples of the past; I had written a book about the hero, the myth in which man has always lived. But in what myth does man live nowadays? In the Christian myth, the answer might be, "Do *you* live in it?" I asked myself. To be honest, the answer was no. For me, it is not what I live by. "Then do we no longer have any myth?" "No, evidently we no longer have any myth." "But then what is your myth—the myth in which you do live?" At this point the dialogue with myself became uncomfortable, and I stopped thinking. I had reached a dead end.

Chapter 7. Myths and Primitives

(7) Myths and Primitives

For Jung, earliest humanity is "primitive" psychologically as well as socially and economically. At birth, humans are entirely unconscious. Only slowly does consciousness — consciousness of the distinction between oneself and the external world — emerge. Not yet distinguishing themselves from the world, primitives project themselves onto it and thereby create a world of gods. So short for Jung is the step from experiencing a world of gods to creating myths about those gods that he is prepared to say that primitives experience myths rather than invent them.

From "Two Kinds of Thinking," CW 5, par. 29

29   Riklin has drawn attention to the dream mechanism in fairy-tales,[1] and Abraham has done the same for myths. He says: "The myth is a fragment of the superseded infantile psychic life of the race"; and again: "The myth is therefore a fragment preserved from the infantile psychic life of the race, and dreams are the myths of the individual."[2] The conclusion that the myth-makers thought in much the same way as we still think in dreams is almost self-evident. The first attempts at myth-making can, of course, be observed in children, whose games of make-believe often contain historical echoes. But one must certainly put a large question-mark after the assertion that myths spring from the "infantile" psychic life of the race. They are on the contrary the most mature product of that young humanity. Just as those first fishy ancestors of man, with their gill-slits, were not embryos, but fully developed creatures, so the myth-making and myth-inhabiting man was a grown reality and not

[1] *Wishfulfilment and Symbolism in Fairy Tales.*
[2] Abraham, *Dreams and Myths*, pp. 36 and 72, modified.

a four-year-old child. Myth is certainly not an infantile phantasm, but one of the most important requisites of primitive life.

From "**Psychological Aspects of the Mother Archetype**," CW 9 i, par. 187

5. CONCLUSION

187   From what has been said it should be clear that in the last analysis all the statements of mythology on this subject as well as the observed effects of the mother-complex, when stripped of their confusing detail, point to the unconscious as their place of origin. How else could it have occurred to man to divide the cosmos, on the analogy of day and night, summer and winter, into a bright day-world and a dark night-world peopled with fabulous monsters, unless he had the prototype of such a division in himself, in the polarity between the conscious and the invisible and unknowable unconscious? Primitive man's perception of objects is conditioned only partly by the objective behaviour of the things themselves, whereas a much greater part is often played by intrapsychic facts which are not related to the external objects except by way of projection.[3] This is due to the simple fact that the primitive has not yet experienced that ascetic discipline of mind known to us as the critique of knowledge. To him the world is a more or less fluid phenomenon within the stream of his own fantasy, where subject and object are undifferentiated and in a state of mutual interpenetration. "All that is outside, also is inside," we could say with Goethe. But this "inside," which modern rationalism is so eager to derive from "outside," has an *a priori* structure of its own that antedates all conscious experience. It is quite impossible to conceive how "experience" in the widest sense, or, for that matter, anything psychic, could originate exclusively in the outside world. The psyche is part of the inmost mystery of life, and it has its own peculiar structure and form like every other organism. Whether this psychic structure and its elements, the archetypes, ever "originated" at all is a metaphysical question and therefore unanswerable. The structure is something given, the precondition that is found to be present in every case. And this is the *mother*, the matrix — the form into which all experience is poured. The *father*, on the other hand, represents the *dynamism* of the archetype, for the archetype consists of both — form and energy.

---

[3] [Cf. above, "Archetypes of the Collective Unconscious," par. 7. — EDITORS.]

From "The Psychology of the Child Archetype," CW 9 i, par. 261

261   The primitive mentality does not *invent* myths, it *experiences* them. Myths are original revelations of the preconscious psyche, involuntary statements about unconscious psychic happenings, and anything but allegories of physical processes.[4]

From "A Psychological View of Conscience," CW 10, par. 836

836   In practice it is indeed very difficult to distinguish conscience from the traditional moral precepts. For this reason it is often thought that conscience is nothing more than the suggestive elect of these precepts, and that it would not exist if no moral laws had been invented. But the phenomenon we call "conscience" is found at every level of human culture. Whether an Eskimo has a bad conscience about skinning an animal with an iron knife instead of the traditional flint one, or about leaving a friend in the lurch whom he ought to help, in both cases he feels an inner reproach, a "twinge of conscience," and in both cases the deviation from an inveterate habit or generally accepted rule produces something like a shock. For the primitive psyche anything unusual or not customary causes an emotional reaction, and the more it runs counter to the "collective representations" which almost invariably govern the prescribed mode of behaviour, the more violent the reaction will be. It is a peculiarity of the primitive mind to endow everything with mythical derivations that are meant to explain it. Thus everything that we would call pure chance is understood to be intentional and is regarded as a magical influence. Such explanations are in no sense "inventions"; they are spontaneous fantasy-products which appear without premeditation in a natural and quite involuntary way; unconscious, archetypal reactions such as are peculiar to the human psyche. Nothing could be more mistaken than to assume that a myth is something "thought up." It comes into existence of its own accord, as can be observed in all authentic products of fantasy, and particularly in dreams. It is the hybris of consciousness to pretend that everything derives from *its* primacy, despite the fact that consciousness itself demonstrably comes from an older unconscious psyche. The unity and continuity of consciousness are such late acquisitions that there is still a fear that they might get lost again.

---

[4] Cf. "The Structure of the Psyche," pars. 330ff.

Chapter 8. Myths and Moderns

(a) The Demythicizing of the External World

Jung accepts the conventional view that science has replaced religion as the explanation of events in the physical world. In psychological terms, the projection of archetypes onto the world has been withdrawn, and the world is now experienced as impersonal and mechanical. Myth suffers the same fate as religion, of which it has traditionally been a part.

From "The Philosophical Tree," CW 13, par. 395

395   In their various ways, the alchemists struggled to come to terms with the lapis-Christ parallel. They did not find a solution, nor was this possible so long as their conceptual language was not freed from projection into matter and did not become psychological. Only in the following centuries, with the growth of natural science, was the projection withdrawn from matter and entirely abolished together with the psyche. This development of consciousness has still not reached its end. Nobody, it is true, any longer endows matter with mythological properties. This form of projection has become obsolete. Projection is now confined to personal and social relationships, to political Utopias and suchlike. Nature has nothing more to fear in the shape of mythological interpretations, but the realm of the spirit certainly has, more particularly that realm which commonly goes by the name of "metaphysics." There mythologems claiming to utter the absolute truth still tumble over one another, and anyone who dresses up his mythologem in solemn enough words believes that he has made a valid statement, and even makes a virtue of not possessing the modesty becoming to our limited human intelligence, which knows that it does not know. Such people even think that God himself is menaced whenever anyone dares to interpret their archetypal projections for what they are, namely, human statements, which no reasonable person

supposes signify nothing, seeing that even the most preposterous statements of the alchemists have their meaning, though
not the one which they themselves, with but few exceptions,
sought to give their symbols, but one which only the future
could formulate. Whenever we have to do with mythologems it
is advisable to assume that they mean more than what they
appear to say. Just as dreams do not conceal something already
known, or express it under a disguise, but try rather to formulate an as yet unconscious fact as clearly as possible, so myths
and alchemical symbols are not euhemeristic allegories that
hide artificial secrets. On the contrary, they seek to translate
natural secrets into the language of consciousness and to declare the truth that is the common property of mankind. By
becoming conscious, the individual is threatened more and
more with isolation, which is nevertheless the *sine qua non* of
conscious differentiation. The greater this threat, the more it is
compensated by the production of collective and archetypal
symbols which are common to all men.

(b) The Continued Existence of Traditional Myths

*Even if science has replaced myth as an explanation of events in
the external world, myth continues to exist today. Minimally,
myth becomes literature. Writers invoke traditional myths not
to explain the world, which remains the purview of science, but
to articulate their visions of their world, visions stemming in
fact from their experience of the unconscious. One step beyond
the invocation of traditional myths is the updating of the symbols used in traditional myths. In Jung's phrase, myth is thereby
"dreamed onwards."*

From "**Psychology and Literature**," CW 15, pars. 151–52

151   It is therefore to be expected that the poet will turn to mythological figures in order to give suitable expression to his experience. Nothing would be more mistaken than to suppose that
he is working with second-hand material. On the contrary, the
primordial experience is the source of his creativeness, but it is
so dark and amorphous that it requires the related mythological imagery to give it form. In itself it is wordless and imageless,
for it is a vision seen "as in a glass, darkly." It is nothing but a
tremendous intuition striving for expression. It is like a whirlwind that seizes everything within reach and assumes visible

form as it swirls upward. Since the expression can never match the richness of the vision and can never exhaust its possibilities, the poet must have at his disposal a huge store of material if he is to communicate even a fraction of what he has glimpsed, and must make use of difficult and contradictory images in order to express the strange paradoxes of his vision. Dante decks out his experience in all the imagery of heaven, purgatory, and hell; Goethe brings in the Blocksberg and the Greek underworld; Wagner needs the whole corpus of Nordic myth, including the Parsifal saga; Nietzsche resorts to the hieratic style of the bard and legendary seer; Blake presses into his service the phantasmagoric world of India, the Old Testament, and the Apocalypse; and Spitteler borrows old names for the new figures that pour in alarming profusion from his muse's cornucopia. Nothing is missing in the whole gamut that ranges from the ineffably sublime to the perversely grotesque.

152   The psychologist can do little to elucidate this variegated spectacle except provide comparative material and a terminology for its discussion. Thus, what appears in the vision is the imagery of the collective unconscious. This is the matrix of consciousness and has its own inborn structure. According to phylogenetic law, the psychic structure must, like the anatomical, show traces of the earlier stages of evolution it has passed through. This is in fact so in the case of the unconscious, for in dreams and mental disturbances psychic products come to the surface which show all the traits of primitive levels of development, not only in their form but also in their content and meaning, so that we might easily take them for fragments of esoteric doctrines. Mythological motifs frequently appear, but clothed in modern dress; for instance, instead of the eagle of Zeus, or the great roc, there is an airplane; the fight with the dragon is a railway smash; the dragon-slaying hero is an operatic tenor; the Earth Mother is a stout lady selling vegetables; the Pluto who abducts Persephone is a reckless chauffeur, and so on. What is of particular importance for the study of literature, however, is that the manifestations of the collective unconscious are compensatory to the conscious attitude, so that they have the effect of bringing a one-sided, unadapted, or dangerous state of consciousness back into equilibrium. This function can also be observed in the symptomatology of neurosis and in the delusions of the insane, where the process of compensation is often perfectly obvious — for instance in the case of people who have anxiously shut themselves off from the world and suddenly discover that their most intimate secrets are known and talked

about by everybody. The compensation is, of course, not always as crass as this; with neurotics it is much more subtle, and in dreams — particularly in one's own dreams — it is often a complete mystery at first not only to the layman but even to the specialist, however staggeringly simple it turns out to be once it has been understood. But, as we know, the simplest things are often the most difficult to understand.

(c) The Revival of Traditional Myths

The next step — the revival of traditional myths — might seem a step backward, but it is really a step forward. While the myths here remain traditional ones, they are revived as living myths and not merely as literary metaphors. Jung's most powerful example is the twentieth-century revival of the worship of the Teutonic god Wotan. Wotan might not have been invoked to explain thunderstorms, but he was invoked by the Nazis and their predecessors to stir German nationalism.

"Wotan," CW 10, pars. 371–99[1]

En Germanie naistront diverses sectes,
S'approchans fort de l'heureux paganisme:
Le cœur captif et petites receptes
Feront retour à payer la vraye disme.
— *Prophéties de Maistre Michel Nostradamus,* 1555

371   When we look back to the time before 1914, we find ourselves living in a world of events which would have been inconceivable before the war. We were even beginning to regard war between civilized nations as a fable, thinking that such an absurdity would become less and less possible in our rational, internationally organized world. And what came after the war was a veritable witches' sabbath. Everywhere fantastic revolutions, violent alterations of the map, reversions in politics to

[1] [First published as "Wotan," *Neue Schweizer Rundschau* (Zurich), n.s., III (March, 1936), 657–69. Republished in *Aufsätze zur Zeitgeschichte* (Zurich, 1946), 1–23. Trans. by Barbara Hannah in *Essays on Contemporary Events* (London, 1947), 1–16; this version has been consulted. The author added footnotes 3, 4, 15, and 16 (first par.) to the London edn. Motto, trans. by H. C. Roberts:
"In Germany shall divers sects arise,
Coming very near to happy paganism.
The heart captivated and small receivings
Shall open the gate to pay the true tithe."
— EDITORS.]

medieval or even antique prototypes, totalitarian states that engulf their neighbours and outdo all previous theocracies in their absolutist claims, persecutions of Christians and Jews, wholesale political murder, and finally we have witnessed a lighthearted piratical raid on a peaceful, half-civilized people.[2]

372   With such goings on in the wide world it is not in the least surprising that there should be equally curious manifestations on a smaller scale in other spheres. In the realm of philosophy we shall have to wait some time before anyone is able to assess the kind of age we are living in. But in the sphere of religion we can see at once that some very significant things have been happening. We need feel no surprise that in Russia the colourful splendours of the Eastern Orthodox Church have been superseded by the Movement of the Godless — indeed, one breathed a sigh of relief oneself when one emerged from the haze of an Orthodox church with its multitude of lamps and entered an honest mosque, where the sublime and invisible omnipresence of God was not crowded out by a superfluity of sacred paraphernalia. Tasteless and pitiably unintelligent as it is, and however deplorable the low spiritual level of the "scientific" reaction, it was inevitable that nineteenth-century "scientific" enlightenment should one day dawn in Russia.

373   But what is more than curious — indeed, piquant to a degree — is that an ancient god of storm and frenzy, the long quiescent Wotan, should awake, like an extinct volcano, to new activity, in a civilized country that had long been supposed to have outgrown the Middle Ages. We have seen him come to life in the German Youth Movement, and right at the beginning the blood of several sheep was shed in honour of his resurrection. Armed with rucksack and lute, blond youths, and sometimes girls as well, were to be seen as restless wanderers on every road from the North Cape to Sicily, faithful votaries of the roving god. Later, towards the end of the Weimar Republic, the wandering role was taken over by the thousands of unemployed, who were to be met with everywhere on their aimless journeys. By 1933 they wandered no longer, but marched in their hundreds of thousands. The Hitler movement literally brought the whole of Germany to its feet, from five-year-olds to veterans, and produced the spectacle of a nation migrating from one place to another. Wotan the wanderer was on the move. He could be seen, looking rather shamefaced, in the meeting-house of a sect of simple folk in North Germany, dis-

[2] Abyssinia.

guised as Christ sitting on a white horse. I do not know if these people were aware of Wotan's ancient connection with the figures of Christ and Dionysus, but it is not very probable.

374 Wotan is a restless wanderer who creates unrest and stirs up strife, now here, now there, and works magic. He was soon changed by Christianity into the devil, and only lived on in fading local traditions as a ghostly hunter who was seen with his retinue, flickering like a will o' the wisp through the stormy night. In the Middle Ages the role of the restless wanderer was taken over by Ahasuerus, the Wandering Jew, which is not a Jewish but a Christian legend. The motif of the wanderer who has not accepted Christ was projected on the Jews, in the same way as we always rediscover our unconscious psychic contents in other people. At any rate the coincidence of anti-Semitism with the reawakening of Wotan is a psychological subtlety that may perhaps be worth mentioning.

375 The German youths who celebrated the solstice with sheep-sacrifices were not the first to hear a rustling in the primeval forest of the unconscious. They were anticipated by Nietzsche, Schuler, Stefan George, and Ludwig Klages.[3] The literary tradition of the Rhineland and the country south of the Main has a classical stamp that cannot easily be got rid of: every interpretation of intoxication and exuberance is apt to be taken back to classical models, to Dionysus, to the *puer aeternus* and the cosmogonic Eros.[4] No doubt it sounds better to academic ears to interpret these things as Dionysus, but Wotan might be a more correct interpretation. He is the god of storm and frenzy, the unleasher of passions and the lust of battle; moreover he is a

[3] Ever since Nietzsche (1844–1900) there has been consistent emphasis on the "Dionysian" aspect of life in contrast to its "Apollonian" opposite. Since "The Birth of Tragedy" (1872), the dark, earthy, feminine side, with its mantic and orgiastic characteristics, has possessed the imagination of philosophers and poets. Irrationality gradually came to be regarded as the ideal; this is found, for example, all through the research of Alfred Schuler (d. 1923) into the mystery religions, and particularly in the writings of Klages (b. 1872 [d. 1956]), who expounded the philosophy of "irrationalism." To Klages, logos and consciousness are the destroyers of creative preconscious life. In these writers we witness the origin of a gradual rejection of reality and a negation of life as it is. This leads in the end to a cult of ecstasy, culminating in the self-dissolution of consciousness in death, which meant, to them, the conquest of material limitations.

The poetry of Stefan George (1868–1933) combines elements of classical civilization, medieval Christianity, and oriental mysticism. George deliberately attacked nineteenth- and twentieth-century rationalism. His aristocratic message of mystical beauty and of an esoteric conception of history had a deep influence on German youth. His work has been exploited by unscrupulous politicians for propaganda purposes.

[4] *Vom kosmogonischen Eros* is the title of one of Klages' main works (first pub. 1922).

superlative magician and artist in illusion who is versed in all secrets of an occult nature.

376   Nietzsche's case is certainly a peculiar one. He had no knowledge of Germanic literature; he discovered the "cultural Philistine"; and the announcement that "God is dead" led to Zarathustra's meeting with an unknown god in unexpected form, who approached him sometimes as an enemy and sometimes disguised as Zarathustra himself. Zarathustra, too, was a soothsayer, a magician, and the storm-wind:

> And like a wind shall I come to blow among them, and with my spirit shall take away the breath of their spirit; thus my future wills it.
> Truly, a strong wind is Zarathustra to all that are low; and this counsel gives he to his enemies and to all that spit and spew:
> "Beware of spitting against the wind."[5]

377   And when Zarathustra dreamed that he was guardian of the graves in the "lone mountain fortress of death," and was making a mighty effort to open the gates, suddenly

> A roaring wind tore the gates asunder; whistling, shrieking, and keening, it cast a black coffin before me.
> And amid the roaring and whistling and shrieking the coffin burst open and spouted a thousand peals of laughter.

378   The disciple who interpreted the dream said to Zarathustra:

> Are you not yourself the wind with shrill whistling, which bursts open the gates of the fortress of death?
> Are you not yourself the coffin filled with life's gay malice and angel-grimaces?[6]

379   In 1863 or 1864, in his poem "To the Unknown God," Nietzsche had written:

> I shall and will know thee, Unknown One,
> Who searchest out the depths of my soul,
> And blowest through my life like a storm,

---

[5] *Thus Spake Zarathustra*, trans. by Kaufmann, p. 211 (mod.).
[6] Ibid., p. 247 (mod.).

Ungraspable, and yet my kinsman!
I shall and will know thee, and serve thee.

380   Twenty years later, in his "Mistral Song," he wrote:

Mistral wind, chaser of clouds,
Killer of gloom, sweeper of the skies,
Raging storm-wind, how I love thee!
Are we not both the first-fruits
Of the same womb, forever predestined
To the same fate?[7]

381   In the dithyramb known as "Ariadne's Lament," Nietzsche is completely the victim of the hunter-god:

Stretched out, shuddering,
Like a half-dead thing whose feet are warmed,
Shaken by unknown fevers,
Shivering with piercing icy frost arrows,
Hunted by thee, O thought,
Unutterable! Veiled! horrible one!
Thou huntsman behind the clouds.
Struck down by thy lightning bolt,
Thou mocking eye that stares at me from the dark!
Thus I lie,
Writhing, twisting, tormented
With all eternal tortures,
Smitten
By thee, cruel huntsman,
Thou unknown — God![8]

382   This remarkable image of the hunter-god is not a mere dithyrambic figure of speech but is based on an experience which Nietzsche had when he was fifteen years old, at Pforta. It is described in a book by Nietzsche's sister, Elizabeth Foerster-Nietzsche.[9] As he was wandering about in a gloomy wood at night, he was terrified by a "blood-curdling shriek from a neighbouring lunatic asylum," and soon afterwards he came face to face with a huntsman whose "features were wild and uncanny." Setting his whistle to his lips "in a valley surrounded by wild scrub," the huntsman "blew such a shrill blast" that

[7] *Werke*, V, pp. 457f. and 495; trans. by R.F.C.H.
[8] *Thus Spake Zarathustra*, Kaufmann trans., p. 365.
[9] *Der werdende Nietzsche*, pp. 84ff.

Nietzsche lost consciousness — but woke up again in Pforta. It was a nightmare. It is significant that in his dream Nietzsche, who in reality intended to go to Eisleben, Luther's town, discussed with the huntsman the question of going instead to "Teutschenthal" (Valley of the Germans). No one with ears to hear can misunderstand the shrill whistling of the storm-god in the nocturnal wood.

383   Was it really only the classical philologist in Nietzsche that led to the god being called Dionysus instead of Wotan — or was it perhaps due to his fateful meeting with Wagner?

384   In his *Reich ohne Raum*, which was first published in 1919, Bruno Goetz saw the secret of coming events in Germany in the form of a very strange vision. I have never forgotten this little book, for it struck me at the time as a forecast of the German weather. It anticipates the conflict between the realm of ideas and life, between Wotan's dual nature as a god of storm and a god of secret musings. Wotan disappeared when his oaks fell and appeared again when the Christian God proved too weak to save Christendom from fratricidal slaughter. When the Holy Father at Rome could only impotently lament before God the fate of the *grex segregatus*, the one-eyed old hunter, on the edge of the German forest, laughed and saddled Sleipnir.

385   We are always convinced that the modern world is a reasonable world, basing our opinion on economic, political, and psychological factors. But if we may forget for a moment that we are living in the year of Our Lord 1936, and, laying aside our well-meaning, all-too-human reasonableness, may burden God or the gods with the responsibility for contemporary events instead of man, we would find Wotan quite suitable as a causal hypothesis. In fact I venture the heretical suggestion that the unfathomable depths of Wotan's character explain more of National Socialism than all three reasonable factors put together. There is no doubt that each of these factors explains an important aspect of what is going on in Germany, but Wotan explains yet more. He is particularly enlightening in regard to a general phenomenon which is so strange to anybody not a German that it remains incomprehensible even after the deepest reflection.

386   Perhaps we may sum up this general phenomenon as *Ergriffenheit* — a state of being seized or possessed. The term postulates not only an *Ergriffener* (one who is seized) but also an *Ergreifer* (one who seizes). Wotan is an *Ergreifer* of men, and, unless one wishes to deify Hitler — which has indeed actually happened — he is really the only explanation. It is true that Wotan shares this quality with his cousin Dionysus, but Di-

onysus seems to have exercised his influence mainly on women. The maenads were a species of female storm-troopers, and, according to mythical reports, were dangerous enough. Wotan confined himself to the berserkers, who found their vocation as the Blackshirts of mythical kings.

387   A mind that is still childish thinks of the gods as metaphysical entities existing in their own right, or else regards them as playful or superstitious inventions. From either point of view the parallel between Wotan *redivivus* and the social, political, and psychic storm that is shaking Germany might have at least the value of a parable. But since the gods are without doubt personifications of psychic forces, to assert their metaphysical existence is as much an intellectual presumption as the opinion that they could ever be invented. Not that "psychic forces" have anything to do with the conscious mind, fond as we are of playing with the idea that consciousness and psyche are identical. This is only another piece of intellectual presumption. "Psychic forces" have far more to do with the realm of the unconscious. Our mania for rational explanations obviously has its roots in our fear of metaphysics, for the two were always hostile brothers. Hence anything unexpected that approaches us from that dark realm is regarded either as coming from outside and therefore as real, or else as an hallucination and therefore not true. The idea that anything could be real or true which does *not* come from outside has hardly begun to dawn on contemporary man.

388   For the sake of better understanding and to avoid prejudice, we could of course dispense with the name "Wotan" and speak instead of the *furor teutonicus*. But we should only be saying the same thing and not as well, for the *furor* in this case is a mere psychologizing of Wotan and tells us no more than that the Germans are in a state of "fury." We thus lose sight of the most peculiar feature of this whole phenomenon, namely, the dramatic aspect of the *Ergreifer* and the *Ergriffener*. The impressive thing about the German phenomenon is that one man, who is obviously "possessed," has infected a whole nation to such an extent that everything is set in motion and has started rolling on its course towards perdition.

389   It seems to me that Wotan hits the mark as an hypothesis. Apparently he really was only asleep in the Kyffhäuser mountain until the ravens called him and announced the break of day. He is a fundamental attribute of the German psyche, an irrational psychic factor which acts on the high pressure of civilization like a cyclone and blows it away. Despite their cranki-

ness, the Wotan-worshippers seem to have judged things more correctly than the worshippers of reason. Apparently everyone had forgotten that Wotan is a Germanic datum of first importance, the truest expression and unsurpassed personification of a fundamental quality that is particularly characteristic of the Germans. Houston Stewart Chamberlain is a symptom which arouses suspicion that other veiled gods may be sleeping elsewhere. The emphasis on the Germanic race (vulgarly called "Aryan"), the Germanic heritage, blood and soil, the Wagalaweia songs,[10] the ride of the Valkyries, Jesus as a blond and blue-eyed hero, the Greek mother of St. Paul, the devil as an international Alberich in Jewish or Masonic guise, the Nordic aurora borealis as the light of civilization, the inferior Mediterranean races — all this is the indispensable scenery for the drama that is taking place and at bottom they all mean the same thing: a god has taken possession of the Germans and their house is filled with a "mighty rushing wind." It was soon after Hitler seized power, if I am not mistaken, that a cartoon appeared in *Punch* of a raving berserker tearing himself free from his bonds. A hurricane has broken loose in Germany while we still believe it is fine weather.

390   Things are comparatively quiet in Switzerland, though occasionally there is a puff of wind from the north or south. Sometimes it has a slightly ominous sound, sometimes it whispers so harmlessly or even idealistically that no one is alarmed. "Let sleeping dogs lie" — we manage to get along pretty well with this proverbial wisdom. It is sometimes said that the Swiss are singularly averse to making a problem of themselves. I must rebut this accusation: the Swiss do have their problems but they would not admit it for anything in the world, even though they see which way the wind is blowing. We thus pay our tribute to the time of storm and stress in Germany, but we never mention it, and this enables us to feel vastly superior.

391   It is above all the Germans who have an opportunity, perhaps unique in history, to look into their own hearts and to learn what those perils of the soul were from which Christianity tried to rescue mankind. Germany is a land of spiritual catastrophes, where nature never makes more than a presence of peace with world-ruling reason. The disturber of the peace is a wind that blows into Europe from Asia's vastness, sweeping in on a wide front from Thrace to the Baltic, scattering the

---

[10] [After the meaningless refrains sung by the Rhine maidens in Wagner's *Ring* cycle: "*Weia! Waga! Wagala weia!,*" etc. — EDITORS.]

nations before it like dry leaves, or inspiring thoughts that shake the world to its foundations. It is an elemental Dionysus breaking into the Apollonian order. The rouser of this tempest is named Wotan, and we can learn a good deal about him from the political confusion and spiritual upheaval he has caused throughout history. For a more exact investigation of his character, however, we must go back to the age of myths, which did not explain everything in terms of man and his limited capacities but sought the deeper cause in the psyche and its autonomous powers. Man's earliest intuitions personified these powers as gods, and described them in the myths with great care and circumstantiality according to their various characters. This could be done the more readily on account of the firmly established primordial types or images which are innate in the unconscious of many races and exercise a direct influence upon them. Because the behaviour of a race takes on its specific character from its underlying images we can speak of an archetype "Wotan."[11] As an autonomous psychic factor, Wotan produces effects in the collective life of a people and thereby reveals his own nature. For Wotan has a peculiar biology of his own, quite apart from the nature of man. It is only from time to time that individuals fall under the irresistible influence of this unconscious factor. When it is quiescent, one is no more aware of the archetype Wotan than of a latent epilepsy. Could the Germans who were adults in 1914 have foreseen what they would be today? Such amazing transformations are the effect of the god of wind, that "bloweth where it listeth, and thou hearest the sound thereof, but canst not tell whence it cometh, nor whither it goeth." It seizes everything in its path and overthrows everything that is not firmly rooted. When the wind blows it shakes everything that is insecure, whether without or within.

392   Martin Ninck has recently published a monograph[12] which is a most welcome addition to our knowledge of Wotan's nature. The reader need not fear that this book is nothing but a scientific study written with academic aloofness from the subject. Certainly the right to scientific objectivity is fully preserved, and the material has been collected with extraordinary thoroughness and presented in unusually clear form. But over and above all this one feels that the author is vitally interested in it, that the chord of Wotan is vibrating in him too. This is no

[11] One should read what Bruno Goetz (*Deutsche Dichtung*, pp. 36ff. and 72ff.) has to say about Odin as the German wanderer-god. Unfortunately I only read this book after I had finished my article.
[12] *Wodan und germanischer Schicksalsglaube.*

criticism—on the contrary it is one of the chief merits of the book, which without this enthusiasm might easily have degenerated into a tedious catalogue.

393   Ninck sketches a really magnificent portrait of the German archetype Wotan. He describes him in ten chapters, using all the available sources, as the berserker, the god of storm, the wanderer, the warrior, the *Wunsch-* and *Minne-*god, the lord of the dead and of the *Einherier*,[13] the master of secret knowledge, the magician, and the god of the poets. Neither the Valkyries nor the *Fylgja*[14] are forgotten, for they form part of the mythological background and fateful significance of Wotan. Ninck's inquiry into the name and its origin is particularly instructive. He shows that Wotan is not only a god of rage and frenzy who embodies the instinctual and emotional aspect of the unconscious. Its intuitive and inspiring side also manifests itself in him, for he understands the runes and can interpret fate.

394   The Romans identified Wotan with Mercury, but his character does not really correspond to any Roman or Greek god, although there are certain resemblances. He is a wanderer like Mercury, for instance, rules over the dead like Pluto and Kronos, and is connected with Dionysus by his emotional frenzy, particularly in its mantic aspect. It is surprising that Ninck does not mention Hermes, the god of revelation, who as *pneuma* and *nous* is associated with the wind. He would be the connecting link with the Christian pneuma and the miracle of Pentecost. As Poimandres (the shepherd of men) Hermes is an *Ergreifer* like Wotan. Ninck rightly points out that Dionysus and the other Greek gods always remained under the supreme authority of Zeus, which indicates a fundamental difference between the Greek and the Germanic temperament. Ninck assumes an inner affinity between Wotan and Kronos, and the latter's defeat may perhaps be a sign that the Wotan-archetype was once overcome and split up in prehistoric times. At all events, the Germanic god represents a totality on a very primitive level, a psychological condition in which man's will was almost identical with the god's and entirely at his mercy. But the Greeks had gods who helped man against other gods; indeed, All-Father Zeus himself is not far from the ideal of a benevolent, enlightened despot.

---

[13] [*Wunsch*, magical wish; *Minne*, remembrance, love; *Einherier*, the dead heroes in Valhalla (*Meyers Konversations-Lexikon*).—EDITORS.]
[14] [*Fylgja*, attendant spirit in the form of an animal (Hastings, *Encyclopedia*).]

395   It was not in Wotan's nature to linger on and show signs of old age. He simply disappeared when the times turned against him, and remained invisible for more than a thousand years, working anonymously and indirectly. Archetypes are like river beds which dry up when the water deserts them, but which it can find again at any time. An archetype is like an old water-course along which the water of life has flowed for centuries, digging a deep channel for itself. The longer it has flowed in this channel the more likely it is that sooner or later the water will return to its old bed. The life of the individual as a member of society and particularly as part of the State may be regulated like a canal, but the life of nations is a great rushing river which is utterly beyond human control, in the hands of One who has always been stronger than men. The League of Nations, which was supposed to possess supranational authority, is regarded by some as a child in need of care and protection, by others as an abortion. Thus the life of nations rolls on unchecked, without guidance, unconscious of where it is going, like a rock crashing down the side of a hill, until it is stopped by an obstacle stronger than itself. Political events move from one impasse to the next, like a torrent caught in gullies, creeks, and marshes. All human control comes to an end when the individual is caught in a mass movement. Then the archetypes begin to function, as happens also in the lives of individuals when they are confronted with situations that cannot be dealt with in any of the familiar ways. But what a so-called Führer does with a mass movement can plainly be seen if we turn our eyes to the north or south of our country.

396   The ruling archetype does not remain the same forever, as is evident from the temporal limitations that have been set to the hoped-for reign of peace, the "thousand-year Reich." The Mediterranean father-archetype of the just, order-loving, benevolent ruler has been shattered over the whole of northern Europe, as the present fate of the Christian Churches bears witness. Fascism in Italy and the civil war in Spain show that in the south as well the cataclysm has been far greater than one expected. Even the Catholic Church can no longer afford trials of strength.

397   The nationalist God has attacked Christianity on a broad front. In Russia he is called technology and science, in Italy, Duce, and in Germany, "German Faith," "German Christianity," or the State. The "German Christians"[15] are a contra-

---

[15] A National Socialist movement inside the Protestant Church, which tried to eliminate all vestiges of the Old Testament from Christianity.

diction in terms and would do better to join Hauer's "German
Faith Movement."[16] These are decent and well-meaning people
who honestly admit their *Ergriffenheit* and try to come to terms
with this new and undeniable fact. They go to an enormous
amount of trouble to make it look less alarming by dressing it
up in a conciliatory historical garb and giving us consoling
glimpses of great figures such as Meister Eckhart, who was also
a German and also *ergriffen*. In this way the awkward question
of who the *Ergreifer* is is circumvented. He was always "God."
But the more Hauer restricts the world-wide sphere of Indo-
European culture to the "Nordic" in general and to the *Edda* in
particular, and the more "German" this faith becomes as a
manifestation of *Ergriffenheit*, the more painfully evident it is
that the "German" god is the god of the Germans.

398   One cannot read Hauer's book[17] without emotion, if one regards it as the tragic and really heroic effort of a conscientious
scholar who, without knowing how it happened to him, was
violently summoned by the inaudible voice of the *Ergreifer* and
is now trying with all his might, and with all his knowledge and
ability, to build a bridge between the dark forces of life and the
shining world of historical ideas. But what do all the beauties
of the past from totally different levels of culture mean to the
man of today, when confronted with a living and unfathomable
tribal god such as he has never experienced before? They are
sucked like dry leaves into the roaring whirlwind, and the

[16] Wilhelm Hauer (b. 1881), first a missionary and later professor of Sanskrit at the
University of Tübingen, was the founder and leader of the "German Faith Movement." It tried to establish a "German Faith" founded on German and Nordic writings and traditions, e.g., those of Eckhart and Goethe. This movement sought to
combine a number of different and often incompatible trends: some of its members
accepted an expurgated form of Christianity, others were opposed not only to Christianity in any form but to every kind of religion or god. One of the common articles
of faith, which the movement adopted in 1934, was: "The German Faith Movement
aims at the religious renaissance of the nation out of the hereditary foundations of
the German race."
   The spirit of this movement may be contrasted with a sermon preached by Dr.
Langmann, an evangelical clergyman and high dignitary of the Church, at the funeral
of the late Gustloff. Dr. Langmann gave the address "in S.A. uniform and jackboots."
He sped the deceased on his journey to Hades, and directed him to Valhalla, to the
home of Siegfried and Baldur, the heroes who "nourish the life of the German people
by the sacrifice of their blood"—like Christ among others. "May this god send the
nations of the earth *clanking on their way* through history." "Lord bless our struggle.
Amen." Thus the reverend gentleman ended his address, according to the *Neue
Zürcher Zeitung* (1936, no. 249). As a service held to Wotan it is no doubt very
edifying—and remarkably tolerant towards believers in Christ! Are our Churches
inclined to be equally tolerant and to preach that Christ shed his blood for the salvation of mankind, like Siegfried, Baldur, and Odin among others?! One can ask unexpectedly grotesque questions these days.
[17] *Deutsche Gottschau: Grundzüge eines deutschen Glaubens* [German Vision of
God: Basic Elements of a German Faith].

rhythmic alliterations of the *Edda* become inextricably mixed up with Christian mystical texts, German poetry, and the wisdom of the *Upanishads*. Hauer himself is *ergriffen* by the depths of meaning in the primal words lying at the root of the Germanic languages, to an extent that he certainly never knew before. Hauer the Indologist is not to blame for this, nor yet the *Edda*; it is rather the fault of *kairos* — the present moment in time — whose name on closer investigation turns out to be Wotan. I would therefore advise the German Faith Movement to throw aside their scruples. Intelligent people will not confuse them with the crude Wotan-worshippers whose faith is a mere presence. There are people in the German Faith Movement who are intelligent enough not only to *believe* but to *know* that the god of the *Germans* is Wotan and not the Christian God. This is a tragic experience and no disgrace. It has always been terrible to fall into the hands of a living god. Yahweh was no exception to this rule, and the Philistines, Edomites, Amorites, and the rest, who were outside the Yahweh experience, must certainly have found it exceedingly disagreeable. The Semitic[18] experience of Allah was for a long time an extremely painful affair for the whole of Christendom. We who stand outside judge the Germans far too much as if they were responsible agents, but perhaps it would be nearer the truth to regard them also as *victims*.

399   If we apply our admittedly peculiar point of view consistently, we are driven to conclude that Wotan must, in time, reveal not only the restless, violent, stormy side of his character, but also his ecstatic and mantic qualities — a very different aspect of his nature. If this conclusion is correct, National Socialism would not be the last word. Things must be concealed in the background which we cannot imagine at present, but we may expect them to appear in the course of the next few years or decades. Wotan's reawakening is a stepping back into the past; the stream was dammed up and has broken into its old channel. But the obstruction will not last for ever; it is rather a *reculer pour mieux sauter*, and the water will overleap the obstacle. Then at last we shall know what Wotan is saying when he "murmurs with Mimir's head."

> Fast move the sons   of Mim, and fate
> Is heard in the note   of the Gjallarhorn;

[18] [Using the word to connote those peoples within the Semitic language-group. — Trans.]

Loud blows Heimdall,   the horn is aloft,
In fear quake all   who on Hel-roads are.

Yggdrasil shakes   and shivers on high
The ancient limbs,   and the giant is loose;
Wotan murmurs   with Mimir's head
But the kinsman of Surt   shall slay him soon.

How fare the gods?   how fare the elves?
All Jotunheim groans,   the gods are at council;
Loud roar the dwarfs   by the doors of stone,
The masters of the rocks: would you know yet more?

Now Garm howls loud   before Gnipahellir;
The fetters will burst,   and the wolf run free;
Much do I know,   and more can see
Of the fate of the gods,   the mighty in fight.

From the east comes Hrym   with shield held high;
In giant-wrath   does the serpent writhe;
O'er the waves he twists,   and the tawny eagle
Gnaws corpses screaming;   Naglfar is loose.

O'er the sea from the north   there sails a ship
With the people of Hel,   at the helm stands Loki;
After the wolf   do wild men follow,
And with them the brother   of Byleist goes.[19]

From "The Fight with the Shadow," CW 10, pars. 447–49

447   As early as 1918, I noticed peculiar disturbances in the unconscious of my German patients which could not be ascribed
to their personal psychology. Such non-personal phenomena always manifest themselves in dreams as mythological motifs that
are also to be found in legends and fairytales throughout the
world. I have called these mythological motifs *archetypes*: that
is, typical modes or forms in which these collective phenomena
are experienced. There was a disturbance of the collective unconscious in every single one of my German patients. One can
explain these disorders causally, but such an explanation is apt
to be unsatisfactory, as it is easier to understand archetypes by
their aim rather than by their causality. The archetypes I had

[19] *Voluspo* (*The Poetic Edda*, trans. by Bellows, pp. 20f.; line 7 mod.).

observed expressed primitivity, violence, and cruelty. When I had seen enough of such cases, I turned my attention to the peculiar state of mind then prevailing in Germany. I could only see signs of depression and a great restlessness, but this did not allay my suspicions. In a paper which I published at that time, I suggested that the "blond beast" was stirring in an uneasy slumber and that an outburst was not impossible.[20]

448   This condition was not by any means a purely Teutonic phenomenon, as became evident in the following years. The onslaught of primitive forces was more or less universal. The only difference lay in the German mentality itself, which proved to be more susceptible because of the marked proneness of the Germans to mass psychology. Moreover, defeat and social disaster had increased the herd instinct in Germany, so that it became more and more probable that Germany would be the first victim among the Western nations — victim of a mass movement brought about by an upheaval of forces lying dormant in the unconscious, ready to break through all moral barriers. These forces, in accordance with the rule I have mentioned, were meant to be a compensation. If such a compensatory move of the unconscious is not integrated into consciousness in an individual, it leads to a neurosis or even to a psychosis, and the same would apply to a collectivity. Clearly there must be something wrong with the conscious attitude for a compensatory move of this kind to be possible; something must be amiss or exaggerated because only a faulty consciousness can call forth a counter-move on the part of the unconscious. Well, innumerable things were wrong, as you know, and opinions are thoroughly divided about them. Which is the correct opinion will be learned only *ex effectu*; that is, we can only discover what the defects in the consciousness of our epoch are by observing the kind of reaction they call forth from the unconscious.

449   As I have already told you, the tide that rose in the unconscious after the first World War was reflected in individual dreams, in the form of collective, mythological symbols which expressed primitivity, violence, cruelty: in short, all the powers of darkness. When such symbols occur in a large number of individuals and are not understood, they begin to draw these individuals together as if by magnetic force, and thus a mob is formed. Its leader will soon be found in the individual who has the least resistance, the least sense of responsibility and, be-

[20] Cf. "The Role of the Unconscious," par. 17.

cause of his inferiority, the greatest will to power. He will let loose everything that is ready to burst forth, and the mob will follow with the irresistible force of an avalanche.

(d) The Creation of Distinctively Modern Myths

The fullest expression of myth in the modern world is the creation of outright modern myths. Jung's keenest example is the belief in flying saucers. The belief is widespread. It arouses archetypal emotions of awe and fear. It is cited to explain physical events in the world. The saucers are believed to be manned by superhuman personalities. Yet rather than a refutation of science, flying saucers are taken by adherents to be the handiwork of a species more scientifically advanced than we. The sole ingredient missing for a complete myth is a story, one about the creation of the saucers or about their creators. And even it is to be found among some believers.

From "Flying Saucers: A Modern Myth," CW 10, pars. 595–624

1. UFOS AS RUMOURS

595   Since the things reported of Ufos not only sound incredible but seem to fly in the face of all our basic assumptions about the physical world, it is very natural that one's first reaction should be the negative one of outright rejection. Surely, we say, it's nothing but illusions, fantasies, and lies. People who report such stuff—chiefly airline pilots and ground staff—cannot be quite right in the head! What is worse, most of these stories come from America, the land of superlatives and of science fiction.

596   In order to meet this natural reaction, we shall begin by considering the Ufo reports simply as rumours, i.e., as psychic products, and shall draw from this all the conclusions that are warranted by an analytical method of procedure.

597   Regarded in this light, the Ufo reports may seem to the sceptical mind to be rather like a story that is told all over the world, but differs from an ordinary rumour in that it is expressed in the form of visions,[1] or perhaps owed its existence to them in the first place and is now kept alive by them. I would

---

[1] I prefer the term "vision" to "hallucination," because the latter bears the stamp of a pathological concept, whereas a vision is a phenomenon that is by no means peculiar to pathological states.

call this comparatively rare variation a *visionary rumour*. It is closely akin to the collective visions of, say, the crusaders during the siege of Jerusalem, the troops at Mons in the first World War, the faithful followers of the pope at Fatima, Portugal, etc. Apart from collective visions, there are on record cases where one or more persons see something that physically is not there. For instance, I was once at a spiritualistic séance where four of the five people present saw an object like a moon floating above the abdomen of the medium. They showed me, the fifth person present, exactly where it was, and it was absolutely incomprehensible to them that I could see nothing of the sort. I know of three more cases where certain objects were seen in the clearest detail (in two of them by two persons, and in the third by one person) and could afterwards be proved to be non-existent. Two of these cases happened under my direct observation. Even people who are entirely *compos mentis* and in full possession of their senses can sometimes see things that do not exist. I do not know what the explanation is of such happenings. It is very possible that they are less rare than I am inclined to suppose. For as a rule we do not verify things we have "seen with our own eyes," and so we never get to know that actually they did not exist. I mention these somewhat remote possibilities because, in such an unusual matter as the Ufos, one has to take every aspect into account.

598   The first requisite for a visionary rumour, as distinct from an ordinary rumour, for whose dissemination nothing more is needed than popular curiosity and sensation-mongering, is always an *unusual emotion*. Its intensification into a vision and delusion of the senses, however, springs from a stronger excitation and therefore from a deeper source.

599   The signal for the Ufo stories was given by the mysterious projectiles seen over Sweden during the last two years of the war — attributed of course to the Russians — and by the reports about "Foo fighters," i.e., lights that accompanied the Allied bombers over Germany (Foo = *feu*). These were followed by the strange sightings of "Flying Saucers" in America. The impossibility of finding an earthly base for the Ufos and of explaining their physical peculiarities soon led to the conjecture of an extra-terrestrial origin. With this development the rumour got linked up with the psychology of the great panic that broke out in the United States just before the second World War, when a radio play,[2] based on a novel by H. G. Wells, about

---

[2] [*The War of the Worlds*, radio adaptation by Orson Welles (1938). — EDITORS.]

Martians invading New York, caused a regular stampede and numerous car accidents. The play evidently hit the latent emotion connected with the imminence of war.

600   The motif of an extra-terrestrial invasion was seized upon by the rumour and the Ufos were interpreted as machines controlled by intelligent beings from outer space. The apparently weightless behaviour of space-ships and their intelligent, purposive movements were attributed to the superior technical knowledge and ability of the cosmic intruders. As they did no harm and refrained from all hostile acts it was assumed that their appearance over the earth was due to curiosity or to the need for aerial reconnaissance. It also seemed that airfields and atomic installations in particular held a special attraction for them, from which it was concluded that the dangerous development of atomic physics and nuclear fission had caused a certain disquiet on our neighbouring planets and necessitated a more accurate survey from the air. As a result, people felt they were being observed and spied upon from space.

601   The rumour actually gained so much official recognition that the armed forces in America set up a special bureau for collecting, analysing, and evaluating all relevant observations. This seems to have been done also in France, Italy, Sweden, the United Kingdom, and other countries. After the publication of Ruppelt's report the Saucer stories seem to have more or less vanished from the press for about a year. They were evidently no longer "news." That the interest in Ufos and, probably, the sightings of them have not ceased is shown by the recent press report that an American admiral has suggested that clubs be founded all over the country for collecting Ufo reports and investigating them in detail.

602   The rumour states that the Ufos are as a rule lens-shaped, but can also be oblong or shaped like cigars; that they shine in various colours or have a metallic glitter;[3] that from a stationary position they can reach a speed of about 10,000 miles per hour, and that at times their acceleration is such that if anything resembling a human being were steering them he would be instantly killed. In flight they turn off at angles that would be possible only to a weightless object.

603   Their flight, accordingly, resembles that of a flying insect. Like this, the Ufo can suddenly hover over an interesting object for quite a time, or circle round it inquisitively, just as suddenly

[3] Special emphasis should be laid on the *green* fire-balls frequently observed in the southwestern United States.

to dart off again and discover new objects in its zigzag flight. Ufos are therefore not to be confused with meteorites or with reflections from so-called "temperature inversion layers." Their alleged interest in airfields and in industrial installations connected with nuclear fission is not always confirmed, since they are also seen in the Antarctic, in the Sahara, and in the Himalayas. For preference, however, they seem to swarm over the United States, though recent reports show that they do a good deal of flying over the Old World and in the Far East. Nobody really knows what they are looking for or want to observe. Our aeroplanes seem to arouse their curiosity, for they often fly towards them or pursue them. But they also fly away from them. Their flights do not appear to be based on any recognizable system. They behave more like groups of tourists unsystematically viewing the countryside, pausing now here for a while and now there, erratically following first one interest and then another, sometimes shooting to enormous altitudes for inexplicable reasons or performing acrobatic evolutions before the noses of exasperated pilots. Sometimes they appear to be up to five hundred yards in diameter, sometimes small as electric street-lamps. There are large mother-ships from which little Ufos slip out or in which they take shelter. They are said to be both manned and unmanned, and in the latter case are remote-controlled. According to the rumour, the occupants are about three feet high and look like human beings or, conversely, are utterly unlike us. Other reports speak of giants fifteen feet high. They are beings who are carrying out a cautious survey of the earth and considerately avoid all encounters with men or, more menacingly, are spying out landing places with a view to settling the population of a planet that has got into difficulties and colonizing the earth by force. Uncertainty in regard to the physical conditions on earth and their fear of unknown sources of infection have held them back temporarily from drastic encounters and even from attempted landings, although they possess frightful weapons which would enable them to exterminate the human race. In addition to their obviously superior technology they are credited with superior wisdom and moral goodness which would, on the other hand, enable them to save humanity. Naturally there are stories of landings, too, when the saucer-men were not only seen at close quarters but attempted to carry off a human being. Even a reliable man like Keyhoe gives us to understand that a squadron of five military aircraft plus a large seaplane were swallowed up by Ufo mother-ships in the vicinity of the Bahamas, and carried off.

604   One's hair stands on end when one reads such reports together with the documentary evidence. And when one considers
the known possibility of tracking Ufos with radar, then we have
all the essentials for an unsurpassable "science-fiction story."
Every man who prides himself on his sound common sense will
feel distinctly affronted. I shall therefore not enter here into the
various attempts at explanation to which the rumour has given
rise.

605   While I was engaged in writing this essay, it so happened that
two articles appeared more or less simultaneously in leading
American newspapers, showing very clearly how the problem
stands at present. The first was a report on the latest Ufo sight-
ing by a pilot who was flying an aircraft to Puerto Rico with
forty-four passengers. While he was over the ocean he saw a
"fiery, round object, shining with greenish white light," coming
towards him at great speed. At first he thought it was a jet
propelled aircraft, but soon saw that it was some unusual and
unknown object. In order to avoid a collision, he pulled his
aircraft into such a steep climb that the passengers were shot
out of their seats and tumbled over one another. Four of them
received injuries requiring hospital attention. Seven other aircraft strung out along the same route of about three hundred
miles sighted the same object.

606   The other article, entitled "No Flying Saucers, U.S. Expert
Says," concerns the categorical statement made by Dr. Hugh L.
Dryden, director of the National Advisory Committee for Aero-
nautics, that Ufos do not exist. One cannot but respect the un-
flinching scepticism of Dr. Dryden; it gives stout-hearted expression to the feeling that such preposterous rumours are an
offence to human dignity.

607   If we close our eyes a little so as to overlook certain details, it
is possible to side with the reasonable opinion of the majority
in whose name Dr. Dryden speaks, and to regard the thousands
of Ufo reports and the uproar they have created as a visionary
rumour, to be treated accordingly. They would then boil down,
objectively, to an admittedly impressive collection of mistaken
observations and conclusions into which subjective psychic assumptions have been projected.

608   But if it is a case of psychological *projection*, there must be a
psychic cause for it. One can hardly suppose that anything of
such worldwide incidence as the Ufo legend is purely fortuitous
and of no importance whatever. The many thousands of individual testimonies must have an equally extensive causal basis.

When an assertion of this kind is corroborated practically everywhere, we are driven to assume that a corresponding motive must be present everywhere, too. Though visionary rumours may be caused or accompanied by all manner of outward circumstances, they are based essentially on an omnipresent emotional foundation, in this case a psychological situation common to all mankind. The basis for this kind of rumour is an *emotional tension* having its cause in a situation of collective distress or danger, or in a vital psychic need. This condition undoubtedly exists today, in so far as the whole world is suffering under the strain of Russian policies and their still unpredictable consequences. In the individual, too, such phenomena as abnormal convictions, visions, illusions, etc., only occur when he is suffering from a psychic dissociation, that is, when there is a split between the conscious attitude and the unconscious contents opposed to it. Precisely because the conscious mind does not know about them and is therefore confronted with a situation from which there seems to be no way out, these strange contents cannot be integrated directly but seek to express themselves indirectly, thus giving rise to unexpected and apparently inexplicable opinions, beliefs, illusions, visions, and so forth. Any unusual natural occurrences such as meteors, comets, "rains of blood," a calf with two heads, and suchlike abortions are interpreted as menacing omens, or else signs are seen in the heavens. Things can be seen by many people independently of one another, or even simultaneously, which are not physically real. Also, the association-processes of many people often have a parallelism in time and space, with the result that different people, simultaneously and independently of one another, can produce the same new ideas, as has happened numerous times in history.

609   In addition, there are cases where the same collective cause produces identical or similar effects, i.e., the same visionary images and interpretations, in the very people who are least prepared for such phenomena and least inclined to believe in them.[4] This fact gives the eyewitness accounts an air of particular credibility: it is usually emphasized that the witness is above suspicion because he was never distinguished for his lively imagination or credulousness but, on the contrary, for his cool judgment and critical reason. In just these cases the unconscious has to resort to particularly drastic measures in order to

---

[4] Aimé Michel remarks that Ufos are mostly seen by people who do not believe in them or who regard the whole problem with indifference.

make its contents perceived. It does this most vividly by projection, by extrapolating its contents into an object, which then reflects back what had previously lain hidden in the unconscious. Projection can be observed at work everywhere, in mental illness, in ideas of persecution and hallucinations, in so-called normal people who see the mote in their brother's eye without seeing the beam in their own, and finally, in extreme form, in political propaganda.

610   Projections have what we might call different ranges, according to whether they stem from merely personal conditions or from deeper collective ones. Personal repressions and things of which we are unconscious manifest themselves in our immediate environment, in our circle of relatives and acquaintances. Collective contents, such as religious, philosophical, political and social conflicts, select projection-carriers of a corresponding kind—Freemasons, Jesuits, Jews, Capitalists, Bolsheviks, Imperialists, etc. In the threatening situation of the world today, when people are beginning to see that everything is at stake, the projection-creating fantasy soars beyond the realm of earthly organizations and powers into the heavens, into interstellar space, where the rulers of human fate, the gods, once had their abode in the planets. Our earthly world is split into two halves, and nobody knows where a helpful solution is to come from. Even people who would never have thought that a religious problem could be a serious matter that concerned them personally are beginning to ask themselves fundamental questions. Under these circumstances it would not be at all surprising if those sections of the community who ask themselves nothing were visited by "visions," by a widespread myth seriously believed in by some and rejected as absurd by others. Eye-witnesses of unimpeachable honesty announce the "signs in the heavens" which they have seen "with their own eyes," and the marvellous things they have experienced which pass human understanding.

611   All these reports have naturally resulted in a clamorous demand for explanation. Initial attempts to explain the Ufos as Russian or American inventions soon came to grief on their apparently weightless behaviour, which is unknown to earth-dwellers. Human fantasy, already toying with the idea of space-trips to the moon, therefore had no hesitation in assuming that intelligent beings of a higher order had learnt how to counteract gravitation and, by dint of using interstellar magnetic fields as sources of power, to travel through space with the speed of light. The recent atomic explosions on the earth, it was conjec-

tured, had aroused the attention of these so very much more advanced dwellers on Mars or Venus, who were worried about possible chain-reactions and the consequent destruction of our planet. Since such a possibility would constitute a catastrophic threat to our neighbouring planets, their inhabitants felt compelled to observe how things were developing on earth, fully aware of the tremendous cataclysm our clumsy nuclear experiments might unleash. The fact that the Ufos neither land on earth nor show the least inclination to get into communication with human beings is met by the explanation that these visitors, despite their superior knowledge, are not at all certain of being well received on earth, for which reason they carefully avoid all intelligent contact with humans. But because they, as befits superior beings, conduct themselves quite inoffensively, they would do the earth no harm and are satisfied with an objective inspection of airfields and atomic installations. Just why these higher beings, who show such a burning interest in the fate of the earth, have still not found some way of communicating with us after ten years — despite their knowledge of languages — remains shrouded in darkness. Other explanations have therefore to be sought, for instance that a planet has got into difficulties, perhaps through the drying up of its water supplies, or loss of oxygen, or overpopulation, and is looking for a *pied-à-terre*. The reconnaissance patrols are going to work with the utmost care and circumspection, despite the fact that they have been giving a benefit performance in the heavens for hundreds, if not thousands, of years. Since the second World War they have appeared in masses, obviously because an imminent landing is planned. Recently their harmlessness has been doubted. There are also stories by so-called eyewitnesses who declare they have seen Ufos landing with, of course, English-speaking occupants. These space-guests are sometimes idealized figures along the lines of technological angels who are concerned for our welfare, sometimes dwarfs with enormous heads bursting with intelligence, sometimes lemur-like creatures covered with hair and equipped with claws, or dwarfish monsters clad in armour and looking like insects.

612   There are even "eyewitnesses" like Mr. Adamski, who relates that he has flown in a Ufo and made a round trip of the moon in a few hours. He brings us the astonishing news that the side of the moon turned away from us contains atmosphere, water, forests, and settlements, without being in the least perturbed by the moon's skittishness in turning just her unhospitable side towards the earth. This physical monstrosity of a story was actu-

ally swallowed by a cultivated and well-meaning person like Edgar Sievers.[5]

613   Considering the notorious camera-mindedness of Americans, it is surprising how few "authentic" photos of Ufos seem to exist, especially as many of them are said to have been observed for several hours at relatively close quarters. I myself happen to know someone who saw a Ufo with hundreds of other people in Guatemala. He had his camera with him, but in the excitement he completely forgot to take a photo, although it was daytime and the Ufo remained visible for an hour. I have no reason to doubt the honesty of his report. He has merely strengthened my impression that Ufos are somehow not photogenic.

614   As one can see from all this, the observation and interpretation of Ufos have already led to the formation of a regular legend. Quite apart from the thousands of newspaper reports and articles there is now a whole literature on the subject, some of it humbug, some of it serious. The Ufos themselves, however, do not appear to have been impressed; as the latest observations show, they continue their way undeterred. Be that as it may, one thing is certain: they have become a *living myth*. We have here a golden opportunity of seeing how a legend is formed, and how in a difficult and dark time for humanity a miraculous tale grows up of an attempted intervention by extra-terrestrial "heavenly" powers — and this at the very time when human fantasy is seriously considering the possibility of space travel and of visiting or even invading other planets. We on our side want to fly to the moon or to Mars, and on their side the inhabitants of other planets in our system, or even of the fixed stars, want to fly to us. We at least are conscious of our space-conquering aspirations, but that a corresponding extra-terrestrial tendency exists is a purely mythological conjecture, i.e., a projection.

615   Sensationalism, love of adventure, technological audacity, intellectual curiosity may appear to be sufficient motives for our futuristic fantasies, but the impulse to spin such fantasies, especially when they take such a serious form — witness the sputniks — springs from an underlying cause, namely a situation of distress and the vital need that goes with it. It could easily be conjectured that the earth is growing too small for us, that humanity would like to escape from its prison, where we are threatened not only by the hydrogen bomb but, at a still deeper

[5] Cf. *Flying Saucers über Südafrika* (1955).

level, by the prodigious increase in the population figures, which give cause for serious concern. This is a problem which people do not like to talk about, or then only with optimistic references to the incalculable possibilities of intensive food production, as if this were anything more than a postponement of the final solution. As a precautionary measure the Indian government has granted half a million pounds for birth-control propaganda, while the Russians exploit the labour-camp system as one way of skimming off the dreaded excess of births. Since the highly civilized countries of the West know how to help themselves in other ways, the immediate danger does not come from them but from the underdeveloped peoples of Asia and Africa. This is not the place to discuss the question of how far the two World Wars were an outlet for this pressing problem of keeping down the population at all costs. Nature has many ways of disposing of her surplus. Man's living space is, in fact, continually shrinking and for many races the optimum has long been exceeded. The danger of catastrophe grows in proportion as the expanding populations impinge on one another. Congestion creates fear, which looks for help from extra-terrestrial sources since it cannot be found on earth.

616   Hence there appear "signs in the heavens," superior beings in the kind of space ships devised by our technological fantasy. From a fear whose cause is far from being fully understood and is therefore not conscious, there arise explanatory projections which purport to find the cause in all manner of secondary phenomena, however unsuitable. Some of these projections are so obvious that it seems almost superfluous to dig any deeper.[6] But if we want to understand a mass rumour which, it appears, is even accompanied by collective visions, we must not remain satisfied with all too rational and superficially obvious motives. The cause must strike at the roots of our existence if it is to explain such an extraordinary phenomenon as the Ufos. Although they were observed as rare curiosities in earlier centuries, they merely gave rise to the usual local rumours.

617   The universal mass rumour was reserved for our enlightened, rationalistic age. The widespread fantasy about the destruction of the world at the end of the first millennium was metaphysical in origin and needed no Ufos in order to appear rational. Heaven's intervention was quite consistent with the *Weltanschauung* of the age. But nowadays public opinion

---

[6] Cf. Eugen Böhler's enlightening remarks in *Ethik und Wirtschaft* (Industrielle Organisation, Zurich, 1957).

would hardly be inclined to resort to the hypothesis of a metaphysical act, otherwise innumerable parsons would already
have been preaching about the warning signs in heaven. Our
Weltanschauung does not expect anything of this sort. We
would be much more inclined to think of the possibility of
psychic disturbances and interventions, especially as our psychic equilibrium has become something of a problem since the
last World War. In this respect there is increasing uncertainty.
Even our historians can no longer make do with the traditional procedures in evaluating and explaining the developments that have overtaken Europe in the last few decades, but
must admit that psychological and psychopathological factors
are beginning to widen the horizons of historiography in an
alarming way. The growing interest which the thinking public
consequently evinces in psychology has already aroused the
displeasure of the academies and of incompetent specialists. In
spite of the palpable resistance to psychology emanating from
these circles, psychologists who are conscious of their responsibilities should not be dissuaded from critically examining a
mass phenomenon like the Ufos, since the apparent impossibility of the Ufo reports suggests to common sense that the
most likely explanation lies in a psychic disturbance.

618   We shall therefore turn our attention to the psychic aspect of
the phenomenon. For this purpose we shall briefly review the
central statements of the rumour. Certain objects are seen in the
earth's atmosphere, both by day and by night, which are unlike
any known meteorological phenomena. They are not meteors,
not misidentified fixed stars, not "temperature inversions," not
cloud formations, not migrating birds, not aerial balloons, not
balls of fire, and certainly not the delirious products of intoxication or fever, nor the plain lies of eyewitnesses. What as a
rule is seen is a body of *round* shape, disk-like or spherical,
glowing or shining fierily in different colours, or, more seldom,
a cigar-shaped or cylindrical figure of various sizes.[7] It is reported that occasionally they are invisible to the naked eye but
leave a "blip" on the radar screen. The round bodies in particular are figures such as the unconscious produces in dreams, visions, etc. In this case they are to be regarded as *symbols* representing, in visual form, some thought that was not thought

[7] The more rarely reported cigar-form may have the Zeppelin for a model. The obvious phallic comparison, i.e., a translation into sexual language, springs naturally to
the lips of the people. Berliners, for instance, refer to the cigar-shaped Ufo as a "holy
ghost," and the Swiss military have an even more outspoken name for observation
balloons.

consciously, but is merely potentially present in the unconscious in invisible form and attains visibility only through the process of becoming conscious. The visible form, however, expresses the meaning of the unconscious content only approximately. In practice the meaning has to be completed by amplificatory interpretation. The unavoidable errors that result can be eliminated only through the principle of "waiting on events"; that is to say we obtain a consistent and readable text by comparing sequences of dreams dreamt by different individuals. The figures in a rumour can be subjected to the same principles of dream interpretation.

619   If we apply them to the round object—whether it be a disk or a sphere—we at once get an analogy with the symbol of totality well known to all students of depth psychology, namely the *mandala* (Sanskrit for circle). This is not by any means a new invention, for it can be found in all epochs and in all places always with the same meaning, and it reappears time and again, independently of tradition, in modern individuals as the "protective" or apotropaic circle, whether in the form of the prehistoric "sun wheel," or the magic circle, or the alchemical microcosm, or a modern *symbol of order*, which organizes and embraces the psychic totality. As I have shown elsewhere,[8] in the course of the centuries the mandala has developed into a definitely psychological totality symbol, as the history of alchemy proves. I would like to show how the mandala appears in a modern person by citing the dream of a six-year-old girl. She dreamt *she stood at the entrance of a large, unknown building. There a fairy was waiting for her, who led her inside, into a long colonnade, and conducted her to a sort of central chamber, with similar colonnades converging from all sides. The fairy stepped into the centre and changed herself into a tall flame. Three snakes crawled round the fire, as if circumambulating it.*

620   Here we have a classic, archetypal childhood dream such as is not only dreamt fairly often but is sometimes drawn or painted, without any suggestion from outside, for the evident purpose of warding off disagreeable or disturbing family influences and preserving the inner balance.

621   In so far as the mandala encompasses, protects, and defends the psychic totality against outside influences and seeks to unite the inner opposites, it is at the same time a distinct *individua-*

---

[8] "Concerning Mandala Symbolism," in *The Archetypes and the Collective Unconscious.*

tion symbol and was known as such even to medieval alchemy. The soul was supposed to have the form of a sphere, on the analogy of Plato's world-soul, and we meet the same symbol in modern dreams. This symbol, by reason of its antiquity, leads us to the heavenly spheres, to Plato's "supra-celestial place" where the "Ideas" of all things are stored up. Hence there would be nothing against the naïve interpretation of Ufos as "souls." Naturally they do not represent our modern conception of the psyche, but give an involuntary archetypal or mythological picture of an unconscious content, a *rotundum*, as the alchemists called it, that expresses the totality of the individual. I have defined this spontaneous image as a symbolical representation of the *self*, by which I mean not the ego but the totality composed of the conscious *and* the unconscious.[9] I am not alone in this, as the Hermetic philosophy of the Middle Ages had already arrived at very similar conclusions. The archetypal character of this idea is borne out by its spontaneous recurrence in modern individuals who know nothing of any such tradition, any more than those around them. Even people who might know of it never imagine that their children could dream of anything so remote as Hermetic philosophy. In this matter the deepest and darkest ignorance prevails, which is of course the most unsuitable vehicle for a mythological tradition.

622   If the round shining objects that appear in the sky be regarded as visions, we can hardly avoid interpreting them as archetypal images. They would then be involuntary, automatic projections based on instinct, and as little as any other psychic manifestations or symptoms can they be dismissed as meaningless and merely fortuitous. Anyone with the requisite historical and psychological knowledge knows that circular symbols have played an important role in every age; in our own sphere of culture, for instance, they were not only soul symbols but "God-images." There is an old saying that "God is a circle whose centre is everywhere and the circumference nowhere." God in his omniscience, omnipotence, and omnipresence is a totality symbol *par excellence*, something round, complete, and perfect. Epiphanies of this sort are, in the tradition, often associated with fire and light. On the antique level, therefore, the Ufos could easily be conceived as "gods." They are impressive manifestations of totality whose simple, round form portrays the archetype of the self, which as we know from experience plays the chief role in uniting apparently irreconcilable oppo-

[9] Cf. "The Self," in *Aion*.

sites and is therefore best suited to compensate the split-mindedness of our age. It has a particularly important role to play among the other archetypes in that it is primarily the regulator and orderer of chaotic states, giving the personality the greatest possible unity and wholeness. It creates the image of the divine-human personality, the Primordial Man or Anthropos, a *chên-yên* (true or whole man), an Elijah who calls down fire from heaven, rises up to heaven in a fiery chariot,[10] and is a forerunner of the Messiah, the dogmatized figure of Christ, as well as of Khidr, the Verdant One,[11] who is another parallel to Elijah: like him, he wanders over the earth as a human personification of Allah.

623   The present world situation is calculated as never before to arouse expectations of a redeeming, supernatural event. If these expectations have not dared to show themselves in the open, this is simply because no one is deeply rooted enough in the tradition of earlier centuries to consider an intervention from heaven as a matter of course. We have indeed strayed far from the metaphysical certainties of the Middle Ages, but not so far that our historical and psychological background is empty of all metaphysical hope.[12] Consciously, however, rationalistic enlightenment predominates, and this abhors all leanings towards the "occult." Desperate efforts are made for a "repristination" of our Christian faith, but we cannot get back to that limited world view which in former times left room for metaphysical intervention. Nor can we resuscitate a genuine Christian belief in an after-life or the equally Christian hope for an imminent end of the world that would put a definite stop to the regrettable error of Creation. Belief in this world and in the power of man has, despite assurances to the contrary, become a practical and, for the time being, irrefragable truth.

624   This attitude on the part of the overwhelming majority provides the most favourable basis for a projection, that is, for a manifestation of the unconscious background. Undeterred by rationalistic criticism, it thrusts itself to the forefront in the form of a symbolic rumour, accompanied and reinforced by the

---

[10] Significantly enough, Elijah also appears as an eagle, who spies out unrighteousness on earth from above.

[11] Cf. "Concerning Rebirth," in *The Archetypes and the Collective Unconscious*, pars. 240ff.

[12] It is a common and totally unjustified misunderstanding on the part of scientifically trained people to say that I regard the psychic background as something "metaphysical," while on the other hand the theologians accuse me of "psychologizing" metaphysics. Both are wide of the mark: I am an empiricist, who keeps within the boundaries set for him by the theory of knowledge.

appropriate visions, and thus activates an archetype that has always expressed order, deliverance, salvation, and wholeness. It is characteristic of our time that the archetype, in contrast to its previous manifestations, should now take the form of an object, a technological construction, in order to avoid the odiousness of mythological personification. Anything that looks technological goes down without difficulty with modern man. The possibility of space travel has made the unpopular idea of a metaphysical intervention much more acceptable. The apparent weightlessness of the Ufos is, of course, rather hard to digest, but then our own physicists have discovered so many things that border on the miraculous: why should not more advanced star-dwellers have discovered a way to counteract gravitation and reach the speed of light, if not more?

(e) Myth as Never Superseded

Jung ventures beyond the evidence of myths in modernity to assert that the yearning for myth is so strong that it will always find fulfillment. Jung does not quite make the yearning panhuman, for he allows for resistance to it by an elite—but even then only by an act of will. In assessing Jung's view of myth's prospects, one must distinguish two issues: how important for him are the functions fulfilled by myth, and how important for him is myth to the fulfillment of them? Myth for Jung is indispensable only if he is maintaining not merely that the functions it serves are indispensable but also that it alone serves them or serves them best.

From "**Two Kinds of Thinking**," CW 5, par. 30

30   It might be objected that the mythological proclivities of children are implanted by education. This objection is futile. Has mankind ever really got away from myths? Everyone who has his eyes and wits about him can see that the world is dead, cold, and unending. Never yet has he beheld a God, or been compelled to require the existence of such a God from the evidence of his senses. On the contrary, it needed the strongest inner compulsion, which can only be explained by the irrational force of instinct, for man to invent those religious beliefs whose absurdity was long since pointed out by Tertullian. In the same way one can withhold the material content of primitive myths from a child but not take from him the need for

mythology, and still less his ability to manufacture it for himself. One could almost say that if all the world's traditions were cut off at a single blow, the whole of mythology and the whole history of religion would start all over again with the next generation. Only a very few individuals succeed in throwing off mythology in epochs of exceptional intellectual exuberance — the masses never. Enlightenment avails nothing, it merely destroys a transitory manifestation, but not the creative impulse.

Chapter 9. Earlier Psychological Interpretations of Myth

Jung never claims that modern psychology, Freudian or Jung-
ian, is the first to recognize the psychological nature of myth.
On the contrary, he is eager to trace a hoary tradition of psy-
chological interpretation all the way back to the Stoics and to
the Church Fathers. For millennia, he contends, the subject
matter of myth has been recognized by some to be inner rather
than outer — or, more often, inner as well as outer. Modern psy-
chology is for him distinctive in differentiating the inner, psy-
chological subject matter from the outer, physical or metaphysi-
cal one, but it constitutes the latest, not the first, stage of the
psychology of myth.

From "The Personification of the Opposites," CW 14, par.
170

170   In interpreting the words "your understanding increases in
my sister," etc., it is well to remember that a philosophical interpretation of myths had already grown up among the Stoics,
which today we should not hesitate to describe as psychological. This work of interpretation was not interrupted by the development of Christianity but continued to be assiduously practised in a rather different form, namely in the hermeneutics of
the Church Fathers, which was to have a decided influence on
alchemical symbolism. The Johannine interpretation of Christ
as the pre-worldly Logos is an early attempt of this kind to put
into other words the "meaning" of Christ's essence. The later
medievalists, and in particular the natural philosophers, made
the Sapientia Dei the nucleus of their interpretation of nature
and thus created a new nature-myth. In this they were very
much influenced by the writings of the Arabs and of the Har-

ranites, the last exponents of Greek philosophy and gnosis, whose chief representative was Tabit ibn Qurra in the tenth century. One of these writings, the "Liber Platonis quartorum," is a dialogue in which Thebed (Tabit) speaks in person. In this treatise the intellect as a tool of natural philosophy plays a role that we do not meet again until the sixteenth century, in Gerhard Dorn. Pico della Mirandola appeals to the psychological interpretation of the ancients and mentions that the "Greek Platonists" described Sol as διάνοια[1] and Luna as δόξα,[2] terms that are reminiscent of Simon's Nous and Epinoia.[3] Pico himself defines the difference as that between "scientia" and "opinio."[4] He thinks that the mind (animus), turning towards the spirit (spiritus) of God, shines and is therefore called Sol. The spirit of God corresponds to the aquae superiores, the "waters above the firmament" (Gen. 1:7). But in so far as the human mind turns towards the "waters under the firmament" (aquae inferiores), it concerns itself with the "sensuales potentiae," "whence it contracts the stain of infection" and is called Luna.[5] In both cases it is clearly the human spirit or psyche, both of which have, however, a double aspect, one facing upwards to the light, the other downwards to the darkness ruled by the moon ("The sun to rule the day, the moon also to govern the night"). "And while," says Pico, "we wander far from our fatherland and abide in this night and darkness of our present life, we make most use of that which turns us aside to the senses, for which reason we think many things rather than know them,"[6] — a pessimistic but no doubt accurate view that fully accords with the spiritual benightedness and sinful darkness of this sublunary world, which is so black that the moon herself is tarnished by it.

From "The Conjunction," CW 14, par. 677

677   The second step on the way to the production of this substance was the reunion of the spirit with the body. For this procedure there were many symbols. One of the most important was the chymical marriage, which took place in the retort.

[1] 'Thought, intellect, mind'.
[2] 'Opinion, view, notion'. Pico adds: "According to the principles of their teaching." "Heptaplus," Opera omnia, Lib. IV, cap. IV, p. 32.
[3] In the same place Pico mentions that Plato and "certain younger" philosophers interpreted Sol as "active intellect, but the Moon [as] potential intellect."
[4] Ibid.
[5] Ibid.
[6] Ibid.

The older alchemists were still so unconscious of the psychological implications of the opus that they understood their own symbols as mere allegories or—semiotically—as secret names for chemical combinations, thus stripping mythology, of which they made such copious use, of its true meaning and using only its terminology. Later this was to change, and already in the fourteenth century it began to dawn on them that the lapis was more than a chemical compound. This realization expressed itself mainly in the Christ-parallel.[7] Dorn was probably the first to recognize the psychological implications for what they were, so far as this was intellectually possible for a man of that age. Proof of this is his demand that the pupil must have a good physical and, more particularly, a good moral constitution.[8] A religious attitude was essential.[9] For in the individual was hidden that "substance of celestial nature known to very few," the "incorrupt medicament" which "can be freed from its fetters, not by its contrary but by its like." The "spagyric medicine" whereby it is freed must be "conformable to this substance." The medicine "prepares" the body so that the separation can be undertaken. For, when the body is "prepared," it can be separated more easily from "the other parts."

[7] Early references are given in *Psychology and Alchemy*, pars. 453f.
[8] "It is impossible for a man of evil life to possess the treasure that is concealed from the sons of wisdom, and he is unfit to acquire it or to search it out, much less to find it" ("Phil. medit.," p. 457).
[9] "I have thought it right to admonish the disciples to implore the divine aid, and [to remind them] of the need for the most careful diligence in preparing themselves for the reception of this grace" (ibid.).

Chapter 10. Myth and Religion

Jung maintains that, in the wake of science, it is no longer pos-sible for moderns to continue to read the Bible literally, full as it is of miracles and other supernatural events. But Jung main-tains just as strongly that it is neither necessary nor, more, ben-eficial for moderns to read the Bible literally. For its true mean-ing is psychological. Rather than an obstacle to the retention of the Bible, the rise of science provides the opportunity to recog-nize what its true meaning, like that of any other sacred scrip-ture, has always been. Rather than discarded, the Bible needs only to be reinterpreted. Most fortuitously, the psychological meaning of the Bible is not only its true, eternal meaning but also the sole acceptable modern meaning of it. The appeal of the New Testament in particular, to which Jung devotes more attention than to the Old, has always been psychological, which for Jung means mythical. For Jung, not Jesus the man but Jesus the symbol has always been the true inspiration for Christians. Jesus is at once a symbol of several overlapping archetypes—the god archetype, the god/man archetype, the savior archetype—and a model of the lifelong quest for individ-uation. Jung's scorn for the effort by the theologian Rudolf Bultmann to make the New Testament palatable to modern Christians by "demythologizing" it is ironic. For despite Bultmann's indisputably misleading term "demythologizing," he no less than Jung is seeking to uncover the true, eternal, symbolic, mythological core to the life of Jesus masked by the false, contingent, literal, historical shell.

From "The Undiscovered Self (Present and Future)," CW 10, par. 521

521   In early times and until comparatively recently there was, therefore, talk of "powers ordained by God" (Romans 13:1). Today this conception is antiquated. The Churches stand for traditional and collective convictions which in the case of many

of their adherents are no longer based on their own inner experience but on *unreflecting belief*, which is notoriously apt to disappear as soon as one begins thinking about it. The content of belief then comes into collision with knowledge, and it often turns out that the irrationality of the former is no match for the ratiocinations of the latter. Belief is no adequate substitute for inner experience, and where this is absent even a strong faith which came miraculously as a gift of grace may depart equally miraculously. People call faith the true religious experience, but they do not stop to consider that actually it is a secondary phenomenon arising from the fact that something happened to us in the first place which instilled πίστις into us — that is, trust and loyalty. This experience has a definite content that can be interpreted in terms of one or other of the denominational creeds. But the more this is so, the more the possibilities of these conflicts with knowledge mount up, which in themselves are quite pointless. That is to say, the standpoint of the creeds is archaic; they are full of impressive mythological symbolism which, if taken literally, comes into insufferable conflict with knowledge. But if, for instance, the statement that Christ rose from the dead is to be understood not literally but symbolically, then it is capable of various interpretations that do not conflict with knowledge and do not impair the meaning of the statement. The objection that understanding it symbolically puts an end to the Christian's hope of immortality is invalid, because long before the coming of Christianity mankind believed in a life after death and therefore had no need of the Easter event as a guarantee of immortality. The danger that a mythology understood too literally, and as taught by the Church, will suddenly be repudiated lock, stock and barrel is today greater than ever. Is it not time that the Christian mythology, instead of being wiped out, was understood symbolically for once?

From "The Undiscovered Self (Present and Future)," CW 10, pars. 551–52

551   Nothing is more characteristic and symptomatic in this respect than the gulf that has opened out between *faith* and *knowledge*. The contrast has become so enormous that one is obliged to speak of the incommensurability of these two categories and their way of looking at the world. And yet they are concerned with the same empirical world in which we live, for even the theologians tell us that faith is supported by facts that became historically perceptible in this known world of ours —

namely that Christ was born as a real human being, worked many miracles and suffered his fate, died under Pontius Pilate, and rose up in the flesh after his death. Theology rejects any tendency to take the assertions of its earliest records as written myths and, accordingly, to understand them symbolically. Indeed, it is the theologians themselves who have recently made the attempt — no doubt as a concession to "knowledge" — to "demythologize" the object of their faith while drawing the line quite arbitrarily at the crucial points. But to the critical intellect it is only too obvious that myth is an integral component of all religions and therefore cannot be excluded from the assertions of faith without injuring them.

552   The rupture between faith and knowledge is a symptom of the *split consciousness* which is so characteristic of the mental disorder of our day. It is as if two different persons were making statements about the same thing, each from his own point of view, or as if one person in two different frames of mind were sketching a picture of his experience. If for "person" we substitute "modern society," it is evident that the latter is suffering from a mental dissociation, i.e., a neurotic disturbance. In view of this, it does not help matters at all if one party pulls obstinately to the right and the other to the left. This is what happens in every neurotic psyche, to its own deep distress, and it is just this distress that brings the patient to the analyst.

From "**Psychology and Religion,**" CW 11, par. 146

146   The life of Christ is understood by the Church on the one hand as an historical, and on the other hand as an eternally existing, mystery. This is especially evident in the sacrifice of the Mass. From a psychological standpoint this view can be translated as follows: Christ lived a concrete, personal, and unique life which, in all essential features, had at the same time an archetypal character. This character can be recognized from the numerous connections of the biographical details with worldwide myth-motifs. These undeniable connections are the main reason why it is so difficult for researchers into the life of Jesus to construct from the gospel reports an individual life divested of myth. In the gospels themselves factual reports, legends, and myths are woven into a whole. This is precisely what constitutes the meaning of the gospels, and they would immediately lose their character of wholeness if one tried to separate the individual from the archetypal with a critical scalpel. The life of Christ is no exception in that not a few of the great figures of

history have realized, more or less clearly, the archetype of the hero's life with its characteristic changes of fortune. But the ordinary man, too, unconsciously lives archetypal forms, and if these are no longer valued it is only because of the prevailing psychological ignorance. Indeed, even the fleeting phenomena of dreams often reveal distinctly archetypal patterns. At bottom, all psychic events are so deeply grounded in the archetype and are so much interwoven with it that in every case considerable critical effort is needed to separate the unique from the typical with any certainty. Ultimately, every individual life is at the same time the eternal life of the species. The individual is continuously "historical" because strictly time-bound; the relation of the type to time, on the other hand, is irrelevant. Since the life of Christ is archetypal to a high degree, it represents to just that degree the life of the archetype. But since the archetype is the unconscious precondition of every human life, its life, when revealed, also reveals the hidden, unconscious ground-life of every individual. That is to say, what happens in the life of Christ happens always and everywhere. In the Christian archetype all lives of this kind are prefigured and are expressed over and over again or once and for all. And in it, too, the question that concerns us here of God's death is anticipated in perfect form. Christ himself is the typical dying and self-transforming God.

From "Foreword to White's *God and the Unconscious*" CW 11, pars. 450–51[1]

450   Psychopathology and medical psychotherapy are, when viewed superficially, far removed from the theologian's particular field of interest, and it is therefore to be expected that no small amount of preliminary effort will be required to establish a terminology comprehensible to both parties. To make this possible, certain fundamental realizations are required on either side. The most important of these is an appreciation of the fact that the object of mutual concern is the psychically sick and suffering human being, who is in need of consideration as much from the somatic or biological standpoint as from the spiritual or religious. The problem of neurosis ranges from disturbances in the sphere of instinct to the ultimate questions and decisions

[1] [Originally trans. (by Fr. White) from the German ms. for publication in the book by Fr. Victor White, O.P. (London, 1952; Chicago, 1953). The foreword was there subscribed May 1952. It has been slightly revised, on the basis of the original ms. — Editors.]

affecting our philosophy of life. Neurosis is not an isolated, sharply defined phenomenon; it is a reaction of the *whole* human being. Here a pure therapy of the symptoms is obviously even more definitely proscribed than in the case of purely somatic illnesses; these too, however, always have a psychic component or accompanying symptom even though they are not psychogenic. Modern medicine has just begun to take account of this fact, which the psychotherapists have been emphasizing for a long time. In the same way, long years of experience have shown me over and over again that a therapy along purely biological lines does not suffice, but requires a spiritual complement. This becomes especially clear to the medical psychologist where the question of *dreams* is concerned; for dreams, being statements of the unconscious, play no small part in the therapy. Anyone who sets to work in an honest and critical frame of mind will have to admit that the correct understanding of dreams is no easy matter, but one that calls for careful reflection, leading far beyond purely biological points of view. The indubitable occurrence of archetypal motifs in dreams makes a thorough knowledge of the spiritual history of man indispensable for anyone seriously attempting to understand the real meaning of dreams. The likeness between certain dream-motifs and mythologems is so striking that they may be regarded not merely as similar but even as identical. This recognition not only raises the dream to a higher level and places it in the wider context of the mythologem, but, at the same time, the problems posed by mythology are brought into connection with the psychic life of the individual. From the mythologem to the religious statement it is only a step. But whereas the mythological figures appear as pale phantoms and relics of a long past life that has become strange to us, the religious statement represents an immediate "numinous" experience. It is a *living mythologem.*

451   Here the empiricist's way of thinking and expressing himself gets him into difficulties with the theologian. The latter — when he is either making a dogma of the Gospel or "demythologizing" it — won't hear anything of "myth" because it seems to him a devaluation of the religious statement, in whose supreme truth he believes. The empiricists, on the other hand, whose orientation is that of natural science, does not connect any notions of value with the concept "myth." "Myth," for him, means "a statement about processes in the unconscious," and this applies equally to the religious statement. He has no means of deciding whether the latter is "truer" than the mythologem,

for between the two he sees only one difference: the difference
in living intensity. The so-called religious statement is still numinous, a quality which the myth has already lost to a great
extent. The empiricist knows that rites and figures once "sacred" have become obsolete and that new figures have become
"numinous."

From "**Answer to Job**," CW 11, par. 648

648   In view of these portentous impossibilities, it has been assumed, perhaps as the result of a growing impatience with the
difficult factual material, that Christ was nothing but a myth, in
this case no more than a fiction. But myth is not fiction: it consists of facts that are continually repeated and can be observed
over and over again. It is something that happens to man, and
men have mythical fates just as much as the Greek heroes do.
The fact that the life of Christ is largely myth does absolutely
nothing to disprove its factual truth—quite the contrary. I
would even go so far as to say that the mythical character of a
life is just what expresses its universal human validity. It is perfectly possible, psychologically, for the unconscious or an archetype to take complete possession of a man and to determine
his fate down to the smallest detail. At the same time objective,
non-psychic parallel phenomena can occur which also represent
the archetype. It not only seems so, it simply is so, that the
archetype fulfils itself not only psychically in the individual, but
objectively outside the individual. My own conjecture is that
Christ was such a personality. The life of Christ is just what it
had to be if it is the life of a god and a man at the same time. It
is a *symbolum*, a bringing together of heterogenous natures,
rather as if Job and Yahweh were combined in a single personality. Yahweh's intention to become man, which resulted from
his collision with Job, is fulfilled in Christ's life and suffering.

From "**Rex and Regina**," CW 14, par. 474

474   In the myth of the phoenix as reported by Pliny we again
meet the worm: ". . . from its bones and marrow is born first a
sort of maggot, and this grows into a chicken."[2] This version is
repeated in Clement of Rome,[3] Artemidorus,[4] Cyril of Jerusa-

---

[2] *Natural History*, X, ii (trans. by Rackham, III, p. 294).
[3] *The Apostolic Constitutions*, V, 7 (trans. by Smith and others, p. 134).
[4] *Onirocriticon*, lib. IV, cap. 47.

lem,[5] St. Ambrose,[6] and Cardan.[7] In order to understand the phoenix myth it is important to know that in Christian hermeneutics the phoenix is made an allegory of Christ, which amounts to a reinterpretation of the myth.[8] The self-burning of the phoenix corresponds to Christ's self-sacrifice, the ashes to his buried body, and the miraculous renewal to his resurrection.[9] According to Horapollo (4th cent.), whose views were taken over by later writers,[10] the phoenix signifies the soul and its journey to the land of rebirth.[11] It stands for the "long-lasting restitution of things" (ἀποκατάστασιν πολυχρόνιον); indeed, it is renewal itself.[12] The idea of apocatastasis or restitution (Acts 3:21) and re-establishment in Christ (Ephesians 1:10, DV)[13] may well have helped the assimilation of the phoenix allegory, quite apart from the main motif of renewal.

From "Jung and Religious Belief," CW 18, pars. 1665–66

1665   A myth remains a myth even if certain people believe it to be the literal revelation of an eternal truth, but it becomes moribund if the living truth it contains ceases to be an object of belief. It is therefore necessary to renew its life from time to time through a *new interpretation*. This means re-adapting it to

---

[5] *Catecheses Mystagogicae*, XVIII, 8 (ed. Reischl and Rupp, II, pp. 307ff.).
[6] *De Excessu fratris*, lib. II, cap. 59 (ed. Faller, p. 281), and *Hexaemeron*, V, cap. 23 (Migne, *P.L.*, vol. 14, col. 238).
[7] *De subtilitate*, p. 602.
[8] The fact that the myth was assimilated into Christianity by interpretation is proof, first of all, of the myth's vitality; but it also proves the vitality of Christianity, which was able to interpret and assimilate so many myths. The importance of hermeneutics should not be under-estimated: it has a beneficial effect on the psyche by consciously linking the distant past, the ancestral heritage which is still alive in the unconscious, with the present, thus establishing the vitally important connection between a consciousness oriented to the present moment only and the historical psyche which extends over infinitely long periods of time. As the most conservative of all products of the human mind, religions are in themselves the bridges to the ever-living past, which they make alive and present for us. A religion that can no longer assimilate myths is forgetting its proper function. But its spiritual vitality depends on the continuity of myth, and this can be preserved only if each age translates the myth into its own language and makes it an essential content of its view of the world. The *Sapientia Dei* which reveals itself through the archetype always ensures that the wildest deviations shall return to the middle position. Thus the fascination of philosophical alchemy comes very largely from the fact that it was able to give new expression to nearly all the most important archetypes. Indeed, as we have seen already, it even tried to assimilate Christianity.
[9] Numerous examples of these parallels can be found in Picinellus, *Mundus Symbolicus*, I, pp. 322ff.
[10] Cf. the edition of his *Hieroglyphica* in Caussin, *De Symbolica Aegyptorum sapientia* (1618), p. 142.
[11] *The Hieroglyphics of Horapollo* (trans. by Boas), p. 75 (Book I, No. 34).
[12] Ibid., p. 96 (Book II, No. 57): "For when this bird is born, there is a renewal of things."
[13] Likewise Col. 1:20, and in a certain sense Rom. 8:19ff.

the changing spirit of the times. What the Church calls "prefig-urations" refer to the original state of the myth, while the Christian doctrine represents a new interpretation and re-adap-tation to a Hellenized world. A most interesting attempt at re-interpretation began in the eleventh century,[14] leading up to the schism in the sixteenth century. The Renaissance was no more a rejuvenation of antiquity than Protestantism was a return to the primitive Christianity: it was a new interpretation necessitated by the devitalization of the Catholic Church.

1666   Today Christianity is devitalized by its remoteness from the spirit of the times. It stands in need of a new union with, or relation to, the atomic age, which is a unique novelty in history. The myth needs to be retold in a new spiritual language, for the new wine can no more be poured into the old bottles than it could in the Hellenistic age. Even conservative Jewry had to produce an entirely new version of the myth in its Cabalistic Gnosis. It is my practical experience that psychological under-standing immediately revivifies the essential Christian ideas and fills them with the breath of life. This is because our worldly light, i.e., scientific knowledge and understanding, coincides with the symbolic statement of the myth, whereas previously we were unable to bridge the gulf between knowing and believing.

From **Memories, Dreams, Reflections,** pp. 332–33

Our myth has become mute, and gives no answers. The fault lies not in it as it is set down in the Scriptures, but solely in us, who have not developed it further, who, rather, have suppressed any such attempts. The original version of the myth offers am-ple points of departure and possibilities of development. For example, the words are put into Christ's mouth: "Be ye there-fore wise as serpents, and harmless as doves." For what pur-pose do men need the cunning of serpents? And what is the link between this cunning and the innocence of the dove? "Except ye become as little children . . ." Who gives thought to what children are like in reality? By what morality did the Lord jus-tify the taking of the ass which he needed in order to ride in triumph into Jerusalem? How was it that, shortly afterward, he put on a display of childish bad temper and cursed the fig tree? What kind of morality emerges from the parable of the unjust steward and what profound insight, of such far-reaching signifi-

---

[14] [Cf. Aion, pars. 139ff.]

cance for our own predicament, from the apocryphal logion: "Man, if thou knowest what thou dost, thou art blessed; but if thou knowest not, thou art accursed and a transgressor of the law"?[15] What, finally, does it mean when St. Paul confesses: "The evil which I would not, that I do"? I will not discuss the transparent prophecies of the Book of Revelation, because no one believes in them and the whole subject is felt to be an embarrassing one.

The old question posed by the Gnostics, "Whence comes evil?" has been given no answer by the Christian world, and Origen's cautious suggestion of a possible redemption of the devil was termed a heresy. Today we are compelled to meet that question; but we stand empty-handed, bewildered, and perplexed, and cannot even get it into our heads that no myth will come to our aid although we have such urgent need of one. As the result of the political situation and the frightful, not to say diabolic, triumphs of science, we are shaken by secret shudders and dark forebodings; but we know no way out, and very few persons indeed draw the conclusion that this time the issue is the long-since-forgotten *soul of man*.

A further development of myth might well begin with the outpouring of the Holy Spirit upon the apostles, by which they were made into sons of God, and not only they, but all others who through them and after them received the *filiatio* — sonship of God — and thus partook of the certainty that they were more than autochthonous *animalia* sprung from the earth, that as the twice-born they had their roots in the divinity itself. Their visible, physical life was on this earth; but the invisible inner man had come from and would return to the primordial image of wholeness, to the eternal Father, as the Christian myth of salvation puts it.

Just as the Creator is whole, so His creature, His son, ought to be whole. Nothing can take away from the concept of divine wholeness. But unbeknownst to all, a splitting of that wholeness ensued; there emerged a realm of light and a realm of darkness. This outcome, even before Christ appeared, was clearly prefigured, as we may observe *inter alia* in the experience of Job, or in the widely disseminated Book of Enoch, which belongs to immediate pre-Christian times. In Christianity, too, this metaphysical split was plainly perpetuated: Satan, who in the Old Testament still belonged to the intimate entourage of Yahweh, now formed the diametrical and eternal

---

[15] *Codex Bezae ad Lucam* 6, 4.

opposite of the divine world. He could not be uprooted. It is therefore not surprising that as early as the beginning of the eleventh century the belief arose that the devil, not God, had created the world. Thus the keynote was struck for the second half of the Christian aeon, after the myth of the fall of the angels had already explained that these fallen angels had taught men a dangerous knowledge of science and the arts. What would these old storytellers have to say about Hiroshima?

From **Letters**, vol. 2, pp. 84–85

To Dorothee Hoch   (23 September 1952)

   To be sure we are dealing with the meaning and content of mythologems. To be sure "Christ" gave the myth a new meaning for the *man of antiquity.* But when we still go on stressing the newness 2000 years later, we must point out what exactly is the *news for us,* which we *haven't yet heard and understood.* Then we could feel like primitive Christians again. But we hear only the same old words and, like Bultmann, get sick of mythology. *How far is the message new for us?* How far is Christ still unknown to us? We heard ages ago that he exists as a living person exempt from our arbitrariness, and all the rest of it. What we need is a new point of departure, and this cannot be found without the assignment of new meaning. The message is alive only if it creates new meaning. I don't believe at all that it has run dry, rather that theology has. Just how do you make it clear to your listeners that "the death and resurrection of Christ are *their* death and *their* resurrection"? Aren't you equating Christ with the self of man, and isn't this a view which is contested when *I* say it? If the death and resurrection of Christ are my death and resurrection, i.e., if a = b, then b = a. That Christ is the self of man is implicit in the gospel, but the conclusion Christ = self has never been explicitly drawn. This is an assignment of new meaning, a further stage in the incarnation or actualization of Christ. You are drawing near to this insight with rapid steps; indeed, you have already voiced it. And with it Christ becomes a formulable psychological experience: the self is a living person and has always been there. It is an insight upon which Hindu philosophy (the equivalent of Western theology), Buddhism, Taoism, mystical Islamic sects, and Christianity are all agreed. My psychology is a modest contribution to this illustrious assemblage, and from the Christian standpoint you have formulated the essential psychological principle in the words quoted above. Thanks to this insight and inner experience the figure of Christ has come alive for you, and means for you an ultimate and unshakable truth, because it issues from a universally disseminated, collective archetype, which is ἀχειροποίητος.[16] Every Christian should rejoice, but I fear the theologians will make a sour face. I, however, rejoice that the unconscious has put into your mouth the true meaning: θαρρεῖτε μύσται τοῦ θεοῦ σεσοσμένον.[17] As you may know, I have written in detail about this in *Aion* and *Answer to Job* and other works.

From **Letters**, vol. 2, pp. 205–7

To Upton Sinclair   (7 January 1955)

This is a kind-hearted iconoclasm far more deadly than the frankly murderous arrows from M. de Voltaire's quiver: all these mythological assertions are so obviously impossible that their refutation is not even needed. These relics of the dark ages vanish like morning mist before the rising sun, when the idealistic and charming gardener's boy experiments with miracles of the good old kind, or when your authentic Galilean grandmother "Marya" does not even recognize herself or her beloved son in the picture produced by the magic mirror of Christian tradition.

Yet, why should a more or less ordinary story of a good mother and her well-meaning idealistic boy give rise to one of the most amazing mental or spiritual developments of all times? Who or what is its *agens*? Why could the facts not remain as they were originally? The answer is obvious: The story is so ordinary that there would not have been any reason for its tradition, quite certainly not for its world-wide expansion. The fact that the original situation has developed into one of the most extraordinary myths about a divine *heros*, a God-man and his cosmic fate, is not due to its underlying human story, but to the powerful action of pre-existing mythological motifs attributed to the biographically almost unknown Jesus, a wandering miracle Rabbi in the style of the ancient Hebrew prophets, or of the contemporary teacher John the Baptizer, or of the much later Zaddiks of the Chassidim.[18] The immediate source and origin of the myth projected upon the teacher Jesus is to be

[16] = made without hands (Mark 14:58).
[17] "Be of good cheer, mystes of the saved god." Julius Firmicus Maternus, *De errore profanorum religionum* (c. A.D. 346), 23.
[18] The Chassidim (or Hasidim) were a mystical sect of Judaism, founded shortly before the middle of the 18th cent. by the mystic Israel Baal Shem ("Master of the Holy Name"; 1700–1760). The leaders were called Zaddiks (righteous men).

found in the then popular Book of Enoch and its central figure of the "Son of Man" and his messianic mission. From the Gospel texts it is even manifest that Jesus identified himself with this "Son of Man." Thus it is the spirit of his time, the collective hope and expectation, which caused this astounding transformation and not at all the more or less insignificant story of the man Jesus. The true *agens* is the archetypal image of the God-man, appearing in Ezekiel's vision[19] for the first time in Jewish history, but in itself a considerably older figure in Egyptian theology, viz., Osiris and Horus.

The transformation of Jesus, i.e., the integration of his human self into a super- or inhuman figure of a deity, accounts for the amazing "distortion" of his ordinary personal biography. In other words: the essence of Christian tradition is by no means the simple man Jesus whom we seek in vain in the Gospels, but the lore of the God-man and his cosmic drama. Even the Gospels themselves make it their special job to prove that their Jesus is the incarnated God equipped with all the magic powers of a κύριος τῶν πνευμάτων.[20] That is why they are so liberal with miracle gossip which they naïvely assume proves their point. It is only natural that the subsequent post-apostolic developments even went several points better in this respect, and in our days the process of mythological integration is still expanding and spreading itself even to Jesus' mother, formerly carefully kept down to the human rank and file for at least 500 years of early church history. Boldly breaking through the sacrosanct rule about the definability of a new dogmatic truth, viz., that the said truth is only *definibilis* inasmuch as it was believed and taught in apostolic times, *explicite* or *implicite*, the pope has declared the *Assumptio Mariae* a dogma of the Christian creed. The justification he relies on is the pious belief of the masses for more than 1000 years, which he considers sufficient proof of the work of the Holy Ghost. Obviously the "pious belief" of the masses continues the process of projection, i.e., of transformation of human situations into myth.

But why should there be myth at all? My letter is already too long so that I can't answer this last question any more, but I have written several books about it. I only wanted to explain to you my idea that in trying to extract the quintessence of Christian tradition, you have removed it like Prof. Bultmann in his attempt at "demythologizing" the Gospels. One cannot help

[19] Ezekiel 1:26.
[20] = Lord of the spirits.

admitting that the human story is so very much more probable, but it has little or nothing to do with the problem of the myth containing the essence of Christian religion. You catch your priests most cleverly in the disadvantageous position which they have created for themselves by their preaching a concrete historicity of clearly mythological facts. Nobody reading your admirable novel can deny being deeply impressed by the very dramatic confrontation of the original with the mythological picture, and very probably he will prefer the human story to its mythological "distortion."

From **Letters**, vol. 2, pp. 484–85

To Pastor Tanner (12 February 1959)

In consequence, the tenets of belief have to be purified, or made easier, by being relieved of their principal encumbrances, which for the rationalist are their particularly obnoxious "mythological" components. Bultmann's endeavours are obviously intended to serve this purpose. Where they should or could stop is highly questionable. Christ as "Redeemer," for instance, is a mythologem of the first older, and so too is the "Son of God," the "Son of Man," the "Son of the Virgin," etc. "Faith without religion" or "religion without creed" is simply a logical consequence which has got out of Bultmann's control.

But if the believer without religion now thinks that he has got rid of mythology he is deceiving himself: he cannot get by without "myth." *Religio* is by its very nature always an *erga*, a "towards," no matter whether the following accusative be "God," "Redeemer," a philosophical idea or an ethical principle; it is always a "mythic" or transcendental statement. This is naturally also the case when the ultimate principle is called "matter." Only the totally naïve think this is the opposite of "myth." *Materia* is in the end simply a chthonic mother goddess, and the late Pope seems to have had an inkling of this. (Cf. the second Encyclical[21] to the dogma of the Assumption!)

Clearly the anti-mythological trend is due to the difficulties we have in clinging on to our previous mythological tenets of belief. Nowadays they demand too much of the effort to believe. This was not so in earlier centuries, with their very limited knowledge of nature. It needed no *sacrificium intellectus* to believe in miracles, and the report of the birth, life, death, and resurrection of the Redeemer could still pass as biography. All

---

[21] *Ad Caeli Reginam*. Cf. Sinclair, 7 Jan. 55, n. 7.

this has radically changed in recent times under the compelling influence of scientific rationalism, and the aversion of the younger generation for mythology seems the natural outcome of the premise: we are tired of the excessive effort of having to believe, because the object of belief is no longer inherently convincing. The dogma of the Trinity, the divine nature of the Redeemer, the Incarnation through the Holy Ghost, Christ's miraculous deeds and resurrection, are more conducive to doubt than to belief. One dogma after another falls. The "message of the Crucified and Risen Christ" is just not understood any more, but is, at most, felt as a well-meant object lesson in ethics that is conceded to have some practical utility. From here it is but a short step to the view that certain ethical principles can be acquired without the mythological trimmings.

Part 2. Developments in the Jungian Theory of Myth

Chapter 11. Erich Neumann

In the introduction to The Origins and History of Consciousness, *Erich Neumann outlines his evolutionary view of myth. Myths follow the same line of psychological development as human beings and can be categorized by the stage of development they evince. Neumann, like many other Jungians, seeks to give Jungian psychology a scientific underpinning.*

Introduction to **The Origins and History of Consciousness,** pp. xv–xxiv

The following attempt to outline the archetypal stages in the development of consciousness is based on modern depth psychology. It is an application of the analytical psychology of C. G. Jung, even where we endeavor to amplify this psychology, and even though we may speculatively overstep its boundaries.

Unlike other possible and necessary methods of inquiry which consider the development of consciousness in relation to external environmental factors, our inquiry is more concerned with the internal, psychic, and archetypal factors which determine the course of that development.

The structural elements of the collective unconscious are named by Jung "archetypes" or "primordial images." They are the pictorial forms of the instincts, for the unconscious reveals itself to the conscious mind in images which, as in dreams and fantasies, initiate the process of conscious reaction and assimilation.

These fantasy-images undoubtedly have their closest analogues in mythological types. We must therefore assume that they correspond to certain *collective* (and not personal) structural elements of the human psyche in general, and, like the morphological elements of the human body, are *inherited*.[1]

---

[1] Jung, "The Psychology of the Child Archetype," p. 155.

The archetypal structural elements of the psyche are psychic organs upon whose functioning the well-being of the individual depends, and whose injury has disastrous consequences:

> Moreover, they are the unfailing causes of neurotic and even psychotic disorders, behaving exactly like the neglected or maltreated physical organs or organic functional systems.[2]

It is the task of this book to show that a series of archetypes is a main constituent of mythology, that they stand in an organic relation to one another, and that their stadial[3] succession determines the growth of consciousness. In the course of its ontogenetic development, the individual ego consciousness has to pass through the same archetypal stages which determined the evolution of consciousness in the life of humanity. The individual has in his own life to follow the road that humanity has trod before him, leaving traces of its journey in the archetypal sequence of the mythological images we are now about to examine. Normally the archetypal stages are lived through without disturbance, and the development of consciousness proceeds in them just as naturally as physical development proceeds in the stages of bodily maturation. As organs of the psyche's structure the archetypes articulate with one another autonomously, like the physical organs, and determine the maturation of the personality in a manner analogous to the biological hormone-components of the physical constitution.

Besides possessing an "eternal" significance, the archetype also has an equally legitimate historical aspect. Ego consciousness evolves by passing through a series of "eternal images," and the ego, transformed in the passage, is constantly experiencing a new relation to the archetypes. Its relation to the eternality of the archetypal images is a process of succession in time — that is to say, it takes place in stages. The ability to perceive, to understand, and to interpret these images changes as ego consciousness changes in the course of man's phylogenetic and ontogenetic history; consequently the relativity of the eternal image to the evolving ego consciousness becomes more and more pronounced.

The archetypes that determine the stages of conscious development form only a segment of archetypal reality as a whole. But by availing ourselves of the evolutionary or synoptic view

---

[2] Ibid., p. 157.
[3] [An adjective derived from Lat. *stadium* in the biological sense of "stage of development." — TRANS.]

we can make out a kind of guiding line running through limitless symbolism of the collective unconscious which helps us to orient ourselves in the theory and practice of depth psychology.

An investigation of the archetypal stages also affords a better psychological orientation in a number of ancillary subjects, e.g., the history of religion, anthropology, folk psychology, and the like. All these can then be brought together on a psycho-evolutionary basis which would promote a deeper understanding.

Surprisingly enough, these specialized sciences have not so far allowed themselves to be sufficiently enriched by depth psychology, and least of all by Jungian psychology. In spite of that, the psychological starting point of these disciplines emerges more and more plainly, and it is beginning to become obvious that the human psyche is the source of all cultural and religious phenomena. Hence a final reckoning with depth psychology cannot be evaded much longer.

We must emphasize that our exposition of myth is not based on any specialized branch of science, whether archaeology, comparative religion, or theology, but simply and solely on the practical work of the psychotherapist, whose concern is the psychic background of modern man. The connection between his psychology and the deeper layers of humanity still alive in him is therefore the real starting point and subject of this work. The seductive and systematic method of exposition here adopted may at first obscure the topical and therapeutic significance of our findings, but anyone familiar with psychic events at the deepest level will recognize the importance and relevance of these connections, whose detailed illustration by modern empirical material is reserved for later examination.

As is well known, the "comparative" method of analytical psychology collates the symbolic and collective material found in individuals with the corresponding products from the history of religion, primitive psychology, and so on, and in this way arrives at an interpretation by establishing the "context." This method we now supplement by the evolutionary approach, which considers the material from the standpoint of the stage reached by the developing consciousness, and hence by the ego in its relations with the unconscious. Our work therefore links up with that fundamental early work of Jung's, *The Psychology of the Unconscious*, even though we may be obliged to make certain emendations. Whereas in Freudian psychoanalysis the evolutionary approach led only to a concretistic and narrowly personalistic theory of libido, analytical psychology has so far failed to pursue this line of inquiry any further.

The emergence of the collective human background as a

transpersonal reality has forced us to recognize the relativity of our own position. The multiplicity of forms and phenomena in which the infinite diversity of the human psyche is expressed, the wealth of cultures, values, patterns of behavior, and world views produced by the vitality of man's psychic structure, must make any attempt at a general orientation seem, at the outset, a perilous venture. Yet such an attempt has to be made, even with the knowledge that our specifically Western orientation is only one among many. The evolution of consciousness as a form of creative evolution is the peculiar achievement of Western man. Creative evolution of ego consciousness means that, through a continuous process stretching over thousands of years, the conscious system has absorbed more and more unconscious contents and progressively extended its frontiers. Although from antiquity right down to recent times we see a new and differently patterned canon of culture continually superseding the previous one, the West has nevertheless succeeded in achieving an historical and cultural continuity in which each canon gradually came to be integrated. The structure of modern consciousness rests on this integration, and at each period of its development the ego has to absorb essential portions of the cultural past transmitted to it by the canon of values embodied in its own culture and system of education.

The creative character of consciousness is a central feature of the cultural canon of the West. In Western culture, and partly also in the Far East, we can follow the continuous, though often fitful, development of consciousness over the last ten thousand years. Here alone has the canon of stadial development, collectively embodied in mythological projections, become a model for the development of the individual human being; here alone have the creative beginnings of individuality been taken over by the collective and held up as the ideal of all individual development. Wherever this type of creative ego consciousness has developed, or is still developing, the archetypal stages of conscious evolution are in force. In stationary cultures, or in primitive societies where the original features of human culture are still preserved, the earliest stages of man's psychology predominate to such a degree that individual and creative traits are not assimilated by the collective. Indeed, creative individuals possessed of a stronger consciousness are even branded by the collective as antisocial.[4]

The creativity of consciousness may be jeopardized by reli-

---

[4] Mead, *Sex and Temperament in Three Primitive Societies*, pp. 228 f.

gious or political totalitarianism, for any authoritarian fixation of the canon leads to sterility of consciousness. Such fixations, however, can only be provisional. So far as Western man is concerned, the assimilative vitality of his ego consciousness is more or less assured. The progress of science and the increasingly obvious threat to humanity from unconscious forces impel his consciousness, from within and without, to continual self-analysis and expansion. The individual is the bearer of this creative activity of the mind and therefore remains the decisive factor in all future Western developments. This holds true regardless of the fact that individuals co-operate and mutually determine the spiritual democracy in which they live.

Any attempt to outline the archetypal stages from the standpoint of analytical psychology must begin by drawing a fundamental distinction between personal and transpersonal psychic factors. Personal factors are those which belong to one individual personality and are not shared by any other individual, regardless of whether they are conscious or unconscious. Transpersonal factors, on the other hand, are collective, supra- or extra-personal, and are to be regarded not as *external* conditions of society, but as *internal* structural elements. The transpersonal represents a factor that is largely independent of the personal, for the personal, both collectively and individually, is a late product of evolution.

Every historical inquiry — and every evolutionary approach is in this sense historical — must therefore begin with the transpersonal. In the history of mankind as in the development of the individual there is an initial preponderance of transpersonal factors, and only in the course of development does the personal realm come into view and achieve independence. The individualized conscious man of our era is a late man, whose structure is built on early, pre-individual human stages from which individual consciousness has only detached itself step by step.

The evolution of consciousness by stages is as much a collective human phenomenon as a particular individual phenomenon. Ontogenetic development may therefore be regarded as a modified recapitulation of phylogenetic development.

This interdependence of collective and individual has two psychic concomitants. On the one hand, the early history of the collective is determined by inner primordial images whose projections appear outside as powerful factors — gods, spirits, or demons — which become objects of worship. On the other hand, man's collective symbolisms also appear in the individual, and the psychic development, or misdevelopment, of each individual is governed by the same primordial images which determine man's collective history.

Since we have undertaken to expound the whole canon of mythological stages, their sequence, their interconnections, and their symbolism, it is not only permissible but imperative to draw the relevant material from different spheres of culture and different mythologies, irrespective of whether or not all stages are present in any one culture.[5]

We do not therefore maintain that all the stages of conscious development are to be found always, everywhere, and in every mythology, any more than the theory of evolution maintains that the evolutionary stages of every animal species are repeated in man's evolution. What we do maintain is that these developmental stages arrange themselves in an orderly sequence and thus determine all psychic development. Equally we maintain that these archetypal stages are unconscious determinants and can be found in mythology, and that only by viewing the collective stratification of human development together with the individual stratification of conscious development can we arrive at an understanding of psychic development in general, and individual development in particular.

Again, the relation between the transpersonal and the personal — which plays a decisive role in every human life — is prefigured in human history. But the collective aspect of this relationship does not mean that unique or recurrent historical events are inherited, for up to the present there has been no scientific proof of the inheritance of acquired characteristics. For this reason analytical psychology considers the structure of the psyche to be determined by a priori transpersonal dominants — archetypes — which, being essential components and organs of the psyche from the beginning, mold the course of human history.

The castration motif, for instance, is not the result of the inheritance of an endlessly repeated threat of castration by a primordial father, or rather by an infinity of primordial fathers. Science has discovered nothing that could possibly support such a theory, which moreover presupposes the inheritance of acquired characteristics. Any reduction of the castration threat, parricide, the "primal scene" of parental intercourse, and so

---

[5] A thorough investigation of the archetypal stages in individual spheres of culture and mythology would be exceedingly interesting, because the absence or overemphasis of individual stages would enable us to draw important conclusions about the cultures concerned. Such an inquiry will doubtless be undertaken at a later date.

on, to historical and personalistic data, which presumes to paint the early history of humanity in the likeness of a patriarchal bourgeois family of the nineteenth century, is scientifically impossible.[6]

It is one of the tasks of this book to show that, in regard to these and similar "complexes," we are really dealing with symbols, ideal forms, psychic categories, and basic structural patterns whose infinitely varied modes of operation govern the history of mankind and the individual.[7]

The development of consciousness in archetypal stages is a transpersonal fact, a dynamic self-revelation of the psychic structure, which dominates the history of mankind and the individual. Even deviations from the path of evolution, their symbology and symptomatology, must be understood in relation to the prior archetypal pattern.

In the first part of our exposition — The Mythological Stages in the Evolution of Consciousness — the accent lies on the wide distribution of the mythological material, and on demonstrating the connections between the symbols and the various strata of conscious development. Only against this background can we understand the normal developments of the psyche, as well as the pathological phenomena in which collective problems constantly appear as the basic problems of human existence and so must be understood in that light.

Besides uncovering the evolutionary stages and their archetypal connections, our inquiry also has a therapeutic aim, which is both individual and collective. The integration of personal psychic phenomena with the corresponding transpersonal symbols is of paramount importance for the further development of consciousness and for the synthesis of the personality.[8]

The rediscovery of the human and cultural strata from which

---

[6] See The Origins and History of Consciousness, p. 53, note 16.

[7] It is in this sense that we use the terms "masculine" and "feminine" throughout the book, not as personal sex-linked characteristics, but as symbolic expressions. When we say masculine or feminine dominants obtrude themselves at certain stages, or in certain cultures or types of person, this is a psychological statement which must not be reduced to biological or sociological terms. The symbolism of "masculine" and "feminine" is archetypal and therefore transpersonal; in the various cultures concerned, it is erroneously projected upon persons as though they carried its qualities. In reality every individual is a psychological hybrid. Even sexual symbolism cannot be derived from the person, because it is prior to the person. Conversely, it is one of the complications of individual psychology that in all cultures the integrity of the personality is violated when it is identified with either the masculine or the feminine side of the symbolic principle of opposites.

[8] Here we would only emphasize the material content of the symbols. The healing and "whole-making" effect of the emotional components of the collective unconscious is discussed in Part II.

these symbols derive is in the original sense of the word *"bildend"* — "informing." Consciousness thus acquires images (*Bilder*) and education (*Bildung*), widens its horizon, and charges itself with contents which constellate a new psychic potential. New problems appear, but also new solutions. As the purely personal data enter into association with the transpersonal, and the collective human aspect is rediscovered and begins to come alive, new insights, new possibilities of life, add themselves to the narrowly personalistic and rigid personality of the sick-souled modern man.

Our aim is not confined to pointing out the correct relation of the ego to the unconscious, and of the personal to the transpersonal. We have also to realize that the false, personalistic interpretation of everything psychic is the expression of an unconscious law which has everywhere constrained modern man to misinterpret his true role and significance. Only when we have made it clear to what degree the reduction of the transpersonal to the personal springs from a tendency which once had a very deep meaning, but which the crisis of modern consciousness has rendered wholly meaningless and nonsensical, will our task be fulfilled. Only when we have recognized how the personal develops out of the transpersonal, detaches itself from it but, despite the crucial role of ego consciousness, always remains rooted in it, can we restore to the transpersonal factors their original weight and meaning, lacking which a healthy collective and individual life is impossible.

This brings us to a psychological phenomenon which will be fully discussed in Part II, under the "law of secondary personalization." This maintains that contents which are primarily transpersonal and originally appeared as such are, in the course of development, taken to be personal. The secondary personalization of primary transpersonal contents is in a certain sense an evolutionary necessity, but it constellates dangers which for modern man are altogether excessive. It is necessary for the structure of personality that contents originally taking the form of transpersonal deities should finally come to be experienced as contents of the human psyche. But this process ceases to be a danger to psychic health only when the psyche is itself regarded suprapersonally, as a numinous world of transpersonal happenings. If, on the other hand, transpersonal contents are reduced to the data of a purely personalistic psychology, the result is not only an appalling impoverishment of individual life — that might remain merely a private concern — but also a congestion of the collective unconscious which has disastrous consequences for humanity at large.

Psychology, having penetrated to the collective layer in its investigation of the lower levels of the individual psyche, is faced with the task of evolving a collective and cultural therapy adequate to cope with the mass phenomena that are now devastating mankind. One of the most important objectives of any depth psychology in the future is its application to the collective. It has to correct and prevent the dislocation of collective life, of the group, by applying its specific points of view.[9]

The relation of the ego to the unconscious and of the personal to the transpersonal decides the fate not only of the individual, but of humanity. The theater of this encounter is the human mind. In the present work, a substantial part of mythology is seen as the unconscious self-delineation of the growth of consciousness in man. The dialectic between consciousness and the unconscious, its transformation, its self-liberation, and the birth of human personality from this dialectic form the theme of Part I.

[9] Cf. my *Depth Psychology and a New Ethic.*

Chapter 12. Marie-Louise von Franz

In the first chapter of Patterns of Creativity Mirrored in Creation Myths, *Marie-Louise von Franz stresses the difference between creation myths and hero myths.* Creation myths are far more abstract and impersonal than hero myths, for they describe the birth of the whole world and not merely of an individual. Still, their symbolic meaning is the same as that of hero myths, at least of hero myths of the first half of life. The creation of the world symbolizes the creation of ego consciousness, which can be defined as the recognition of the difference between oneself and the world.*

From **Patterns of Creativity Mirrored in Creation Myths**, pp. 5–19

CHAPTER I

The Creation Myth

In these lectures I shall try to interpret motifs that occur frequently in creation myths. Creation myths are of a different class from other myths — hero myths, or fairy tales for instance — for when they are told there is always a certain *solemnity* that gives them a central importance; they convey a mood which implies that what is said will concern the basic things of existence, something more than is contained in other myths. Therefore, one may say that as far as the feeling and emotional mood which accompanies them is concerned, creation myths are the deepest and most important of all myths. In many primitive religions the telling of the creation myth forms an essential teaching in the *ritual of initiation*. They are told to the young initiates as the most important part of the tribal tradition. In many other ways also, as we shall see later, they refer to the most basic problems of human life, for they are concerned with the ultimate meaning, not only of *our* existence, but of the existence of the whole cosmos.

Because the origin of nature and of human existence is a complete mystery to us, the unconscious has produced many models of this event. The same thing happens wherever the human mind touches the borders of the unknown. If, for example, you look at maps of antiquity, let us say maps of Greece, Greece is shown more or less in the centre of the map, but on the borderline things become a bit distorted and unknown; the upper part of Yugoslavia tends towards the upper part of Italy, and then at the end of a known area there is simply a drawing of the Uroboros, the snake which eats its own tail, which on old maps also represents the Ocean. As decoration, at the corners of the maps, there are pictures of animals or monsters, or of the four winds. In the Middle Ages the area of the known world was always shown in the centre surrounded by all-embracing symbols and sometimes even demonic figures: the four winds blowing towards the centre, heads with a blowing mouth, or something similar. These maps demonstrate *ad oculos* that *wherever known reality stops, where we touch the unknown, there we project an archetypal image.*

The same applies in the case of medieval astronomical charts. In the Middle Ages they drew all the constellations they knew and outside them the cosmos was surrounded by the Zodiac snake, the snake on which were all the signs of the Zodiac; beyond that lay the unknown. There again the snake which bites its own tail, the Uroboros motif, comes up where man reaches the end of his conscious knowledge. In late antiquity, the beginnings of chemistry show that people also had certain knowledge of the elements and some technical knowledge, but when it came to the end of known facts, they again projected this archetypal image, the symbol of the Uroboros, to characterize the mystery of unknown matter. In alchemy it was the symbol of the *prima materia,* of the original matter of the world.

Most of the questions as to the origin and substance of our cosmos have now been resolved for us, but in spite of the increase of technical instruments, unknown factors still remain. There are archetypal models and projections of modern science which I shall discuss later, but we are still confronted with completely puzzling facts and with contradictory theories. Other civilizations have not been less naive than we, for they too fell into this hole of the unknown, and when confronted with a mystery they projected mythological symbols out of which, among other things, the creation myths arose.

In order to explain what projection means, I would like to

call your attention, like a pedantic schoolmaster, back to Jung's definition of projection. One sees again and again that projection has not been really understood, but always gives rise to all sorts of misinterpretation. Jung says in his definitions at the end of *Psychological Types*:

> Projection means the expulsion of a subjective content into an object; it is the opposite of *introjection*. Accordingly it is a process of *dissimilation* (v. *assimilation*), by which a subjective content becomes alienated from the subject and is, so to speak, embodied in the object. The subject gets rid of painful, incompatible contents by projecting them, as also of positive values which, for one reason or another — self-depreciation, for instance — are inaccessible to him. (Now comes the sentence which is important for us): *Projection results from the archaic identity of subject and object, but is properly so called only when the need to dissolve the identity with the object has already arisen.* This need arises when the identity becomes a disturbing factor, i.e., when the absence of the projected content is a hindrance to adaptation and its withdrawal into the subject has become desirable. (CW 6, §783)

We sometimes use the term projection in talking about primitive societies, saying that their myths and gods are projections of archetypal images. This leads to confusion, because in the society within which those gods are still psychologically alive the necessity has not yet arisen for the withdrawal of the projection. So there you really still have a state of archaic identity. It is only because *we* do not believe, say, in the gods of the Shilluk of the Upper Nile that we may now speak of projection, but that is an indirect application of the term. We often clash with ethnologists, who say that it is not *only* a projection, that they have lived with such primitive people, and for them the gods are a living reality, that you cannot just call them "only a projection." Such scientists have simply misunderstood how we use the word "projection."

There is another reason why I would like to comment on this, but first I want to go on to the term of archaic identity which Jung uses and defines in the same book:

> I use the term *identity* to denote a psychological conformity. It is always an unconscious phenomenon since a conscious conformity would necessarily involve a consciousness of two dissimilar things, and, consequently, a separation of subject

and object, in which case the identity would already have been abolished. Psychological identity presupposes that it is unconscious. It is a characteristic of the primitive mentality and the real foundation of *participation mystique*, which is nothing but a relic of the original non-differentiation of subject and object, and hence of the primordial unconscious state. It is also a characteristic of the mental state of early infancy and, finally, of the unconscious of the civilized adult, which, in so far as it has not become a content of consciousness, remains in a permanent state of identity with objects. . . . It is not an *equation*, but an *a priori likeness* which was never the object of consciousness.

(CW 6, §741–742)

Thus we must assume that in relatively early stages of our development there was no difference between our unconscious psyche and the outer world; they were in a state of *complete equality*, i.e., archaic identity. Then certain mysterious psychic processes, mutations, took place which disturbed the peace of this identity and forced us to withdraw certain representations and see that they were inner not outer facts. We then always replace the idea about the outer facts with a new "projection," of which we do not yet see its subjective aspect.

As you will see when we study several creation myths, it is sometimes revealed very clearly to us that they represent unconscious and pre-conscious processes which describe not the origin of our cosmos, but *the origin of man's conscious awareness of the world*. This means that before I become consciously aware of the world as a whole, or of a part of my surroundings, a lot happens in my unconscious. The pre-conscious processes that take place in a human being before this awareness befalls him can be observed in dreams and in unconscious material: as an analyst you can sometimes see a fortnight ahead, or even longer, that now a new form of consciousness is approaching, but the dreamer has not as yet any realisation of it. It is like an annunciation of a process in consciousness which appears in the dream but has not yet taken place within reality. A fortnight later the dreamer will come and say: "Now I understand, now I have realised something," but you saw in the dream that this new understanding, this sudden realisation, was prepared some time ago in pre-conscious processes. I give this now as an *a priori* statement but hope to demonstrate it in a convincing way when we look at the creation myths.

What we cannot any longer see is that such processes also

should mirror the origin of our outer cosmic world. This is because the old identity has been disturbed and other new projections have been produced — projections which seem to *us* to represent "objective" scientific models of the outer world. These new models have pushed away the old ones and thus we see the old ones as projections. If I may use a drawing, the process of projections is very much like this:

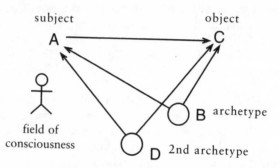

A, the human being or the ego in the centre of his field of consciousness, looks at an object, he being the subject. When there is an original projection it means that an archetype has been constellated in the unconscious, B. The subject stares at the object, C, and can make no sense of it, but wonders what the Hell it is! Then he gets an idea and conceives of the object as being so and so, but he is not aware of the fact that the archetype, B, has been constellated in his unconscious and has conveyed to him the model of the idea from which he recognizes C; he sees only that the object coincides with his idea. This is what constitutes the cognition process as a whole.

Now, this mode of apperception is all right as long as it works. If, for instance, I say that Mr. X. seems to me to be a genius and he continually behaves as if he were and never does anything to contradict my opinion, then nobody will ever convince me that he is not a genius. But if one day he behaves like a complete idiot (that is the factor of the disturbance), then I will say: "Now why, and how, did I ever get the idea that this man was a genius?" But only when there is a disturbance, a not coinciding, do I begin to realise that something has happened which must have disturbed my ideas. This is the case which Jung mentions: the projection does not fit anymore. For instance, I want to be convinced that an object is like this or that, but my idea does not fit; there are a lot of factors which, as one says in modern natural science, do not converge, there is no convergence of result. In the Hubble idea of the expanding universe the other results of atomic investigation do not coincide and you have no convergence of results, you begin to wonder if this is not just a speculative idea, or, in our language, a projection of Hubble's. But as long as the results seem to converge in the same direction, as long as the object seems really to behave in accordance with my mental model, I have no reason to withdraw the projection. I will be naively convinced that I know the quality of the object itself.

So one reason for withdrawing a projection is that the idea of the object does not fit the facts, that something limps somewhere and does not coincide with the facts. The other very frequent possibility is that another archetype constellates (D): a second archetype pushes itself forward in the unconscious and puts another model, or idea, into the subject's mind, and another projection onto the object. The subject then jumps to this new idea claiming that *this* is the truth and the former idea was an error, an illusion — a projection. Looking back, one calls it a projection, but as long as one is caught in it, as long as the archetype is validly constellated in one's unconscious and conscious, one will never call it a projection but will consider it to be true cognition. The subject then feels that he is talking about true facts as honestly as he can. This shifting of archetypes naturally generally coincides with outer changes in conditions so that certain theories do not fit them any longer. As long as we feel subjectively that we are not talking about projections but about the true quality of the object — a special aspect of our western mentality — then we call it the scientific truth.

Easterners are so introverted that even when they feel convinced they yet have a certain doubt and are capable of putting a question mark against their "true convictions," but we are sure we are talking about the outer object so long as our projections seem to fit them. We are now under the domination of a new archetypal constellation which for the moment is working and with which all the objective qualities seem to fit. Where there is what Bavink called convergence of scientific results, where everything seems to fit into the picture and one cannot think of any facts which contradict the model we have in mind, this is, for the time being, our truth. Being less critical as a whole, and having only a fragmentary knowledge of outer facts, or only a partial knowledge compared to ours, the primitives have produced cosmogonic explanations of the origin of existence which to us are absolutely transparent projections.

Please keep this fact in mind, because we cannot understand these myths if we simply call them projections of pre-conscious processes without understanding "projection" accurately in the sense I have tried to describe.

Before trying to understand the creation myths, we have also to remember another fact, namely that *we cannot speak about any kind of reality except in its form as a content of our consciousness.* The only reality we can talk about is the reality of which we are aware. If it is difficult for you to understand this then imagine that you had a dream at night and do not recall it in the morning. If there was no observer proving that you dreamt, then the dream has no existence. You can *assume* that it existed, or that it did not, you can say anything you like arbitrarily about it, but, scientifically speaking, you cannot say that it existed or that it did not. All of this means that no factor which has not somewhere entered the field of conscious awareness of some human subject can be talked about as being real. The only facts we can talk about as real are those which have somehow, somewhere entered the field of awareness of a human being. All the rest is arbitrary speculation. Naturally in the morning one can *assume* one has had a dream and forgotten it, but it cannot be talked about as a *fact*.

In practical terms we may say, therefore, that the only reality we can talk about, or with which we are really concerned, is the *image* of reality in our field of consciousness. The spontaneous argument of the extravert, who is by temperament terribly object bound, will be to say: "Yes, but there *is* a reality, only we cannot talk about it." There we can only say that if he likes to assume it, he may, but it is a sheer subjective assumption. If you take a stand and say: "I believe that there is a reality beyond my field of consciousness," that is a belief which springs from certain temperamental needs, and if somebody else prefers not to believe it you have no right to cut his head off. Therefore, if the Indians prefer to say that there is no reality beyond what enters the field of their consciousness, we have no right to say that they are fools. We can simply say that that does not suit our temperamental disposition, that we prefer to deal with things as if we believed there is a reality which is transcendent to our consciousness, though we cannot deal with it directly. Here we enter the field of metaphysical and religious beliefs and assumptions where everyone is free to make his assumptions; but we have left the field of discussible scientific fact. It is therefore understandable that stories which are supposed to describe the origin of the real world are completely intertwined and mixed up with factors which we would rather call *stories of the pre-conscious processes in the origin of human consciousness.*

Where do we see creation myths nowadays, or elements, or typical motifs of creation myths in our practical analytical work and in dreams? The most visible form of it can be observed in *schizophrenic material*, where a schizophrenic episode is often prepared by dreams of world destruction. In modern terms it is generally an atomic explosion, or the end of the world, the stars fall down—absolutely apocalyptic images; or, one wakes up and everybody is dead, one's surroundings are going to pieces, the surface of the world splits open, and so on. This generally announces that the consciousness of this human being is in a state of explosion or is going to explode, and his reality awareness will soon disappear; his subjective world will actually go to pieces. But very often when a schizophrenic episode begins to fade, or to pass out of its acute phase, then in fantasies and dreams the motifs of creation myths come up and the world is re-created from a very small germ, just as it is in creation myths. Reality is rebuilt. From my practical experience if you understand these rebuilding symbols, if you understand what is going on when such symbols come up after an episode, and as a therapist can support them adequately and join in with them and deal with them properly, you can sometimes help in the rebuilding of a new conscious personality that the return of the tide will not smash up again.

I remember a case where this took place, though it was not quite so bad; it was not a clinical schizophrenia. It was a borderline situation, a woman who, in complete animus possession, had smashed up her relationship with a man to whom she had a terrific transference. She was a walking animus and had nothing but her animus to live on. Complete destruction of her feminine personality had gone on for many years (a schizophrenic disposition), and she was within an ace of going off her head. A colleague who treated her with me proposed internment, considering that she would either commit suicide or do something crazy, like murder the man who had seemingly disappointed her so badly. Before agreeing to internment I wanted to see her myself, and when I did I realised at once that I could no longer make any contact. She stared past me with glaring eyes, and I could not reach her emotionally. I had the feeling she did not hear me, which was later confirmed when she told me that she had not heard a word of what I said. She was in such a state that her awareness, her consciousness was completely gone. In my despair I finally said to her: "No dreams, no dreams in such a desperate situation?" She said: "Just a fragment: I saw an egg and a voice said 'the mother and the daughter'." I was as happy as could be and went off telling her all the creation myths and of how the world is reborn from a world egg. I said that this showed the germ of a new possibility of life and that all would come right, that we had only to wait until everything came out of the egg, etc. I talked myself into a terrific enthusiasm, saying that "the mother and the daughter" naturally referred to the Eleusinian mysteries, and I told her about this and of the rebirth of the feminine world where the new consciousness would be a feminine consciousness, and so on. I saw that while I was talking she became quite quiet; finally I put my hand on her arm and said: "Do you feel any better?" She smiled at me for the first time and said she did. I asked her if she thought she could go to bed and not do anything silly and she said, Yes, she thought she could! And so it proved, and the difficult episode was bridged. Later she told me that she was in such a black hole and her consciousness was so far gone that she didn't understand a word of what I had said. She only realised that *I* understood her dream motif and understood it positively and so, on the way home, she said to herself, "Well, it *can* be understood, and it seems to be O.K." So you see I had understood what was going on. I couldn't convey it to her, her ego complex was already too far gone, but even the fact that she felt that somebody understood was sufficient to bridge an exceedingly dangerous situation. There you see how important it is to know about these pre-conscious archetype processes.

I have had the experience that generally you cannot convey the meaning of such creation myths to people when they are right in the darkness, because the material, as you will see, and that will probably disappoint you very much in this Course, describes processes which are very remote from consciousness. In contrast to other mythologies, the themes do not give you that intimate reaction of understanding something and being able to apply it to your own case, which you have when you listen to interpretations of fairy tales, or hero myths, where you have an emotional and feeling bridge with the material. The motifs of creation myths seem weird and extremely abstract, and are therefore very difficult to bring up into consciousness. Because the meaning is so remote, when you try to convey it to other people it is difficult to give them the feeling that they have understood. I must therefore warn you that if you want to stick out these lectures you will have to do a lot of abstract thinking and follow a difficult mental operation, because creation myths really contain very difficult material.

What you can observe in borderline cases, namely the destruction of consciousness and of the awareness of reality and the rebuilding of a new consciousness, is only the extreme case, the exaggeration, of something which you can also find in normal situations. You find creation myth motifs *whenever the unconscious is preparing a basically important progress in consciousness*. The psychological development of a human being seems to follow the pattern of the physical growth of children, who do not grow continuously but in fits and starts. The growth of consciousness also tends to make sudden jumps forward: there are periods where the field of awareness enlarges suddenly to a great extent. Whenever the enlargement of consciousness or the rebuilding of consciousness is very sudden, people speak of getting an "illumination" or revelation. When it is more continuous, they do not notice it so much and have only an agreeable feeling that they are growing, that they are moving in the flow of life and that life is interesting, but they do not have this feeling of sudden illumination or awakening. Whenever the progress of consciousness takes a big jump forward there are preparatory dreams, generally with creation myth motifs in them.

Last but not least, you have to know the motifs of creation myths if ever you analyse a *creative personality*. To analyse creative people is a great problem because often such people think they are neurotic or are in a neurotic crisis, and show every sign of this, but when you look at their dream material it shows that they are not neurotic because of a maladjustment to the outer or inner facts of life, but because they are haunted by a creative idea and should do something creative. They are haunted by a creative task; outwardly they behave exactly as other neurotic people do, and very often diagnose themselves as neurotic on account of it. Now the difficulty is that you cannot make the invention for the other! Let us say that a physicist who should invent something comes to you, his unconscious wants that of him. You cannot do it for him! For one thing, you probably do not know enough about physics and besides, it would then be your invention and *invenere* means to step into something, to discover something new, and you cannot do that for another person. Thank God, for you would steal the most valuable experience of his life if you did. So you have to accompany the other on his painful way. He says: "Yes, but *what* have I to find out?" Well, I don't know either, but he has to find out something! But he says that if I can't tell him what it is, that does not help him. But you must have enough scientific material on hand to be able to show him that now a creative act is taking place, that a new world is about to be born, that something new wants to enter consciousness. There are certain preparatory processes which must be understood, because from them you can at least derive some indications as to the direction the invention will take and can spare your analysand a painful waste of time. You can serve him like a dog who sniffs and says: "Not there, not that track, but rather over there!" Thus you can circumscribe intuitively the direction in which his creative inner process is moving, so that he need not waste his time for years in chasing wrong tracks but can sooner come close to the original world-creating event which has constellated in his psyche.

This is tremendously important if you think how widespread is the belief that psycho-analysis, and Jungian analysis too, is destructive to the creative personality. A number of artists and creative scientists avoid contact with us because they believe that we, in a reductive analytical way, are going to destroy their creativeness. Rilke said, when he was pressed to go in for a Freudian analysis, that he was afraid that by driving out his devils his angels would be driven out as well, and therefore he refused analysis. I would say that this fear of the creative personality to go into analytical treatment, or to be interested in analysis, is justified to the extent that not enough analysts know about the creative processes in the psyche, and misunderstanding it, use reductive neurosis-cure methods when they should rather take the attitude of supporting a new birth of consciousness. The creative personality, when weighed down and depressed by a creative task, *does* very often behave like an awful neurotic, in a maladjusted and impossible way. To correct a little, or to cut off neurotic behavior a little, and at the same time not to destroy the creative kernel of the process is a very delicate task. There it is very important to know the material so that one can recognise the processes. You will see that the creation myths will help us to find such material.

Mircea Eliade has written a book which was first published as *The Myth of the Eternal Return* and has now been republished in the Harper Torchbook series and called *Cosmos and History*. On reading it you will find that creation myths in many civilizations have been repeated under specific conditions. Cosmogonic myths and mythology, in India for instance, are used every time a new house is built. Eliade gives an example:

'The astrologer shows in what spot in the foundation is exactly above the head of the snake (that is a star constellation) that supports the world. The mason fashions a little wooden peg from the wood of the Khadira tree, and with a coconut drives the peg into the ground at this particular spot, in such a way as to peg the head of the snake securely down'. . . . A foundation stone is placed above the peg. The cornerstone is thus situated exactly at the "center of the world." But the act of foundation at the same time repeats the cosmogonic act, for to "secure" the snake's head, to drive the peg into it, is to imitate the primordial gesture of Soma (*Rg-Veda*, II, 12, 1) or of Indra when the latter "smote the serpent in his lair". . . (VI, 17, 9). The serpent symbolizes chaos, the formless and non-manifested. Indra comes upon Vrtra (IV, 19, 3) undivided *(aparvan)*, unwakened *(abudkyam)*. . . . (p. 19)

At the moment one lays the foundation of a house, one (as it were) recreates the whole world once again. In the early Middle Ages when the Vikings or the Anglo-Saxons first set foot in a new country, they built an altar and repeated the creation myth, meaning that this country had not formerly existed, and only now that they were there and it had entered their field of consciousness and they had set a conscious order in it, did they create it by coming into it and settling it. What it felt like to the conquered people was not considered. The same repetition of the creation myth is to be found also in many civilizations whenever a town is founded: every town which is founded repeats, so to speak, the cosmogony; a centre is established which is the navel of the world and around which everything is concentrated, and the town is a new order, a new cosmos established from this centre. So the creation myth is either partially enacted once more in ritual or it is solemnly re-told. Another use of the creation myth, where it is still alive within a religion, is to retell it at every New Year festival. I mention the New Year festival not only in our sense of the word, but whenever a new year in any sense begins. Whenever this new time begins, then a creation myth is solemnly re-told, which means, now the world begins again and therefore one has to bring back into one's consciousness everything which happened *in illo tempore*, as Eliade calls it.

Another situation in which the creation myth finds expression is among the Fijians. These islanders repeat it not only at each enthronement of a new king, but also whenever the crops are bad: "Each time that life is threatened and the cosmos, in their eyes, is exhausted and empty, the Fijians feel the need for a return *in principio*; in other words, they expect the regeneration of cosmic life not from its restoration but from its recreation. Hence the essential importance, in rituals and myths, of anything which can signify the 'beginning,' the original, the primordial." There you see confirmed what we can observe whenever a new conscious attitude, a new readjustment to reality from a very basic depth, is needed. If as a conqueror, for instance, you enter an unknown country, you are in a psychologically and psychically dangerous situation; it is a tremendous risk, you have lost your roots, you are not adapted, and therefore you are threatened by physical death and psychological dissociation. Therefore in a new country the conqueror establishes a new cosmos. The New Year ceremonial shows that our conscious awareness of reality and our adjustment to it tends to fade, to become sloppy and a half-unconscious habit instead of a conscious effort, and it ages just as the king symbol ages, as the symbols of religion age. What was once perhaps in one's youth a fervent prayer, said with all one's heart, becomes a mechanical "blah-blah" in later time. This constant threat of relapse into repetition and mechanical continuation and of gliding off into unconsciousness so that the feeling of aliveness fades out of it, has to be fought by this reaction of the whole reality, by going back to the source of consciousness. The Fijians have a less mechanical way of doing the same thing — they don't do it only every New Year, but whenever they feel suddenly that there is an urgent threat to life. Whenever they are threatened by dissociation and panic and social disorder, they try to restore the creation and the whole cosmos by re-telling the creation myth.

Finally, we can still see that when the individual is threatened physically or by complete dissociation, as for instance in the example I gave you, the creation myth is re-told by the unconscious. The unconscious re-tells parts of the creation myth to restore conscious life and the conscious awareness of reality again. There will be one more element in this, namely the analogy of the creation myth to the symbolism of the process of individuation which you see most clearly in alchemical material; this I will mention in my last lecture.

Just a word about the outline of these lectures. The first type I shall speak about is the myth that shows more clearly than others how creation is an awakening towards consciousness: I mean where we can catch *in flagranti* how awakening towards consciousness is identical with the creation of the world. Then I will bring a few examples of the birth of the cosmos through *accidental action*. Third, I will go on to the type where creation is represented as a *movement from above to below* — where spiritual Beings in the Beyond create by coming down or throwing things down. Then I will turn to creation through a *movement from below to above*, such as we find in Emergence-myths where everything comes out of a hole in the earth. Then I will take up the motif of the two creators, namely the *two animals*, or the *twin creatures*, etc. The motif of the *Deus Faber*, namely the Godhead which manufactures the world, as in our Biblical creation myth, will occupy us next. Afterwards I shall take the motif of the *first victim*. Then I will shortly describe the *subjective moods of the creating Being*, for instance creation by laughing, by fear, by crying, and all those creations through a feeling of longing, of yielding, and of love. Then I will discuss briefly a few of the *basic primordial motifs*, namely the *world egg*, the *primordial man* through whose decay the whole cosmos is built, the libido concept by a *creative fire*, a *mana*, a *world energy* from which everything springs. Then I shall briefly discuss why so many creation myths contain innumerable *chains of generations*. These are mostly in the Polynesian and Hawaiian creation myths, but also in the Japanese, and again in the Gnostic creation myths where God produces twin pairs such as life and truth and Logos and Word, and so on, chains and chains of generations of either gods or spirits or other Beings, till reality is born. Then there is the motif of the particles, the *seeds of the world*. Then finally, the *subjective reproduction of creation in meditation* as practised in Alchemy, where making the philosopher's stone was looked on as reproducing the creation of the world on a subjective level. That is the plan of the lectures.

Questions and Remarks

Question: Could not the problem of reducing a personality, which you mentioned in regard to the creative personality, be true for everyone?

Dr. von Franz: Yes, to an extent. Sometimes you can say that the creative part is 80% of the problem, and readjustment 20%; sometimes it is the other way round. Some of it is always there and that is one of the subtleties in analysis. It depends very much on the feeling relationship between analyst and analysand, for if there is too much counter-transference, the analyst tends not to be sufficiently reductive, and if the analyst has a secret depreciation of the analysand he might do him harm by being too reductive and thus destroy his creative possibilities. That is a very delicate situation in which one has sometimes also to rely on one's own dreams. It is like a gardener who has to make up his mind what he is going to weed out and what he is going to support in its growth.

Remark: It strikes me that one has frequently — not only frequently but always — to be on one's toes not to fall into the error, where one might have too strong a transference, of thinking that everybody's kernel of creativity is the main thing and whatever nonsense comes out is creative and therefore must be nurtured.

Dr. von Franz: Yes, an over-maternal analyst, who sits on a lot of phoenix eggs, hatches "phoney" eggs!

Question: Can a genuine creative impulse really be killed? Has not one to distinguish between what is wrong and what is genuine? If someone had a really creative instinct surely that could not be destroyed?

Dr. von Franz: I think the creative instinct is so strong that if the analyst tries to destroy it, the analysand will leave him and analysis. One cannot destroy it — you are quite right. If the analyst has made a wrong attempt to squash it, it causes ill-feeling and a hatred of psychology. It will create bitterness, but I think you are absolutely right, the dynamic strength of a creative disposition will never be suppressed.

Remark: We all have many ideas which are fakes and the difficulty is to know what is real and genuine!

Dr. von Franz: Yes, it might be well to put some sort of acid test to such fake or illusory ideas. Only one can say that there are also human individuals who have no strong creativeness, but have some minor amount of creative fantasy which could enlarge their horizon and make their life more meaningful, so why not let them live! Because, after all, one does feel better if one does not squash the impulse. If every time you want to play with something that is amusing you think that it is childish, then you dry up. It is not a catastrophe, but I think it is a pity to squash minor creative impulses which could be quite an embellishment to life. Generally, thank God, the dreams get wild about it if one wrongly squashes something.

Chapter 13. James Hillman

For James Hillman, as for Jung, myths serve above all to help one understand and experience the archetypes of the unconscious. But for Hillman myths are more than colorful ways of describing psychological states. Myths describe what it is like to be in those states. One grasps myth by fantasizing, or imagining, what it would be like to do what a god in a myth does. In the following selection from his key work, Re-Visioning Psychology, Hillman outlines the use of myth to experience the pathological side of one's personality. By imagining oneself as a god whose myth describes his "falling apart," one encounters the same pathological, ultimately suicidal capacity in one's own personality. But to identify oneself with a single character in a myth is to assume the unitary perspective against which Hillman rails. Rather, one must imagine oneself as all of the characters in the situation. Indeed, one must above all open oneself up to imagination itself.

From Re-Visioning Psychology, pp. 99–112

3. MYTHS

On the assumption that a psychological sickness is an enactment of a pathologizing fantasy, archetypal psychology proceeds to search for the *archai*, the governing principles or root metaphors of the fantasy. Archetypal psychology would attempt to lead the pathologizing into meaning through resemblance with an archetypal background following the principle stated by Plotinus, "All knowing comes by likeness,"[1] and following the method he also initiated called "reversion" (*epistrophé*) — the idea that all things desire to return to the archetypal originals of which they are copies and from which they

---

[1] *The Enneads*, trans. Stephen Mackenna (London: Faber, 1956), I, 8, 1. Compare the idea of resemblance or family in Wittgenstein, cf. F. Zabeeh, "Resemblance" in his *Universals* (The Hague: Nijhoff, 1966), pp. 37–49, where likeness loses its archetypal significance and becomes only a nominalistic language game.

proceed.[2] Pathologizings, too, would be examined in terms of likeness and imagined as having the intentionality of returning to an archetypal background.

What archetypal pattern is like my present behavior and fantasy? Who am I like when I do and feel this way? "Likeness" here refers to the idea that what is concretely manifested in an individual psyche has its likeness in a cluster of archetypal resemblances where the pathologizing I am undergoing finds place, makes sense, has necessity, and to which the pathologizing can "revert." These archetypal resemblances are best presented in myths in which the archetypal persons I am like and the patterns I am enacting have their authentic home ground.

It is to this mythical realm that I return all fantasies. The authentication of the fantasies of sickness is not in nature but in psyche, not in literal sickness but imaginal sickness, not in the psychodynamics of actual configurations past or present, but in mythical figures which are the eternal metaphors of the imagination,[3] the universals of fantasy.[4] These mythical figures, like my afflictions, are "tragical, monstrous, and unnatural,"[5] and their effects upon the soul, like my afflictions, "perturb to excess."[6] Only in mythology does pathology receive an adequate mirror, since myths speak with the same distorted, fantastic language.

Pathologizing is a way of mythologizing. Pathologizing takes one out of blind immediacy, distorting one's focus upon the natural and actual by forcing one to ask what is within it and behind it. The distortion is at the same time an enhancement

---

[2] Proclus, *Elements of Theology*, Prop. 29 ff. on *epistrophé*.

[3] I use the term *metaphorica* as employed by Albertus Magnus in the art of memory, see *Re-Visioning Psychology*, p. 91f, with references to Frances Yates.

[4] G. Vico, *The New Science* (1744), trans. T. G. Bergin and M. H. Fisch (Ithaca, N.Y.: Cornell Univ. Press, 1968), pp. 74, 119 (§§209, 381) where Vico speaks of mythical figures as *universali fantastici*.

[5] T. Taylor, "An Apology for the Fables of Homer" (1804), translation of Proclus' essay on the fables of Homer, found in *Thomas Taylor, the Platonist*, K. Raine and G. M. Harper, eds., Bollingen Series (Princeton, N.J.: Princeton Univ. Press, 1969), p. 460. Taylor attempts to account (as do many moralists and Christian thinkers) for the apparent paradox of a sublime religious philosophy and poetry (of Homer) riddled with pathologized images. The entire passage reads:

> It likewise appears to me, that whatever is tragical, monstrous, and unnatural, in poetical fictions, excites the hearers, in an all-various manner, to the investigation of the truth, attracts us to recondite knowledge, and does not suffer us through apparent probability to rest satisfied with superficial conceptions, but compels us to penetrate into the interior parts of fables, to explore the obscure intention of their authors, and survey what natures and powers they intended to signify to posterity by such mystical symbols.

[6] Vico, *New Science*, p. 117 (§376). The point of these mythical images, according to Vico, is "to perturb to excess."

and a new clarification, reminding the soul of its mythical existence. While in the throes of pathologizing, the psyche is going through a reversion into a mythical style of consciousness. Psychoanalysts have seen this but condemned it as regression to magical, primitive levels. But the psyche reverts not only to escape reality but to find another reality in which the pathologizing makes new sense.

In recent years I have made several forays into the idea of reversion as a primary method of archetypal psychology. A new *method* had become urgent. If a psychology refuses to borrow the developmental and historical, the natural scientific, and the religious approaches to psychological events, then it must find another fundamental method of understanding. Understanding psychological events through the general principle of opposites — depth psychology's main method — is too mechanical. It presents all soul events within a compensatory system of pairs: mind and body, ego and world, spirit and instinct, conscious and unconscious, inner and outer, and so on interminably. But soul events are not part of a general balancing system or a polar energy system or a binary information system. Soul events are not *parts* of any system. They are not reactions and responses to other sorts of events at the opposite end of any fulcrum. They are independent of the tandems in which they are placed, inasmuch as there is an independent primacy of the imaginal that creates its fantasies autonomously, ceaselessly, spontaneously. Myth-making is not compensatory to anything else; nor is soul-making.

So I began by examining various psychological syndromes as if they were mythical enactments, as if they were ways in which the soul is mimetic of an archetypal pattern. Of course this approach in modern times started with Freud. He imagined psychopathology against a background of the Oedipus myth. But Freud's method of reversion took a positivistic course; it became reduction. Instead of leading events back to their base in myth and seeing that pathologizing was ultimately mythical behavior — the soul's return to myth — Freud tried to base the myths on the actual behavior of actual biological families, ultimately reducing the mythical to the pathological.

My first essay in this method was an attempt to deliteralize suicide by grasping the pathologizing fantasy there going on as a metaphorical search for death by a soul caught in a naturalistic literalism called life.[7] The more I went into the subject, the

[7] J. Hillman, *Suicide and the Soul* (1964) (New York: Harper Colophon, 1973).

less satisfactory were the positivistic explanations of it and the more it seemed that the pathologizing in suicide fantasies and behaviors were evidently of compelling necessity to the soul. I came to realize that we could do nothing whatsoever therapeutically about the literal act of suicide unless we understood very closely the fantasy and its intentions of returning the soul from life to death as a metaphor for another sort of existence.

But the task of referring the soul's syndromes to specific myths is complex and fraught with dangers. It must meet the philosophical and theological arguments against remythologizing, arguments which would see our approach as a backward step into magical thinking, a new daemonology, unscientific, un-Christian, and unsound.[8] It must meet as well its own inherent pitfalls, such as those we find in Philip Slater's work, *The Glory of Hera*.[9] Though he indeed recognizes that mythology must be related to psychology for myths to remain vital, his connection between psychological syndromes and myths puts things the wrong way round. He performs a wrong pathologizing upon mythology by explaining Greek myths through social culture and family relations. His is the sociological fallacy: i.e., one reads Greek myths for allegories of sociology. I would read sociology as an enactment of myths. And just here is a redeeming value of Slater's work. It offers an insight into the archetypal background — not of myths, but of his own sociological perspective. His theme is Hera, Goddess of family, state, and society; his approach is that of sociology, the discipline which in our day is a tribute to this Goddess, a Glory of Hera.

But the chief danger lies in taking myths literally even as we aim at taking syndromes mythically. For if we go about reversion as a simple act of matching, setting out with the practical intellect of the therapist to equate mythemes with syndromes, we have reduced archetypes to allegories of disease; we have merely coined a new sign language, a new nominalism. The Gods become merely a new (or old) grid of classificatory terms. Instead of imagining psychopathology as a mythical enactment, we would, *horribile dictu*, have lost the sense of myth through using it to label syndromes. This is the diagnostic perspective rather than the mythical, and we are looking not for a new way to classify psychopathology but for a new way of *experiencing* it. Here the Homeric and classical Greeks themselves provide a

---

[8] A main attack on remythologizing via depth psychology comes from Jaspers, whose argument is presented and refused in my "Deep Subjectivity, Introspection and Daemonology," forthcoming from Spring Publications.
[9] P. Slater, *The Glory of Hera* (Boston: Beacon, 1971).

clue: their medical diagnoses were not in literal terms of myths and Gods, even though their thinking and feeling about affliction and madness was permeated with myths and Gods.[10] So we must take care, remembering that mythical thinking is not direct, practical thinking. Mythical metaphors are not etiologies, causal explanations, or name tags. They are perspectives toward events which shift the experience of events; but they are not themselves events. They are likenesses to happenings, making them intelligible, but they do not themselves happen. They give an account of the archetypal story in the case history, the myth in the mess. Reversion also provides a new access to myths: if they are directly connected to our complexes, they may be insighted through our afflictions. They are no longer stories in an illustrated book. *We* are those stories, and we illustrate them with our lives.

Despite the risk of losing precisely the mythical perspective we are trying to gain, we can point to some of the potentialities in this approach. We can refer the manifestations of depression together with styles of paranoid thought to Saturn and the archetypal psychology of the senex.[11] Saturn in mythology and lore presents the slowness, dryness, darkness, and impotence of depression, the defensive feelings of the outcast, the angle of vision that sees everything askew and yet deeply, the repetitious ruminations, the fixed focus on money and poverty, on fate, and on fecal and anal matters.

Later I explored hysteria and the myths of Dionysus to show the God in that syndrome.[12] I hoped I might grasp why hysteria has always been associated with women, young women especially, and why this women's God, in whose troop were raving dancing girls, was also called Lord of Souls and associated with the depths of the underworld. I suggested that similar mythical phenomena were taking place in the beginnings of depth psychology, for it was hysteria in young women patients that led to the discovery of the unconscious psyche.

In a third study I explored the mythopathology revolving around the figure of Pan and the phenomenology of instinctual drives such as masturbation, rape, and panic.[13] Through the

---

[10] A good deal has been written on the thinking of the ancient Greeks about psychopathology, e.g., E. R. Dodds, *The Greeks and the Irrational* (Boston: Beacon, 1957); George Rosen, *Madness in Society* (London: Routledge, 1968), pp. 71–136; B. Simon and H. Weiner, "Models of Mind and Mental Illness in Ancient Greece," *J. Hist. Behav. Sci.* 2 (1966):303–14.

[11] J. Hillman, "On Senex Consciousness," *Spring 1970*, pp. 146–65.

[12] *MA*, pt. 3.

[13] J. Hillman, "An Essay on Pan," in *Pan and the Nightmare: Two Essays*, with W. H. Roscher.

myths of Pan's behavior, especially in relation with retreating anima figures of reflection (Echo, Syrinx, and the Moon), we can learn much about the compulsion-inhibition patterns of human impulsiveness.

Eros in relation with Psyche, a myth which has been depicted in carvings and painting and tales for more than two thousand years,[14] offers a background to the divine torture of erotic neuroses — the pathological phenomena of a soul in need of love, and of love in search of psychic understanding. This story is particularly relevant for what goes on in the soul-making relationships which have been technically named "transference."

In addition to these examples, it is also possible to insight the ego, and ego psychology, by reverting it to the heroic myths of Hercules, with whose strength and mission we have become so caught that the patterns of Hercules — clubbing animals, refusing the feminine, fighting old age and death, being plagued by Mom but marrying her younger edition — are only now beginning to be recognized as pathology.

There are many avenues open for bringing mythology and pathology together. How little we understand, for instance, about the relation of sensual love and battling activity, the pathologized cycle of battle to bed to battle. But the Mars-Venus myths could give insights. What for instance would the myths of Hera tell about the pathologizings of marriage; and what background can be found in Hera's sons — Ares of battle-rage and Hephaistos the crippled smith — for a woman's angry attempts to smash the marriage bond to create on her own. (Hera brought forth these sons, by the way, without benefit of Zeus, in revenge and on her own.) Or we could look at the high-flying young champions — Bellerophon falling from his white winged horse, Icarus plunging into the sea, Phaëthon hurtling in flames, unable to manage his father's chariot of the sun — to understand the self-destructive behavior of the spirit and the young men in whom the spirit is strong.[15] The tales are endless and so are their possibilities, but no more endless than our pathologies and their possibilities.

This first entry into myth needs an important correction. It commits the ego fallacy by taking each archetypal theme into the ego. We fall into an identity with one of the figures in the tale: I become Zeus deceiving my wife, or Saturn devouring my children, or Hermes thieving from my brother. But this neglects

[14] MA, pt. 1.
[15] J. Hillman, "Senex and Puer," Eranos 36 — 1967 (Zürich, Rhein), pp. 301–60, and "The Great Mother, Her Son, Her Hero, and the Puer," in Fathers and Mothers (New York/Zürich: Spring Publ., 1973), pp. 75–127.

that the whole myth is pertinent and all its mythical figures relevant: by deceiving I am also being deceived, and being devoured, and stolen from, as well as all the other complications in each of these tales. It is egoistic to recognize oneself in only one portion of a tale, cast in only one role.

Far more important than oversimplified and blatant self-recognitions by means of myths is the experiencing of their working *intrapsychically* within our fantasies, and then through them into our ideas, systems of ideas, feeling-values, moralities, and basic styles of consciousness. There they are least apparent, for they characterize the notion of consciousness itself according to archetypal perspectives; it is virtually impossible to see the instrument by which we are seeing. Yet our notion of consciousness may derive from the light and form of Apollo, the will and intention of Hercules, the ordering unity of the senex, the communal flow of Dionysus. When any one of these is assumed by the ego as its identity and declared to be the defining characteristic of consciousness, then the other archetypal styles tend to be called psychopathological.

This leads to a conclusion: psychopathology from the archetypal perspective means that *specific* psychopathologies belong to the various myths and operate as inalienable functions and images within them; psychopathology, as a *general* term, refers to the intervention into polytheistic consciousness of the monotheistic standpoint, forcing the literalizations and identifications that we still commonly call ego. Psychopathology, in general, refers to singleness of vision or an ignorance of fantasies that are always playing through all behavior.

Pathologizing: A Peroration

We are now in a position to form three ideas about the necessity of pathologizing. These ideas also express the dominant themes of this chapter, and the entire book presents variations upon them.

First, archetypal psychology can put its idea of psychopathology into a series of nutshells, one inside the other: within the affliction is a complex, within the complex an archetype, which in turn refers to a God. Afflictions point to Gods; Gods reach us through afflictions. Jung's statement — "the gods have become diseases; Zeus no longer rules Olympus but rather the solar plexus, and produces curious specimens for the doctor's consulting room"[16] — implies that Gods, as in Greek tragedy,

[16] CW 13, §54.

force themselves symptomatically into awareness. Our pathologizing is their work, a divine process working in the human soul. By reverting the pathology to the God, we recognize the divinity of pathology and give the God his due.

From the archetypal perspective the Gods manifest themselves in and through human life, and therefore Greek polytheism, as W. F. Otto said, "contradicts no human experience."[17] Everything belongs — nothing is denied or excluded. Psychopathologies of every sort become part of the divine manifestation. "The gods" writes H. D. F. Kitto, "are never transcendental, external to our universe . . . they are some force within ourselves, some divine instinct. . . ."[18] They are the very sources of our acts and our omissions, according to Kerényi, present not only when invoked or praised.[19] To find them we look to our complexes, recognizing the archetypal power in the complex. For as Jung says, "It is not a matter of indifference whether one calls something a 'mania' or a 'god.' To serve a mania is detestable and undignified, but to serve a god is full of meaning. . . ."[20]

A complex must be laid at the proper altar, because it makes a difference both to our suffering and perhaps to the God who is there manifesting, whether we consider our sexual impotence, for example, to be the effect of the Great Mother's Son who may be served thereby, or Priapus who, neglected, is taking revenge, or Jesus whose genitality is simply absent, or Saturn who takes physical potency and gives lascivious fantasy. Finding the background for affliction calls for familiarity with an individual's style of consciousness, with his pathologizing fantasies, and with myth to which style and fantasy may revert.

To study the complex only personally, or to examine only personally the psychodynamics and history of a case is not enough, since the other half of pathology belongs to the Gods. Pathologies are both facts and fantasies, both somatic and psychic, both personal and impersonal. This view of pathology brings with it a view of therapy such as we find in the Renaissance with Paracelsus, who said:

> . . . The physician must have knowledge of man's other half, that half of his nature which is bound up with astronomical

---

[17] W. F. Otto, *The Homeric Gods*, trans. M. Hadas (New York: Pantheon, 1954), p. 169.
[18] H. D. F. Kitto, "The Idea of God in Aeschylus and Sophocles," in *La Notion du Divin*, Fondation Hardt I (Geneva: Vandoeuvres, 1954), p. 188.
[19] K. Kerényi, *Geistiger Weg Europas* (Zürich: Rhein, 1955), pp. 39–40.
[20] CW 13, §55.

philosophy; otherwise he will be in no true sense man's physician, since Heaven retains within its sphere half of all bodies and all maladies. What is a physician who knows nothing of cosmography?[21]

"Cosmography" here refers to the imaginal realm, the archetypal powers bearing the names of the planets and the myths portrayed by the constellations of the stars. Neglect of this "half," the imaginal or psychic component, the God in the disease, fails the human. To deal fully with any human affair, one must devote half one's thoughts to what is not human. "Maladies" lie also in the archetypes and are part of them.

If Gods reach us through afflictions, then pathologizing makes them immanent, opening the psyche for them to enter; thus pathologizing is a way of moving from transcendental theology to immanent psychology. For immanence is only a doctrine until I am knocked back through symptoms by these dominant powers, and I recognize that in my disturbances there really are forces I cannot control and yet which want something from me and intend something with me.

Of all my psychological events my pathologizing seems at times to be the only happening that is peculiarly mine. Afflictions give me the convincing delusion of being different. My hopes and fears, and even my loves, may all have been put upon me by the world's directions, or by my parents as residues and options of their unlived lives. But my symptoms point to my soul as my soul points to me through them.

Yet the symptoms and quirks are both me and not me — both, most intimate and shameful and a revelation of my deeps, steering my fate through character so that I cannot shrug them off. Yet they are *not* of my intention; they are visitations, alienations, bringing home the personal/impersonal paradox of the soul: what is "me" is also not "mine" — "I" and "soul" are alien to each other because of soul's domination by powers, daimons, and Gods.

The pathological experience gives an indelible sense of soul, unlike those we may get through love or beauty, through nature, community, or religion. The soul-making of pathology has its distinct flavor, salty, bitter; it "skins alive," "wounds," "bleeds," making us excruciatingly sensitive to the movements of the psyche. Pathology produces an intensely focused consciousness of soul, as in undergoing a symptomatic pain —

---

[21] Quoted in J. Seznec, *The Survival of the Pagan Gods*, trans. B. F. Sessions (New York: Harper Torchbook, 1961), p. 58.

sobering, humbling, blinding. It gives the hero a little twinge of heel, the soft spot that reminds the ego of death, of soul. Do you remember Zooey's remark (in Salinger's story) when his sister asks him about his symptom? "*Yes*, I have an ulcer, for Chrissake. This is Kaliyuga, buddy, the Iron Age. Anybody over sixteen without an ulcer's a goddam spy."[22] In my symptom is my soul.

What pathologizing does for the individual's psychology it does as well for the field of psychology: it keeps us close to the actuality of the psyche, preventing metaphysical and scientific escapes. Already a generation ago Erwin Minkowski pointed out:

> . . . Psychopathology has had the great merit of leading me and my philosopher-psychiatrist colleagues back to the concrete reality of our patients' lives again and again . . . thus protecting us from the dangers of pure philosophy. It was never a question of transposing purely and simply the data and methods used by a given philosophy into the realm of psychopathological facts. That would have led to a 'hyper-philosophizing' of psychopathology . . . it would have risked deforming psychopathology entirely.[23]

This sensate, concrete physical reality of soul was refound in this century through the psychological occupation with pathologizing. The descent into soul via pathologizing is what the last three score years and ten of analysis has taught. It has been the chief lesson of the entire psychotherapeutic movement. Any postanalytical hermeneutic for the soul must have learnt this lesson so as to include its meaning. The rediscovery of soul through psychopathology reigns supreme over all psychotherapy's other achievements: cultural, social, methodological, philosophical. Where earlier psychology tried to see through religion for its psychopathological content, we are now trying to see through psychopathology for its religious content.

---

[22] J. D. Salinger, *Franny and Zooey* (Boston: Little, Brown, 1961), p. 140. Zooey (need I point out that his name means life in Greek?) *did not want his symptom psychoanalyzed into an explanation.* Compare Jung, "The Symbolic Life" (transcript from shorthand notes by D. Kitchin, Guild Lecture 80 [London: Guild of Pastoral Psychology, 1954], p. 17): "And so we dismiss our souls—'Oh, I am bound by a fixation to my mother, and if I see that I have all kinds of impossible fancies about my mother, I am liberated from that fixation.' *If the patient succeeds, he has lost his soul.* Every time you accept that explanation you lose your soul. You have not helped your soul; you have replaced your soul by an explanation, a theory."
[23] Eugène Minkowski, *Le Temps vecu: Études phénoménologiques et psychopathologiques* (Paris: Coll. de l'Evolution psychiatrique, 1933), now *Lived Time: Phenomenological and Psychopathological Studies*, trans. N. Metzel (Evanston, Ill.: Northwestern Univ. Press, 1970), p. xxxix.

Our complexes are not only wounds that hurt and mouths that tell our myths, but also eyes that see what the normal and healthy parts cannot envision. André Gide said that illness opens doors to a reality which remains closed to the healthy point of view. One understands what he meant about the psychological acuity and richness of a culture during periods of historical decay; but why is the same phenomenon of psychological depth in periods of personal decay—ageing, neurosis, depression—not recognized with the same respect?

The soul sees by means of affliction. Those who are most dependent upon the imagination for their work—poets, painters, fantasts—have not wanted their pathologizing degraded into the "unconscious" and subjected to clinical literalism. ("The unconscious," and submitting the pathologized imagination to therapy, found favor with less imaginative professions: nurses, educationalists, clinical psychologists, social workers.) The crazy artist, the daft poet and mad professor are neither romantic clichés nor antibourgeois postures. They are metaphors for the intimate relation between pathologizing and imagination. Pathologizing processes are a source of imaginative work, and the work provides a container for the pathologizing processes. The two are inextricably interwoven in the work of Sophocles and Euripides, Webster and Shakespeare, Goya and Picasso, Swift and Baudelaire, O'Neill and Strindberg, Mann and Beckett—these but an evident few.

The wound and the eye are one and the same. From the psyche's viewpoint, pathology and insight are not opposites— as if we hurt because we have no insight and when we gain insight we shall no longer hurt. No. Pathologizing is itself a way of seeing; the eye of the complex gives the peculiar twist called "psychological insight." We become psychologists because we see from the psychological viewpoint, which means by benefit of our complexes and their pathologizings.

Normal psychology insists that this twisted insight is pathological. But let us bear in mind that normal psychology does not admit pathologizing unless dressed in its patient's uniform. It has a special house called abnormal. And let us also bear in mind that the ego's normative view of the psyche is a cramped distortion. If we studied soul through art, biography, myth; or through the history of wars, politics and dynasties, social behavior and religious controversy; then normal and abnormal might have to switch houses. But normal academic psychology eschews these fields and compiles its statistics so often from undergraduates who have not yet had the chance to experience the range of their madness.

The deeper reason for steering clear of analysis is that it may disturb the myth in the madness by excising its pathological parts in the name of clinical improvement. If our psychological lives are under the governance of mythical patterns because Gods are moving in our complexes, then the pathologizing going on in our lives cannot be extracted without deforming the myth and preventing reversion to it. The implication is that each archetype has its pathological themes and that each pathological theme has an archetypal perspective. Archetypal psychopathology finds the pathological inherently necessary to the myth: Christ must have his crucifixion; Dionysus must be childish and attract titanic enemies; Persephone must be raped; Artemis must kill him who comes too close.

Myths include the phenomena that are discredited in normative psychology, where they are called abnormal, bizarre, absurd, self-destructive, and sick. If we pursue this difference between usual psychology and mythology, we see clearly how *mythology saves the phenomena of psychopathology.* Psychology finds place for these phenomena of the soul only by discrediting them; mythology credits them just as they are, finding them necessary to its account. It makes no excuse, for it presents nothing wrong. It is not the myth that is wrong but our ignorance of its workings in us. The fallacies are circumvented; they do not even arise — neither the normative, the clinical, nor the moralistic. Because archetypal psychology looks to myth for its base, it too regards the pathologized phenomena of the psyche as necessary to a complete account of any psychic complexity. Without psychopathology there is no wholeness; in fact, psychopathology is a differentiation of that wholeness.

The healthy, normal parts of the soul — or what might better be called its unimaginative and literalistic fantasies — are never quite able to accept the ultimate reflection each of us makes about our individual course of depth analysis.

There is an irreversible trend of pathologizing in the soul. I am curiously dependent upon it, and when it is lost to me, my sense of soul too wavers and fades. I experience the necessity of pathologizing as a need of soul. It is like an immutable and incorruptible core, for though it moves and goes through changes, it is never transformed, is permanently bound to all my psychological life, providing the base ground, the primal material for all my psychic processes, for soul-making itself. It is irredeemable because the category of redemption does not here apply; it belongs authentically to the soul's mythical essence; as such, pathologizing is essential to my myths and my soul.

Second, these conclusions about pathologizing reflect our historical culture. Although these ideas are drawn from the same sources as Freud and Jung and in the main follow their thinking, yet these ideas reflect the movement of pathologizing beyond Freud and Jung.

Consciousness today is closer to its pathology. Psychopathology is no longer held behind asylum walls. The sickness fantasy is now so dominant that one sees disintegration, pollution, insanities, cancerous growth, and decay wherever one looks. Pathology has entered our speech and we judge our fellows and our society in terms once reserved for psychiatric diagnoses. And the ego falls apart.

No longer is ego able to cope by *will power* with tough problems in a *real* world of *hard* facts. Our falling apart is an imaginal process, like the collapse of cities and the fall of heroes in mythical tales — like the dismemberment of Dionysian loosening which releases from oversight constraint, like the dissolution and decay in alchemy. The soul moves, via the pathologized fantasy of disintegration, out of too-centralized and muscle-bound structures which have become ordinary and normal, and so normative that they no longer correspond with the psyche's needs for nonego imaginal realities which "perturb to excess."[24]

Is it history or culture or society that has forced the recognition of pathologizing on us? It seems the psyche itself insists on pathologizing the strong ego and all its supportive models, disintegrating the "I" with images of psychopathic hollowness in public life, fragmentation and depersonalization in music and painting, hallucinations and pornographies in private visions, violence, cruelty, and the absurd surrealisms of urban wars, racisms, causes, freakishness in dress and speech. These images, like the pathologized *metaphorica* in the memory art, alchemy, and myth, twist and shock the "I" out of its integrative identity, out of its innocence and its idealization of human being, open-

---

[24] Vico, *New Science*, p. 117 (§376). There is a distinction between *acting out* "shocking truths" which perturb the psyche to excess and the metaphorical mode of imagination. It is not that we have to do violent, excessive things in order to move the psyche. This is the Romantic's way of seeking perturbations and excess — "living dangerously." Nor must the shocking fantasy be literalized by psychiatry into violent physical treatments such as suggested by Celsus (who gave us the term "insanity") in ancient Rome and by Cerletti (who invented electroshock — as well as artillery fuses, by the way) in modern Rome. Curiously, therapy regards physical shocks to be therapeutic while still regarding the shocking events in myth, dreams, and fantasies as pathological. An excessively strong pathologized image that does violence to our nature might be better understood as the psyche's self-induced shock treatment, preferable to coarser modes of its clinical enactment.

ing it to the underworld of psychic being. It is not the psyche itself that insists upon a revision of psychology in terms not of peaks but of parts?

Falling apart makes possible a new style of reflection within the psyche, less a centered contemplation of feeling collected around a still point, thoughts rising on a tall stalk, than insights bouncing one off the other. The movements of Mercury among the multiple parts, fragmentation as moments of light. Truth is the mirror, not what's in it or behind it, but the very mirroring process itself: psychological reflections. An awareness of fantasy that cracks the normative cement of our daily realities into new shapes.

This style, with which we are engaged in both the form and the content of these chapters, could not have come into being had the normal control apparatus of the old ego not fragmented, making possible a new sophistication of multiple mirroring, where beginning and end do not matter, where premises are themselves conclusions and conclusions open into discontinuities, repetitions with variations. The very style of doing psychology — of thinking and feeling and writing it — incorporate pathologizing. And so it must, if a psychology book is to reflect and evoke the psyche.

The style of consciousness today is pathologized and draws its awareness from the pathography that is our actual lives. "Consciousness" means psychic reflection of the *psychic* world about us and is part of adaptation to that reality. As that reality darkens and divides, consciousness can no longer be described with heroic metaphors of light, decision, intention, and central control. *Ego consciousness as we used to know it no longer reflects reality.* Ego has become a delusional system. "Heightened" consciousness today no longer tells it from the mountain of Nietzsche's superman, an overview. Now it is the underview, for we are down in the multitudinous entanglements of the marshland, in anima country, the "vale of Soul-making."[25] So heightened consciousness now refers to moments of intense uncertainty, moments of ambivalence. Hence the task of depth psychology now is the careful exploration of the parts into which we fall, releasing the Gods in the complexes, bringing home the realization that all our knowing is in part only, because we know only through the archetypal parts playing in us, now in this complex and myth, now in that; our life a dream, our complexes our *daimones*.

[25] See *Re-Visioning Psychology*, Introduction, p. i, for origins of this phrase in Keats and also Blake.

I mentioned earlier how our fantasies carry events to an incurable possibility, to meningitis or cancer, or to suicide. The "incurable possibility" is nothing less than death. So for a *third* reason pathologizing is a royal road of soul-making. It takes each complex to its ultimate term, to its final unknown, the depths where we can penetrate no further, never knowing what's "the matter." The complex that gnaws and makes us peculiar also makes us particular distinct individuals—for that is what "peculiar" means. For life, the complex is but a symptom to be rid of. But because the inhibition, the distortion, and the affliction point to death, the complex becomes a center around which one's psychic life constellates. It is not upon life that our ultimate individuality centers, but upon death.[26] Its kingdom, Greek myths of Hades and Tartarus say, is the world under and within all life, and there souls go home.[27] There, psychic existence is without the natural perspective of flesh and blood, so that pathologizing by taking events to death takes them into their ultimate meaning for soul. One has one's death, each his own, alone, singular, toward which the soul leads each piece of life by pathologizing it. Or perhaps it is pathologizing that unerringly leads the soul into the deepest ontological reflection. Symptoms are death's solemn ambassadors, deserving honor for their place, and life mirrored in its symptoms sees there its death and remembers soul. Pathologizing returns us to soul, and to lose the symptom means to lose this road to death, this way of soul.

Plato and his followers presented three main modes of soul-making: eros, dialectics, and mania.[28] There is a fourth: thanatos. We find a basis for this connection between soul-making and death in Plato's own description of the dying Socrates in a dialogue (*Phaedo*) which examines the nature and reality of *psyché* even while dwelling upon the pathologized details of hemlock poisoning. The soul is led to knowledge of itself (to true ideas in Platonic language) through love, through intellectual discipline, and as Hegel too saw, through madness.[29] But equal with these is pathologizing as the mode of reflection in terms of invisibles and unknowables, the fantasies of psychic

[26] Cf. M. de Unamuno, *Tragic Sense of Life* (1921), trans. J. E. C. Flitch (New York: Dover, 1954), p. 269.

[27] I have presented at length some of the phenomenology of the realm of Hades and its psychological significance in "The Dream and the Underworld," *Eranos* 42—1973.

[28] Cf. Paul Friedländer, *Plato*, 3 vols., trans. H. Meyerhoff, Bollingen Series (New York and Princeton, N.J.: Pantheon and Princeton Univ. Press, 1958–69)1:29–31.

[29] See *Re-Visioning Psychology*, p. 369a on Hegel and insanity.

existence, what is below and after the actions of life and is deeper than they—that is, what is symbolically attributed to death.

Like Socrates in the *Phaedo*, although for a period which extended through his whole adult life, Freud examined the nature and reality of the psyche, all the while reflecting upon his own death and that of his friends and family, on the nature of death, on the physical pathology of his body, and the pathologizing going on in his patients and colleagues.[30] His pathologizing was contemporaneous with the creation of depth psychology, which laid the groundwork for soul-making again in our era.

By beginning with the symptom, "a thing that is more foreign to the ego," pathologizing turns the entire psyche upon a new pivot: death becomes the center, and with it fantasies that lead right out of life. Pathologizing is not only a metaphorical language but a way of translation, a way of turning something literally known, usual, and trivial like the psychopathologies of everyday life into something unknown and deep. As such, pathologizing is a hermeneutic which leads events into meaning. Only when things fall apart do they open up into new meanings; only when an everyday habit turns symptomatic, a natural function becomes an affliction, or the physical body appears in dreams as a pathologized image, does a new significance dawn. As the psyche is never invulnerable to these movements, so it is never cured. Therewith archetypal realizations may enter. So too an archetypal psychology can never leave its base in pathography.

The deepening and interiorizing that goes on through pathologizing lends neurosis an extraordinary feeling of significance, that through it we are elected, separated from merely ordinary people. This appraisal, deriving itself from neurosis, is of course neurotic (nothing makes us more commonly normal than our "abnormalities"). But the sense of significance points beyond neurosis, beyond this symptom and that complaint which so many others have too.

The feeling of election through the complex is above all a psychic statement, which says that a pathologized awareness is

---

[30] Cf. M. Schur, *Freud: Living and Dying* (New York: Internat. Univ. Press, 1972). Freud's pathologizings included: fainting spells, colon and bladder difficulties, some heart trouble, his smoking addiction and dreadfully painful cancer of the mouth, his cocaine period, the afflictions reported in his letters to Fliess, his "depersonalization" experience on the Acropolis—and his obsessive ideas about the date of his own death. Beyond all these concrete manifestations was his "pathologized eye"; his speculative imagination required pathologizing.

fundamental to the sense of individuality. It tells of a difference, not between kinds of people, but between styles of consciousness, natural and psychic, literal and imaginal. Having forced the reality of the imaginal upon one, pathologizing leaves one marked by its imprint. A piece of the person has been struck by the Gods and drawn into a myth and now cannot let go of its mad requirements. The boar has wounded Ulysses' thigh; the daemon of the crossing point has broken Jacob's hip. I am an individual, by virtue not of my common wounds but of what comes through them to me, the archetypes of my myths in which lie my madness, fate, and death.

By clinging faithfully to the pathological perspective which is the differential root of its discipline, distinguishing it from all others, depth psychology maintains its integrity, becoming neither humanistic education, spiritual guidance, social activity, nor secular religion. By refusing the temptations and sentimentalities that would leave sickness and queerness behind, depth psychology retains even the disparaging terms of its textbooks. For to abandon the words so weighted with sickness, so negative in connotation, would again split the psyche from its pathology. The value of these words lies precisely in keeping psyche pathologized. Neither literalistically real, nor the empty nomina of a professional convention, these words are metaphorical expressions for our psychic condition, sources of reflection, ways of finding oneself into a myth.

By remembering its own genealogy myth — that it was born from the psychopathology of French and Austrian hysteria and Swiss schizophrenia, outcast afflictions which then made no sense and were held in disrepute — depth psychology keeps in touch with souls *in extremis*, with the afflicted, the abnormal, the refused. By maintaining itself in this perspective through pathologizing, in touch with the fantasy of sickness that everyone else would prefer to cure or to deny, depth psychology is inevitably both traditional and revolutionary.

We are traditional because we return all things to their deepest principles, the *archai*, the limiting roots holding down and in. They determine by recurring with fatalistic regularity, little caring for place or time. We are revolutionary because these same *archai* are the radicals of existence. They will out, always. They force the claims of the dispossessed soul upon the ruling consciousness of each place and time.

Index

Library of Congress Cataloging-in-Publication Data

Jung, C. G. (Carl Gustav), 1875–1961.
   Jung on mythology / selected and introduced by Robert A. Segal.
     p.   cm. — (Encountering Jung)
   Includes bibliographical references and index.
   ISBN 0-691-01736-0 (pbk. : alk. paper)
   1. Myth. 2. Mythology. 3. Psychiatry and religion. 4. Jung,
C.G. (Carl Gustav), 1875–1961. I. Segal, Robert Alan. II. Title.
III. Series: Jung, C. G. (Carl Gustav), 1875–1961. Selections.
English. 1995.
BL304.J86 1998
291.1'3 — dc21
                                     97-51807